W9-BBD-407

BELABORED PROFESSIONS

Belabored

NARRATIVES OF AFRICAN AMERICAN WORKING WOMANHOOD

Professions

XIOMARA SANTAMARINA

The University of North Carolina Press

Chapel Hill

Set in Arnhem type by Tseng Information Systems, Inc.
Manufactured in the United States of America

The paper in this book meets the guidelines for permanence and durability of the Committee on Production Guidelines for Book Longevity of the Council on Library Resources.

Library of Congress Cataloging-in-Publication Data
Santamarina, Xiomara.
Belabored professions : narratives of African American working womanhood / Xiomara Santamarina.
p. cm.
Includes bibliographical references and index.
ISBN 0-8078-2981-1 (cloth : alk. paper)
ISBN 0-8078-5648-7 (pbk. : alk. paper)
1. American prose literature—African American authors—History and criticism. 2. American prose literature—Women authors—History and criticism. 3. American prose literature—19th century—History and criticism. 4. Women and literature—United States—History—19th century. 5. African American women—Biography—History and criticism. 6. African American women—Intellectual life—19th century. 7. African American women in the professions—History. 8. African American women—Employment—History. 9. Autobiography—African American authors. 10. African American women in literature. 11. Autobiography—Women authors. 12. Narration (Rhetoric) I. Title.
PS366.A35S26 2005
818'.408099287'08996073—dc22 2005010229

Portions of this work were published earlier as "Black Hairdresser and Social Critic: Eliza Potter and the Labors of Femininity," *American Literature* 77.1 (March 2005), 151–77, and "Behind the Scenes of Black Labor: Elizabeth Keckley and the Scandal of Publicity," *Feminist Studies* 28.3 (Fall 2002), 515–36.

cloth 09 08 07 06 05 5 4 3 2 1
paper 09 08 07 06 05 5 4 3 2 1

For Dan, Isabel, and Sebe

CONTENTS

ILLUSTRATIONS

PREFACE
IT IS NO DISGRACE FOR EITHER SEX TO ENGAGE IN AN HONORABLE EMPLOYMENT

DEAR ANGLO: *You will, no doubt, tell us why persons who labor are so generally neglected by others more fortunate?*

We have been taught in childhood that it is honorable to work. And now when we remember the disadvantages under which we find a miserable existence as "proscribed Americans," we discover no extenuation for the sin of those who proscribe each other for such a noble cause, i.e., working for their living. Many a young lady at service is made to feel most keenly the unnatural distinction made between them and those who were blessed with trades. There are others in our communities, both male and female, who do nothing but dress and promenade, and are raised in idleness, kept in ignorance and luxury, yet these are the "lions of society." If we appreciate the idle, do we not foster all of its consequent evils? When our reformers will rebuke these distinctions, and the "Anglo" lend its valuable aid, the world will learn that it is no disgrace for either sex to engage in an honorable employment.

"One Who Works," Weekly Anglo-African *(June 30, 1860)*

The letter by "One Who Works" that appeared in an antebellum African American newspaper posed the following questions for its readers: why should an "honorably" employed woman laboring in the "noble cause" of "working for [her] living" be made to feel inferior to "idle" folk who look down on "young lad[ies] at service"? And why should employment that makes one economically independent be viewed in deprecating terms and not as "honorable"? Provoked by this misrepresentation, "One Who Works" publicly repudiated the social disadvantages associated with domestic service. In her rebuke of the community's "idle" and its "lions of society," as well as its "reformers," "One Who Works" denounced widely held assumptions about servants' low status by emphasizing the economic independence and "honorable" nature of working for a living. As "proscribed Americans" struggling in difficult circumstances, she suggested somewhat ironically, African American readers especially should value the independence-granting capacities of paid domestic labor and rebuke those—including reformers who should know better—biased against those "at service."

This working woman's complaint is distinctive for many reasons: it displays frank irritation at the patronizing putting down of her work by those perceived as the "lions of society" and talks back to these class superiors, displaying intraracial class tensions. But of particular interest here is the type of appeal this worker makes to her readers about the domestic labor at the root of this conflict: "One Who Works" does not plead for sympathy as a victim of racial and sexual discrimination (though she recognizes the "proscribed" status of African Americans); she promotes her service labor on the basis of what it does for her as honorable, self-supporting work. "One Who Works" indignantly disciplines those presumed to be her social superiors by describing herself and her labor as being at the center, and not at the margins, of legitimizing discourses that view work that enables one to earn a living as "honorable employment."

Belabored Professions explores four women's autobiographies that testify, like the letter from "One Who Works," to the symbolically powerful yet highly contested nature of black women's self-supporting labor during the antebellum period. Written by former slaves and freeborn black women, these autobiographies recast their authors' often-disparaged labor as socially and culturally valuable to the nation. They profess the meanings of African American women's work and illuminate these women's contributions to and participation in moral discourses about social legitimacy, despite the disadvantaged status of black women workers in the antebellum nation. Together, these texts constitute an archive of black "working womanhood" that speaks to the representational possibilities that black women's labor offered for mediating contradictory discourses of class, citizenship, race, and femininity during a period of economic, political, and cultural transformations. Although cultural perceptions of black working women emphasized their abject status as "drudges," as degendered beings performing manual labor, or as hypersexualized slave chattel, these women as autobiographers demanded that their readers recognize the centrality of self-supporting labor to their gendered and raced subjectivity.

For modern readers, the texts at the center of this study—Sojourner Truth's *Narrative of Sojourner Truth* (1850), Harriet Wilson's *Our Nig* (1859), Eliza Potter's *A Hairdresser's Experience in High Life* (1859), and Elizabeth Keckley's *Behind the Scenes* (1868)—yield new perspectives on the nineteenth-century emergence of the vital African American autobiographical tradition. They dramatize the degree to which black working women shaped rhetorics for labor, race, and femininity that spoke to the possibilities for independence attainable through their wage labor. To date, these possibilities remain largely overlooked and, indeed, are far from axiomatic, despite their somewhat common-sense nature: contemporary critical discussions still view nineteenth-century African American cultural production through the lenses of reform discourses in which the self-supporting labor of black women is downplayed and black women's "work" is framed almost exclusively through abolition and reform—through black women's roles as "doers of the word." As her rebuke of reformers makes clear, "One Who Works" foregrounds the potentially constricted or narrow basis of framing black women's labor through these lenses. Likewise, these working women's texts demand that we reach beyond, even as we acknowledge, understandings of black women's contributions to the reform genres of spiritual and slave autobiography and shed light on the tenuous yet often fruitful possibilities for legitimation embodied in black women's labor. For when these women reclaimed their economic and symbolic productivity as workers and as citizens, they revealed the roots of ideologies about republican freedom and true womanhood in the material circumstances of racial, gender, and class subordination.

As autobiographers, these women publicized the conditions and products of their work in all its aspects: free, slave, interracial, and yes, profoundly gendered. Like "One Who Works," they repudiated widely held beliefs about the degendering nature of self-supporting labor and rearticulated their femininity in the context of such labor as independent, respectable, and honorable. Yet when these women took up this kind of corrective publicity, they were not entirely freed from the burdens associated with their disparaged labor; their professions of value are "belabored," not simply because they are about labor, but because in belaboring or "exploiting" their exploitation they necessarily encountered and negotiated the limits of rewriting their domination as an opportunity for legitimation. When they intervened in debates about the value of black labor they forged historically specific, or conjunctural, descriptions of work that simultaneously contested and reproduced contradictory languages of labor. These stories of powerful but problematic negotiations of labor, race, and femininity constitute the "professions" at the center of this work.

ACKNOWLEDGMENTS

"Perfection is not an accident," my father used to tell me as a child, over and over again, in that tendentious I'm-handing-down-wisdom mode that so many fathers have. Like so many children, I was less than grateful. While I would obligingly smile and pretend I wasn't tired of hearing this advice, I was fully aware that it was some sloppy performance of mine that had prompted the remark. Chagrined, I would go back to the task at hand, lamenting, "Why do I have to have the hardest-working person in the whole world for MY father?" Today, I regret that my father isn't alive to take credit for getting me over the hump of this first scholarly effort and for passing on the intellectual curiosity and commitment that drove me to it. There is no doubt in my mind that I wouldn't have taken the first step on this path had he not encouraged me, at every turn, to make the absolute most of any opportunity that came my way. Fortunately, for me, he was not alone in offering his generosity and support. I have been the lucky beneficiary of myriad contributions from family, colleagues, and students while working on this project.

This work began as a dissertation at the University of Chicago under the brilliant directorship of Lauren Berlant and Kenneth Warren. The University of Chicago generously supported my work on this project as a student and then again as a Whiting Humanities Postdoctoral Fellow at the Franke Humanities Institute. I am grateful to Jim Chandler, head of the Institute, and all the other postdoctoral fellows, for providing crucial feedback. Also at Chicago, I'd like to thank Cathy Cohen at the "Race Center" and the members of the Department of English Students of Color, along with Jacqueline Stewart, Terri Francis, Rolland Murray, Pat Chu, and Yolanda Padilla, who offered support and encouragement on those terrible days when I felt I would surely die as a graduate student. Ken Warren, in particular, continues to be the perfect role model for both rigorous critique and affability, as he has been since I-can't-remember-when during our Northwestern days. His generous intellectual collegiality is unsurpassed.

For unstinting friendship and support at the University of Michigan, I'd like to thank Kelly Askew and Sandra Gunning, who offered much-needed encouragement during difficult times, even when they hardly had time for themselves. I'm very fortunate to work in Ann Arbor with a stimulating cohort of colleagues: Patsy Yaeger, Adela Pinch, Valerie Traub, Sidonie Smith, Gregg Crane, Julian Levinson, Lisa Makman, Anita Norich, June Howard, David Halperin, Maria Sanchez, Andrea Zemgulys, and the JFF crew. Other wonderful colleagues include Marlon Ross, Simon Gikandi, Jonathan Freedman, Sara Blair, Kevin Gaines, Penny Von Eschen, James Jackson, Frieda Ekotto, Dorceta Taylor, Michele Mitchell, Hannah Rosen, Rebecca Scott, and Carroll Smith-Rosenberg. The University of Michigan provided leave time and generous research funds that enabled me to finish this project.

I'd also like to acknowledge the contributions of others, including Frances Smith Foster, Nellie McKay, and Farah Griffin, all of whom offered timely encouragement and wisdom, as well as Glenn Hendler, Wendy Motooka, and Elizabeth Freeman, who extended unfailingly keen insights. Thanks to Duke University Press and Feminist Studies, Inc., for permission to reprint portions of Chapters 3 and 4 that appeared previously in *Feminist Studies* and *American Literature*. At the University of North Carolina Press, I'd like to thank Sian Hunter for her optimism and know-how. A million thanks also to Bob Levine, senior colleague extraordinaire.

I am grateful, above all, to my mother, Xiomara, and my family for their support during this impossibly long journey. My brother, Everard, was always quick to lend a hand with gracious humor and love (the laughs were key) and provided vital assistance in the last stages of preparing the manuscript. I owe him big time. Finally, this book is fondly dedicated to Dan Maier and our children, Isabel and Sebe, my own favorite "labors of love." *Os quiero mucho.*

BELABORED PROFESSIONS

Until we realize our ideal, we are going to idealize our real.

—Nannie Helen Burroughs, president, Women's Convention (National Baptist Convention), 1909

To portray the limits of . . . necessities and the realization, complete or partial, of all possibilities, that is the true business of the historian.

—C. L. R. James, 1938

INTRODUCTION
FROM FIELDS TO WHITE HOUSE

Four very different African American working women and texts are at the heart of this exploration of antebellum race, labor, and femininity. These autobiographers were born enslaved and free between 1797 and 1827 and lived and worked in different regions of the United States. They worked under northern and southern slavery, as free laborers in the South, in the North, and in the "West" of the day (the Western Reserve of Ohio), and they performed wide-ranging labor, from enslaved and indentured farm labor to domestic work as laundresses, nurses, and servants; from itinerant manual work to skilled artisanal labor as hairdresser and dressmaker for elite white women; as social arbiter for social climbers in Cincinnati; and even as "confidante" to a First Lady. Yet given this wide range of statuses and labor practices, in their texts, Sojourner Truth, Harriet Wilson, Eliza Potter, and Elizabeth Keckley all reclaim the value of their productivity, deconstruct the degraded nature of black women's labor, and reconnect this self-supporting labor to recognized norms for social legitimacy. When they chose this ground as the basis for their own advocacy, these women deliberately deployed the "power within their powerlessness" as workers to negotiate their cultural devaluation as black women.[1]

Perhaps the best known of these women in her day and ours, Sojourner Truth (1797–1883), is credited with the famous address to the Akron, Ohio, Women's Rights Convention in 1851 that stands as the most recognizable instance of such a deliberate rhetorical deployment of labor. Born in upstate New York, Truth worked as a slave until age thirty, when she was emancipated in 1827 under New York State's emancipation laws. Though she worked mostly as a domestic servant between her emancipation and the occasion of the speech that launched her new midlife career as an activist, a central aspect of this speech (as recorded at that time by the *Anti-Slavery Bugle*) emphasized the link she established between her agricultural labor and the civic recognition to which she felt entitled: "I want to say a few words about this matter. I am a woman's rights. I have as much muscle as any man, and can do as much work as any man. I have plowed and reaped and husked and chopped and mowed, and can any man do more than that?"[2] Truth's description of her field labor resisted her transformation into one of the degraded creatures that her listeners could easily have associated with the exploited slave woman of antislavery discourse; instead, it emphasized her productivity with an inventory of different farm tasks: plowing, reaping, husking, chopping, and mowing.

This inventory of tasks illustrates how Truth represented herself as entitled to equality, not simply on the basis of being a woman, but as a formerly enslaved *working* woman. For Truth—who performed both domestic and farm labor while a slave—her history of field labor, in particular, functioned to prove she had "as much muscle" as a man and could perform "as much work as any man." Despite the negative connotations attached to black women's field labor, Truth supported her claim to being "woman's rights" on the basis of this working productivity.[3] She chose to describe the labor she had performed as a member of one of the nation's most disparaged populations not to accede to that exploitation, but precisely as a basis for demanding civic recognition. When she did this, Truth located her enslaved agricultural labor in relation to Jeffersonian agrarian ideals that linked farming to civic virtue, ironically troping her own self-reliant figure as enslaved working woman to appear as a raced and gendered version of the early national "husbandman." Through this trope, Truth appealed to and contested the amnesia over the roles slaves and women played in producing this figure of republican virtue.[4]

Truth's work history as enslaved agricultural worker and as freed, unskilled laborer aptly symbolizes the overdetermined and abject significations associated with the labor performed by black women, enslaved or free, in the antebellum United States. In an industrializing North rife with anxieties about the wide-ranging effects of social and economic transformations, emerging middle-class citizens and white workers found common ground in their pronounced distaste for "nigger work," "working like a nigger," or "slaving" in occupations that were viewed as particularly onerous and lowly.[5] Black women's iconic debasement, produced in part by slavery's "degendering" of women who performed physical labor and by black women's disproportionately large presence in the bottom ranks of female workers (as menial or unskilled labor), meant their work (and not simply their sexual vulnerability as slaves/workers) could be viewed as a symptom of racial and gendered "degradation."[6]

This potent mix of manual labor and degraded black femininity is evident in an anecdote Frederick Law Olmsted related from his travels in the South in the early 1850s:

> We stopped, for some time, on this plantation, near where some thirty men and women were at work, repairing the road. The women were in majority, and were engaged at exactly the same labor as the men; driving the carts, loading them with dirt, and dumping them upon the road; cutting down trees, and drawing wood by hand, to lay across the miry places; hoeing, and shoveling. . . . Clumsy, awkward, gross, elephantine in all their movements; pouting, grinning, and leering at us; sly, sensual, and shameless, in all their expressions and demeanor; I never before had witnessed, I thought, anything more revolting than the whole scene.[7]

Olmsted, writing as a reporter for a northern newspaper, attempted to record objectively the conditions in the South in an effort to persuade southerners of slavery's economic inefficiencies. But his inventory of these women's tasks—cutting, driving, hoeing, and shoveling—concludes with a perspective very different from Truth's: rather than testifying to these women's strength and to the economic benefits accrued from these slave women's versatility, these women's "fit" performance of labor is read as a sign of moral degradation. The leap in Olmsted's logic from the necessary physical exertions inhering in roadwork and the condition of these women's dress to his attribution of sensuality and "shameless" "leering" in what may have been simply their curiosity about his curiosity clearly underscores what appears to have been an almost visceral response to the sight of these women. So negatively do the women affect the antislavery reporter's sensibilities that he naturalizes their "degradation" and represents it as irrevocable: "If these women, and their children after them, were always naturally and necessarily to remain of the character and ca-

Slave women repairing roads in South Carolina.
From Frederick Law Olmsted's Journey in the Seaboard Slave States *(1856). Courtesy of the University of Michigan Library.*

pacity stamped on their faces . . . I don't know that they could be much less miserably situated, or guided more for their own good and that of the world, than they were. They were fat enough, and didn't look as if they were at all overworked, or harassed by cares, or oppressed by a consciousness of their degradation."[8]

Even if today's readers recognize Truth's claim to her field labor as a proud one, Olmsted's remarkable description of these female slaves testifies anew to the high stakes involved in, and the contested nature of, Truth's public assertion of the value of women's manual, field labor. It also shows how *antislavery* insistence on the slave's inefficient labor potentially jeopardized the former slave's protest of her exploitation on the basis of that labor's value. As labor historian Jonathan Glickstein explains, "The antislavery movement's desire that political economy correspond with its sense of morality led it to ignore or screen out those objective developments that undercut this correspondence: above all, perhaps, the evidence of slave labor's actual viability in . . . agricultural enterprise."[9]

Scholars of Truth invoke her famous Akron speech almost exclusively in the context of her later public speaking career, which means that little, if any, connection has ever been made between the speech and the auto/biographical effort, *The Narrative of Sojourner Truth* (1850), that closely preceded it. Though scholars commonly refer to later versions of Truth's collaborated auto/biographies (the 1875 and 1878 versions, in particular) in which accounts of Truth's speaking career figure prominently, the critical neglect of Truth's first effort at self-representation, published in collaboration with abolitionist amanuensis Olive Gilbert, has perpetuated *The Narrative of Sojourner Truth*'s exclusion from the critical tradition of black/slave autobiography (which includes other "as told to" narratives). More important, however, this neglect has prevented recognition of the *literary* origins of Truth's egalitarian speaking persona. If we read *The Narrative of Sojourner Truth* as autobiography, we not only broaden our understanding of Truth's "authorship" of an autobiography; we also recognize the overlooked significance of her rhetorical embodiment as a black female worker. For a hallmark of this little-understood text is Truth's insistence on polemically deploying her productive labor, *while a slave*, as a basis for her membership in the body politic against, and despite, slavery's coercions.[10]

Though Truth is renowned for her independence and polemical public persona, she was not alone in valuing the civic and cultural contributions of black working women's labor. Other antebellum texts published in different parts of the nation introduced readers in "local" public spheres to the working contributions of African Americans. From laundress Chloe Spear to wallpaper hanger Elleanor Eldridge, and from butler Robert Roberts to devoted Catholic barber Pierre Toussaint, the prosperity and success of presumed economically subordinate blacks were central aspects of a black publicity that preceded and, in most cases, existed outside the public spheres of abolitionist reform with which African American cultural production has been exclusively associated.[11] Truth, commonly considered in isolation from other contemporary black women as something of an exception and even as "exotic," appears in this context as referring to and participating in a larger conversation concerned with black workers' contributions to various facets of national life and culture.[12] One of my goals is to sketch the outlines of such a larger conversation and to imagine the questions, methods, and implications that arise from reading texts that are problematic for, and sometimes even indifferent to, the traditions of black protest and reform that have been identified as central to an emergent African American literary tradition.

Like Truth before them, Eliza Potter, Harriet Wilson, and Elizabeth Keckley autobiographically reformulated their agency along the lines of their labor, emphasizing the dignity of their work in *all* its aspects, even as they recognized the constraints and inequities structuring their work practices. Like many workers of the day, white and black, they tried to mediate the negative effects that emerged from the nation's industrialization—rationalized production, skill erosion, the permanent (and increasingly impoverished, or "dependent") status of wage labor—by appealing to often contradictory cultural discourses that bespoke the "dignity of labor" and the civic virtue of those who earned their living "by the sweat of the brow." Even if the day's harsh economic and social realities belied the democratic potential of the (white male) worker's political enfranchisement during the Jacksonian era, there was still a sense in which a consensus about the virtue of self-reliant labor offered workers an opportunity to claim their work as necessary and important to the nation's development.[13] In this way, the autobiographies of Truth, Wilson, and Potter

Elleanor Eldridge. Frontispiece from Memoirs of Elleanor Eldridge *(1838). This singular woodcut is perhaps the earliest positive depiction of an African American working woman. Courtesy of the University of Michigan Library.*

refer to, yet point beyond, the period's problematic rhetorical contexts for black women's labor: they illustrate the overlooked role these women played in the shift from earlier views that validated skilled labor exclusively, to broader views on the dignity of all kinds of wage labor, and to a more universalistic understanding of citizenship that included all wage workers—black, white, male, and female.[14]

As authors, these women spoke out about the symbolic, social, and economic value that they produced under difficult circumstances not to accede to their exploitation as field workers or as domestic or personal servants, but rather to redeem the status of increasingly commodified, deskilled, and devalued labor precisely as a basis for civic recognition. It almost goes without saying: this was an exceptionally difficult task. But to some extent African American working women shared the challenges that white (immigrant and native) women faced working in a culture that simultaneously exploited and demeaned their labor. Contradictory attitudes about women's labor during the antebellum period sparked both black and white women's protests of the devaluation of their work and assertions of their entitlement to the sexual and economic independence their wages afforded them, even as the poorest of wage workers. As one Lowell, Massachusetts, factory woman responded when asked why she continued working in the mills despite the lengthy hours and low wages: "Why [do] we work here? The time we *do* have is our own. The money we earn comes promptly; more so than in any other situation; and our work, though laborious is the same from day to day; we know what it is, and when finished we feel perfectly free."[15] Their exploitation did not constitute an argument against their working, but quite the opposite: it offered them a site from which they could argue for a civic and social entitlement to which they did not otherwise have access as spouses, daughters, and domestic laborers. Consequently, when they described their work, working women invoked republican rights rhetorics that emphasized the independence-producing, or character-building, potential of their wage labor. While these rights languages were eclipsed by the emergence of the "cult of true womanhood" in the 1840s and 1850s,[16] texts like the *Memoirs of Elleanor Eldridge* (1839), in which a white amanuensis argued specifically for the rights of a "colored laboring woman" to fight a white man's theft of her property, stand as an instance of white and black women's earlier, more volatile, discourses about labor.[17] Despite black women's invisibility in accounts of industrializing and collectivizing labor, these autobiographies dramatize the degree to which black working women continued to work within this "tradition" as participants in the late-nineteenth-century radicalizing of labor, leading the way for later formulations valorizing women's "right to labor."[18]

Even as this working publicity points to existing interracial concerns about women's labor, it also displays the specificity of racial difference. This is not surprising, given the material and cultural disadvantages African American working women experienced in comparison to white working women. Black women occupied the narrowest range of occupational opportunity (narrower even than that of immigrant women) over longer periods of their lives than did white working women, many of whom viewed factory or wage labor in terms of temporary participation in the marketplace prior to marriage (although certainly marriage in itself did not guarantee "rising" above labor). That is, even as white women struggled against poverty and the association of labor, femininity, and degradation, they had more "safety nets" in place than black women. Black working women, for example, who married black men—among the poorest workers in the nation—were much more likely to continue working after marriage: for these women, labor, not marriage, was the greater certainty.[19]

More important, unlike most white women, black women performing public labor—as opposed to private, or "domestic" unpaid labor—constantly had to mediate the "public" iconicity that was conferred on them by their racial proximity to slavery, if not their status as slaves or ex-slaves.[20] Even as they "exploited" their own conditions of working exploitation to contest their racial and gendered debasement, this selfsame autobiographical publicity could reinscribe their hypervisibility, not simply as gender deviants, but as representatives of African Americans' racial degeneracy. Even if the labor of white women potentially degendered them, this degradation was not seen as a racial characteristic, or as testifying to the nature of *all* white women. Because of the representational dynamics of racial synecdoche—wherein one ethnically or racially marked individual is perceived to represent the whole race—black women's degradation as workers could and did become easily conflated with notions of blackness—male and female—as racially degenerate.[21]

This last historical fact points to a frequently overlooked, yet critical, irony pertaining to current understandings of abolition as emancipatory and as a prime rhetorical medium for racial legitimation. Inasmuch as the racial integrity of black men was founded in their claims (as heads of households) to the middle-class and patriarchal imperatives of U.S. masculinity, black women's self-supporting labor could undermine their status as the "dependents" of these men and invert the conventional schema of household authority. When Rebecca Brown commended Chloe Spear, an enterprising former slave, for the "habits of industry and economy" that enabled her to earn enough money to buy a house, she spoke of Spear's husband as "being of a different turn of mind from herself and not seriously disposed," as one who "possessed none of the refinement, or economy, for which his companion was so remarkable," and as "taking his rest" while Spear, "after returning from a hard day's work . . . went to washing . . . in the night." In other words, while there is no real evidence in the narrative to mark Spear's husband as indolent, he appears disadvantaged by Spear's industry and lacking in a husband's authority for Brown (the white, female author of Spear's narrative). This inverted dynamic is further exacerbated by the fact that Spear, as a married woman, needed her husband's permission to purchase a house for which she had earned the money.[22] Another narrative, that of Elleanor Eldridge, who was in her day the richest African American in Rhode Island, also speaks to the problematic status of enterprising, married women—in Eldridge's case she was advised by a relative *not* to marry since it was "a WASTE OF TIME." Eldridge never married.[23]

Antebellum African American newspapers amply demonstrate that the ideals of domesticity and the "cult of true womanhood" prevailed in black communities. These communities were concerned with countering stereotypes of feminized slave men and publicly available black women, even when these ideals belied the economic realities in these communities. In copious advice columns, newspaper editors made it clear that black women's respectability and propriety were of paramount importance to the community's efforts at "self-elevation," in effect disparaging the qualities a woman needed to succeed in earning her own living. As one newspaper advised, "one of the chief beauties in a female character is that modest reserve, that retiring delicacy which avoids the public eye, and is disconcerted even at the gaze of admiration." As for intelligence, "A moderate understanding, with diligent and well directed application will go much further than a lively genius," said another article, adding, especially "if attended with that impatience and inattention which too often accompany quick parts." Whereas men "are made to be their own masters" and are "intended by nature, to be the lord of his own household," the nature of women "on the contrary, may be perfectly developed within the domestic circle alone. . . . Her character will not have that high and intellectual tone which distinguishes a highly liberal state of society (and especially the English and American women) but it may possess all goodness and gentleness."[24] With the exception of an occasional story of a female slave who escapes from slavery, black working women and their labors remain largely invisible.[25]

The dominance of abolition-reform discourse in formulating racial equality during the 1850s meant that black working women in general, and these autobiographers in particular, increasingly confronted a dilemma in which their venue for legitimation could be perceived as jeopardizing the whole race—a dilemma that meant the stakes were high when Truth, Potter, Wilson, and Keckley decided to publicize and confront the long history of contradictions, exploitations, and negotiations that characterized the experience of black working women in the United States.

The Problems of Black Women's Labor (Past)

Since colonial days, black women's public agricultural labor (waged and enslaved) was viewed as absolutely necessary to the country's development, yet this same labor could also potentially jeopardize African American men's social legitimacy. In the colonial period, this labor—slave, free, married, or single—was subject to taxation and marked black women's productivity from its inception in the United States as an economic obstruction to the patriarchal masculinity norms that grounded claims to African American racial legitimacy.[26] Since the labor of black women was taxed, in contrast to that of white women, it posed a financial burden on black families that it did not pose for Euro-American families. This racializing asymmetry in tax structures for gendered labor furthermore stigmatized female agricultural labor and linked it to low status and servility. What did this mean for black couples? In the words of one historian, "This stigma, in combination with the genuine financial hardship created by taxes, possibly may have decreased a free black woman's chances of marriage and membership in the kin networks that enhanced social and economic status. Forced to pay extra taxes for an African wife, a free man might have thought twice about marrying her."[27] For black men, once they were prohibited from marrying white women, black women's primary status as labor made it increasingly difficult to achieve the patriarchal family forms that were crucial to men's status in colonial communities.

Unsurprisingly, given this national "prehistory," black working women featured prominently in discourses associating manual and menial labor with women's degradation, a fact to which Olmsted's antislavery account of female slaves attests. Ironically, when abolitionists portrayed black women as middle-class "true women" to counter beliefs in black women's inferiority, they invoked gender ideals and stereotypes of black working women's sexual degradation that were at odds with the economic realities of the free black community. Consequently, when working women autobiographers described the social relations of their work, they not only engaged hegemonic discourses on gender; they also confronted *counter*-hegemonic discourses on reform and abolition that we have perceived to this day as entirely emancipatory and as the main, "default" languages for racial liberation. This is not to discount the role of abolitionist discourse in advancing African Americans' claims to civic entitlement during the antebellum period, but to stress, rather, how these autobiographies complicate our narratives about this period.

Given these historical and rhetorical contexts, black working women who valued their nondomestic or non-reform-oriented paid labor as a means of generating economic independence could be seen as challenging the free black community's emphasis on the bourgeois propriety of its women.[28] While it is hard to find instances of a newspaper singling out and condemning the population of black working women (as I mentioned above, these women would be almost entirely invisible had they not advertised their services as milliners or lodging-house keepers in these papers), this concern with propriety dictated the suspect status of all women's public labor. In a lengthy complaint about ubiquitous working women in Europe, one writer lamented that "the age of chivalry has passed from Europe"; as witness to a wide variety of European women's labor—making mortar, digging cellars, sawing wood, and dragging coal in the "public streets of the metropolis"—this writer advised that these "offices of hardship and notoriety" were "totally incompatible" with "heaven-given womanly nature."[29] Rather than testifying to their initiative and resilience, black working women's self-sufficiency potentially highlighted black men's inability to enact the normative patriarchal identities on which legitimacy in the antebellum public spheres was predicated.[30] As workers, as writers, and as narrators, Sojourner Truth, Eliza Potter, Harriet Wilson, and Elizabeth Keckley needed to negotiate this overdetermined "public" status, not only in relation to white audiences' assumptions about black women's racial inferiority, but in relation to black reformers' efforts to represent black women as middle-class domestic subjects.[31]

African American newspapers' ideological affinity for black women's domesticity at times contradicted the perspective the black press took on the economic realities of freedpeople and the significance of black women's labor. In particular, reformers often cited black workers' severely restricted labor mobility as proof of slavery's effects on the North's social and economic structure. In a capitalizing and racialized class hierarchy, black men were increasingly excluded from skilled trades and almost entirely excluded from the ranks of a growing professional class.[32] African American men's low wages made it difficult for them to support their families and this made the labor of black women, the only group lower than African American men in the economic hierarchy, absolutely necessary.[33] But when Maria Stewart, Frederick Douglass, and Martin Delany, among others, engaged with black workers' restricted mobility, they tended to diagnose it as a racial problem that could be overcome once black men were able to enter the skilled and professional ranks of labor—entirely bypassing discussions of the relevance of black women's labor.

Of course it made obvious sense to insist on making better-paid skilled labor available to black workers (and efforts to found manual labor schools throughout the era manifest this concern), but ironically, in advocating on behalf of black workers consigned to menial employments, reformers at times depicted black workers as acquiescent, and even complacent, in the face of this discrimination. As

Douglass exhorted in 1853 in making the case for black men to abandon menial service jobs, "Now, colored men, what do you mean to do, for you must do something? The American Colonization Society tells you to go to Liberia. Mr. Bibb tells you to go to Canada. Others tell you to go to school. We tell you to go to work; and to work you must go or die. Men are not valued in this country, or in any country, for what they *are*; they are valued for what they can *do*. It is in vain that we talk about being men, if we do not the work of men."[34]

It is anyone's guess how working men would have responded to being told to "do something" and to "go to work," or how one of those men working in menial jobs would feel about being told that "he must make himself useful, and his usefulness will be acknowledged," as if only trade occupations were socially "useful."[35] In another forum, Douglass (perhaps inadvertently) reinforced views about these workers' dependency: "I am yet of the opinion that nothing can be done for the free colored people—remaining in their present employment. These employments—such as waiting at hotels, on steamboats, barbering in large cities, and the like—contribute to no solid character. They require servility, beget dependence, destroy self-reliance, and furnish leisure and temptation to every possible view from smoking cigars to drinking whiskey."[36] In this regard, one historian has pointed to an important ambivalence in black leaders' recognition that the discrimination against the group reinforced the stigma of the labor: "As in the case of other forms of drudge work, critics of 'menial service' labor nevertheless often suggested that there was a quality intrinsic to such work that blighted the character of those who undertook it. Porters and barbers, Douglass argued, were led into improvidence and vice by their attempts to ape the rich whom they served."[37]

Against this background, African American women, excluded from most trades and laboring as manual workers and domestic servants, potentially reinforced prevailing views of blacks' "servility."[38] In another essay published in the *North Star* Douglass again complained of the propensity of blacks to fill menial employments. This time, he made it clear that women shared in the perils attributable to blacks' high concentration in urban areas: in cities, working blacks became "engaged as waiters about hotels, barbers or boot-blacks, and the women washing white people's clothes."[39] In her speeches to the black community, Maria Stewart, a former domestic servant herself, emphasized education and aspirations to "head-work" as a way for black women to escape being "compelled to bury their minds and talents beneath a load of iron pots and kettles. . . . The Americans have practiced nothing but head-work these 200 years, and we have done their drudgery."[40] While her appeal to educate black women was not in itself critical of domestic servants, Stewart's reference to "drudgery" rang a note of resentment echoed by other black leaders that potentially conflated critique of the occupation with criticism of those occupying it.

As the debate at the 1848 Colored Convention in Cleveland makes clear, Douglass's opinions on the peril inhering in these employments were widely shared, and were no doubt themselves influenced by prevalent biases in the black community. Martin Delany, the leader who was perhaps most outspoken on this issue, was so adamantly opposed to black women's serving white men's wives that he managed to provoke the ire of some of the delegates to the convention. Having offered up a resolution in which he "excoriated" those who took domestic service employment in white households, Delany was disciplined by one delegate, J. D. Patterson, who said that "those . . . not in the places of servants, must not cast slurs upon those, who were in such places from necessity."[41] Delany later made clearer the patriarchal imperative underwriting his contempt for black women's domestic service: "Our mothers [are] their nurse-women, our sisters their scrub-women, our daughters their maid-women, and our wives their washer-women. Until colored men, attain to a position above permitting their mothers, sisters, wives and daughters, to do the drudgery and menial offices of other men's wives and daughters; it is useless, it is nonsense, it is pitiable mockery, to talk about equality and elevation in society."[42] Despite a general awareness that black working women had few options available to them, debates about racial "elevation" were largely predicated on the reproduction of a male-headed household in which "wives," "daughters," and "sisters" would be free to perform the (unpaid) domestic labor the race most needed: the labor to "create in the minds of your little girls and boys a thirst for knowledge, the love of virtue, the abhorrence of vice, and the cultivation of a pure heart."[43]

Recent accounts of nineteenth-century debates within northern black communities have traced the latent conservatism in some forms of this "self-elevating" abolitionist-reform discourse and its related "politics of respectability."[44] This was the contradiction "One Who Works" pinpointed in her complaint to the *Weekly Anglo-African*: though everyone recognized that it was more "honorable" to work than to be "idle," as she observed, it was those who best enacted forms of middle-class personhood—those "who do nothing but dress and promenade"—who were deemed the "lions of society." As her rebuke to "our reformers" indicated, these intraracial politics for class could preclude those who did not conform to middle-class gender models from appearing "honorable" or respectable. Consequently, when working women wrote their stories of work, they risked exposing the paradoxical nature of uplift ideologies that equated black working women's low status with their inability to enact middle-class models of domestic femininity. This cultural conundrum—in which emancipatory rhetorics reproduced a different form of subjugation—meant that autobiographical representations of black working women's agency traversed a very contradictory rhetorical terrain in which they featured simultaneously as powerful and problematic: they could be seen as referring to democratic discourses promoting the "dignity of labor," but they could also evoke the potential contradictions at play in the discourses of a transforming economy that continually reorganized—rather than did away with—forms of social hierarchy along lines of middle-class race and gender norms.[45]

Because of their shared emphasis on self-supporting labor, Truth, Wilson, Potter, and Keckley's texts all maintain something of an anomalous, or marginal, status in relation to the protest and reform narratives that form the bulk of the black autobiographical tradition. While critical work in the field of African American literature has long recognized the emergence of slave and black autobiography from the period's abolitionist literary culture, the efforts of those members of the black community who were marginal to abolition or reform efforts have long been overlooked. In this context, Sojourner Truth's isolated activism within the movement in which she figured so prominently illustrates the potentially vexed role working women played among the ranks of the mostly educated and professional black reformers who comprised antebellum America's illustrious abolitionists.[46] This vexed status is palpably evident in Frederick Douglass's account of his 1840s encounter with Truth at the Northampton Association. Though Truth was considered "honest, industrious, and amiable" by the residents of the Northampton, Massachusetts, community, Douglass highlighted the cultural differences that existed between himself and the older woman: "[Truth] seemed to feel it her duty to trip me up in my speeches and to ridicule my efforts to speak and act like a person of cultivation and refinement. . . . She was a genuine specimen of the uncultured negro. She cared very little for elegance of speech or refinement of manners. She seemed to please herself and others best when she put her ideas in the oddest forms. . . . Her quaint speeches easily gave her an audience."[47] Although Truth was renowned for her popular speech, Douglass's comments on her efforts to "trip" him up for his, combined with his invocation of the minstrel-like "genuine" Negro, suggest the potential conflict posed by Truth's popular class style. Most accounts of Truth's difference from her younger abolitionist peers have focused on her unlettered status and independent persona, but I believe the problem (which Truth shared with the other authors I consider) derived from her insistence in framing her life story from a working perspective that potentially conflicted with the middle-class, generic imperatives of the dominant abolitionist paradigm.[48]

In the last few decades, African Americanist–feminist critics and literary scholars have established the central role of nineteenth-century black women in the ranks of abolitionists, correcting years of historical work that overlooked women's participation in and leadership of antislavery movements. These scholars have produced rich accounts of how black women made a place for themselves in a literary public sphere that condemned their appearance, in print and on the platform, before "promiscuous" (mixed sex) audiences.[49] In this vital tradition, the work of religious and abolitionist reformers looms large. Preachers Jarena Lee (1783–?) and Zilpha Elaw (1790–?), former slaves Mary Prince (1788–?) and Harriet Jacobs (1815–97), free-born traveler Nancy Prince (1799–?) and others, used their autobiographies to empower themselves and to affirm black women's status as spiritually and socially "redeemed" by publicizing their spirituality and abolitionist activism.[50]

In their texts, Maria Stewart and Jarena Lee, for example, assumed the right to agitate and to preach, authorizing themselves on the basis of their spirituality or involvement in reform.[51] When they deployed reform and spirituality to counter devaluations of black femininity, Stewart and Lee simultaneously constructed racialized forms of womanhood that allowed them the psychological interiority typically denied black women.[52] In so doing, these women helped set the stage for others, like Nancy Prince and Frances Ellen Watkins Harper, who assumed central roles in later reform efforts of various kinds: emigration to Jamaica, temperance, women's rights, abolition, and uplift. What these activities meant was that for women engaged in activism within the black community, their literary construction of self-worth was most often predicated on representing their efforts as activists on behalf of the "race," stressing their public identities as what would be called, after the war, "race women."[53] It was in this context that a writer in the *North Star* affirmed these women's role as race workers: "Let woman be free to carry forward the great work of regenerating public sentiment."[54] Because nineteenth-century black women featured discursively almost entirely in relation to the work or "labor" of racial reform, and rarely as self-supporting or independent women, black women *workers* are still seen as marginal to the rich literary tradition of black women.

Against this presumption of black women's engagement in advancing the race, even former slave women who risked their standing in the community with their stories of sexual vulnerability could embed their narratives within this activist vein, positioning their publication as a form of self-sacrifice in the name of other slaves, family, or children that they desired to redeem from slavery. This is the case with Harriet Jacobs's text *Incidents in the Life of a Slave Girl* (1861), which has, since its "revival" in the 1970s and 1980s, become the most known and read black woman's text from the period.[55] While Jacobs's description of her difficult sexual history as a slave tested contemporary norms of propriety, we can see *Incidents* as occupying a dialogical literary space that challenges the equation of propriety with privacy but continues in the tradition of a black femininity willing to sacrifice (in this case, one's "character") for other slave women. In this way text and author rearticulate forms of selflessness and duty closely related to dominant understandings of the "domestic woman."[56]

To modern readers accustomed to inferring the sexual abuse of slave women in the silences and oblique accounts common to the period, Jacobs's comparatively frank analysis of slave women's sexual "degradation" and her insistence on the fact that "slavery is far worse for women than for men" contribute to a strong and, at times, single-minded interest in her text. The almost exclusively sexual analysis that drives interest in and criticism of Jacobs's text has had the effect of making *Incidents* appear to represent all antebellum black women's experience of gender; thus it allows us to overlook the ways in which her text might not be representative. Though we might recognize the way that the standing of Jacobs's family in the community, along with her color, made her more the exception than the rule among slave women, the account of gender oppression at the heart of her text so dominates our interpretive frameworks for black women's texts that we have not fully explored how black women might have written about different things, with other sensibilities and audiences in mind, and without necessarily being defensive about their womanhood in the same way as Jacobs.

It is not that Jacobs herself does not represent labor—she does. She assists in caring for the household's children, and at times she speaks of sewing.[57] But, I would argue, the main form of her own labor that she emphasizes, independent and single as she is ("Reader, my story ends with freedom, not with marriage"), is unpaid domestic labor: the labor of saving her children from slavery as a slave mother. Through the domestic work of mothering, Jacobs revises antebellum norms for womanhood so as to include a formerly enslaved woman and to position herself as her readers' equal rather than as their social inferior. In something of a contrast, the only woman who occupies center stage as a worker in *Incidents* is Jacobs's entrepreneurial (emancipated) grandmother, whose "faithful" labor earns her the respect of the town's white women and enables her to acquire her freedom. Though her grandmother obviously commands Jacobs's respect and affection, she is portrayed as an anachronism, apparently unaware of and unwilling to account for the moral, sexual dilemmas that "Linda" confronts, though from what we can see, her own sexual history followed a very similar pattern.[58] And while the goodwill the grandmother generates in the community as a baker of fine crackers is responsible for her eventual emancipation, Jacobs, once in the North, resists her own employer's efforts to buy her to emancipate her. Even if there is a way that "Linda" can relate to and feel proud of her grandmother's independence and self-reliance, grandmother is a figure from a prelapsarian past to which Linda/Jacobs and *Incidents* readers cannot realistically resort. In the end, though Jacobs is critical of and revises norms for domestic subjectivity that make it an impropriety or "crime" for white women to hear what slave women experience, it is her identification with readers through motherhood, not her difference from them as a working woman, that speaks to her participation in sentimental and/or domestic forms of middle-class femininity.[59]

Notwithstanding the revisions enacted by the spiritual-activist model at the heart of black women's autobiographical traditions, the hairdresser, dressmaker, servant, and field worker studied below troubled the boundaries of the "domestic woman" (or "race woman") when they recast gendered (and typically unremunerated) "duty" to include the virtue of paid labor that was completely unrelated to the cause of racial reform. When Potter, Keckley, Wilson, and Truth highlighted the rewards of non-reform-oriented and public labor, they risked being seen as "unfit" for domestic duties and perceived as indecorously independent. Eliza Potter made this vexed connection to sentimental discourses on womanhood clear when she joked sarcastically about succumbing to marriage (on the second page of her text!), saying, "I need not be ashamed to own having committed a weakness, which has, from the beginning of time, numbered the most respectable of the earth among its *victims*."[60] These texts' dynamics outlined the potential anxieties many shared about working women: if successful, the independence they enjoyed could be at odds with propriety. Given the importance of black women's propriety to the antislavery movement and the high stakes involved, abolitionists were unlikely to view even the most remote possibility of impropriety as tolerable.

Yet it is important to note that these women did not recast the ideological parameters of domestic womanhood because they necessarily saw themselves as gender radicals: they were not interested so much in flouting propriety per se as they were in *publicizing*, rather than *apologizing* for, the value of their often-disparaged and invisible work. They wrote their autobiographies in part to establish the value of female independence and female self-reliance as enacting another form of republican virtue. In this manner, their texts mark both the continuities and discontinuities of a black female autobiographical tradition that instantiated notions of black womanhood as multi-dimensional, a black working womanhood that was not "static or a single ideal," to borrow a phrase from Nellie McKay.[61]

The Problems of Black Women's Labor (Present): Why Labor?

As obvious as the contributions of black working women might appear, it is important to note for modern readers that contemporary scholarship has for the most part perpetuated the erasures of laboring subjectivity and contradictions common to nineteenth-century reform discourses on race and gender. In particular, as a result of historical paradigms centered on reform and resistance, these women's efforts to represent their labor continue to be contested and easily misinterpreted. While historians have amply documented free and enslaved women's diverse labor in white and black communities, this evidence still exists in uneasy tension with claims about the oppositional relationship of African American "identity" to work, and about the black community's particular resistance to the degendering often associated with black women's labor in the marketplace.[62] Despite positive assessments of black women's self-supporting labor, even today many scholars agree with influential critic Paul Gilroy that "for the descendants of slaves, work signifies only servitude, misery, and subordination."[63] Another assessment of black working women, "When Your Work Is Not Who You Are," makes a similar argument.[64] In this vein, the low status of black women's labor is often invoked, tautologically, as evidence of its irrelevance to black women's self-production and self-representation. Consequently, the most compelling formulations of black female subjectivity remain those perceived as openly resisting subordinated labor, and black women writers who were neither "race women" or ideologically radical remain invisible.[65]

Cultural and literary race studies have also perpetuated this invisibility: for the most part, they have shied away from discussions of class and race in their explorations of African American texts, perhaps because today many scholars equate a concern with labor with traditional (and to some, outdated) categories of Marxist analysis. Since the late 1980s, trends in African American literary studies have emphasized the literariness of African American texts, turning away from what one eminent scholar termed the "race and superstructure" considerations of the 1970s "Black Aesthetic."[66] But in so doing, many scholars have failed to heed Stuart Hall's admonition to view work and the economic as "the necessary, but not sufficient" condition for understanding the interrelatedness of cultural logics for race, gender, and class.[67] With the exception of labor histories that have explored how the slave served as a figure of oppression for feminists, temperance activists, and white workers, as well as the integral role of race in formations of white labor, the cultural role of labor in discursive constructions of black femininity has been neglected.[68]

These women's autobiographies call for new interpretive perspectives on antebellum black women's labor that can elaborate this labor's specificity and its "literariness" without defining it solely in relation to critical paradigms for resistance or Marxist categories of value that are inadequate to this task. They call for analyses of labor that can trace the meanings produced, evoked, and shaped by historically situated agents and work practices. This means attending to labor's conflicted representational status during a period of profound social, economic, and cultural transformations, a period in which heterogeneous and unstable labor languages afforded these women unrecognized opportunities to redeploy their exploitation and transform it rhetorically in their autobiographies.[69] It calls for deliberate consideration of how these women negotiated the "structural constraints" that limited them as black working women as well as the "conjunctural opportunities" that they could enact.[70] These autobiographies attest to both, constraints and opportunities, and allow us to shed light on the improvisatory nature of these women's rhetorical strategies. How else are we to understand Sojourner Truth's transformation of her coerced enslaved field labor into republicanlike yeoman labor or to discern Harriet Wilson's claim to self-reliance in the ironic titling of *Our Nig*? Only by imagining the cultural relevance of these women's representations of work can we see how they rewrote the terms of their work-related constraints into narratives of "working womanhood." As provisional, or improvised, discursive spaces, these narratives literarily externalize the potential autonomy of black women's independent labor and make visible these women's participation in labor ideologies of "honorable independence," citizenship, and self-reliant femininity, to repeat the claim of "One Who Works."

I have employed economic theories, histories, and sociologies of labor in this analysis of black working women's heterogeneous labor in order to produce a wide-ranging account of this labor's uneven and contradictory status. Located at the intersection of two disparaging rubrics for race, gender, and labor—"nigger work" and "women's work"—this labor's symbolic devaluation was inextricably bound to a national history of exploitation that was related to but not entirely subsumed by slavery's forms of labor. These black women workers intervened in this devaluation by describing their confrontations with economic necessity and coercion as producing social, economic, and cultural value, by making their labor rhetorically visible, and by testifying to the historically and culturally variable nature of labor practices and representations. Their descriptions of the meanings, social relations, and representational economies of their work speak to the very processes through which their labor achieved meaning and cultural intelligibility as "work" or as "vocation," as "servile" and "drudgery," or as "honorable." We can trace these meanings only if we stop assuming the political implications of black women's labor and stop looking for resistance alone; then we might imagine anew how these women claimed the social value of what Marx defined as "alienated" labor, of labor we have not even imagined as "theirs."

My analysis of the cultural role of labor in discursive constructions of black womanhood interrogates, rather than assumes, the manner in which these women cultivated work meanings that were aligned or disaligned, or even "made do," with cultural understandings for race, gender, and work.[71] It does not "reduce" these meanings to the "economic"; rather it perceives these meanings as referring to various forms of capital—symbolic, cultural, social, and economic—as so many different modalities of representation through which these women try to make visible the symbolic surplus value they claim to have generated.[72] Furthermore, because these representations of work referred to multiple systems of value, we cannot assume a priori the class meanings or identifications associated with the work represented. Rather than ascribing simple one-to-one correspondences of these women's status as workers with discrete class positions—either "working" or "middle" class—or trying to delineate some spectrum of these women's "representativeness" in relation to taxonomies for class, race, and gender, I view these women's improvised accounts of work as sometimes refuting and sometimes appealing to the delimiting parameters associated with class-, race-, or gender-based accounts of identity.[73] This approach has allowed me to make sense of how a former slave woman who bought her freedom could still strive to earn the respect of slaveowners (Keckley), or how an exquisitely dressed hairdresser could represent herself as a "poor working woman" (Potter), or how a freed slave could decide to boycott the North's free labor system (Truth). It also enables us to read these texts as testifying to the dynamic and uneven processes of class development that historians have discerned at work in dominant discourses from the period, both inside and outside the black community.[74]

The heterogeneous forms of labor these women describe in their texts call for a flexible accounting of what constitutes "work" and the kinds of value "work" produces. Not surprisingly, for the most part, these working women refute divisions of labor along multiple axes—not simply between axes of race and gender, but within categories for labor. They do not adhere to conventions that denote some labor as skilled "work" in contrast with unskilled mass "labor," to invoke Hannah Arendt's taxonomy,[75] and they resist the prevalent ideological binary of the time that classified labor as either "unproductive" or "productive."[76] In this way, they broke away from the productivist models for racial progress that black leaders espoused when they emphasized African Americans' participation in commodity-producing or professional forms of (mostly male) labor over service work. When Eliza Potter, for example, compares herself to the doctor and the minister in the "Appeal" to her book, she invokes the "face to face" nature and confidentiality of hairdressing as the basis for a professional identity not typically associated with the common hairdresser. She promotes herself as an "expert," not simply in hair, but in "beauty" and in elite women's performances of femininity. That is, like other women who were excluded from the pool of industrial workers, for Potter "work" and an "occupation" were not only activities performed either in factories or in other people's homes: these terms referred to the whole network of social relations structuring their work practices as much as they referred to the assumed end product of their work, whether that was a stylishly dressed head of hair or a middle-class woman's efficiently run house.

Likewise, the wide-ranging kinds of value these women depict as their labor's end-products provide us with a sense of the often shifting and fluid nature of their racial and gender identities. They go beyond conventional descriptions of what their labor produced to provide an inventory of several types of value, ranging from white privilege to self-worth, from black respectability to sexual and racial equality, egalitarian reform, and even alternative family models. In this way as well, they do not rely on any single identitarian category, such as race or gender, to describe the overdetermined and unstable practices comprising black working women's subjectivities. Rather than speaking of "African American femininity," we would be more precise to say we are accounting for a range of "black femininities" and framing these autobiographies in relation to forms of intraracial difference along the multiple axes of race, color, class, and gender.[77] Only in this manner can we begin to account for how black women might have resisted these structures of laboring coercion from within, when upward mobility or "elevation" did not appear to be an option.

Elizabeth Keckley, for example, who worked as a skilled dressmaker while a slave, interpreted her ability to support an entire family (slaveowners included) with her needle as a sign of her worth, not of her collusion with slavery. She perceived herself as contributing to her employers' femininity and, in turn, saw herself as participating in this femininity through the respect and confidence her employers showed her. To Keckley, the social relations of her work proved her claim that she was "worth her salt." Likewise, Sojourner Truth's description of her industriousness as an enslaved field worker refuted her own fellow slaves' observation (as reported by Truth's amanuensis, Olive Gilbert) that she was a "white man's nigger": her hard work for her master originated in her mother's legacy of honesty and spirituality, not in any desire to uphold slavery per se. When Harriet Wilson foregrounded the necessity of what was considered degraded domestic service as the Belmont's "nig," she too refuted the links between service work and degraded femininity to assert her own value as a self-reliant black working woman. Through these formulations of gendered labor and value, Keckley, Truth, Wilson, and Potter made visible the socially productive nature of labor generally deemed symbolically null and void.

Viewed through lenses that attend to the meanings of material work practices, these autobiographies expand our vocabulary and rhetorical strategies for understanding how black working women responded to, refuted, and helped to shape nineteenth-century discourses on racial legitimacy. They display the rich heterogeneity of the antebellum autobiographical tradition and offer new assessments of the multiple perspectives and rhetorical approaches that operated in dialogue with, and sometimes outside of, the values of abolition and uplift, despite the dominance of uplift and reform in the black community on the eve of the Civil War. They not only offer us the opportunity to recover the historical specificity of these women, their work, and their autobiographies; they also offer us another chance to affirm the overlooked contributions that black working women made to nineteenth-century African American, American, and women's literature.

The chapters of *Belabored Professions* pertain to each individual autobiography and map each woman's text in relation to the different discursive moments in which they appeared, ranging from 1850 to 1868. Each provides a different perspective on the contradictions and convergences at work in a nation undergoing multiple transitions: from agrarian to industrial, from slave to free, from regional to national. Each chapter takes on the specific conditions of production that mark its subject's labor as visible or invisible and as problematic or liberatory. Consequently, the chapters do not provide a chronology of black women's writings about work, but rather engage black working women's efforts to make their work rhetorically visible in sometimes overlapping, and at other times contradictory, cultural domains.

I have divided the chapters into two parts—Constraints and Opportunities—to emphasize the different vantage points from which these women tried to mediate their readers' contradictory assumptions about their occupations, and to foreground the historical and rhetorical differences that exist between the domestic workers and the skilled women working in the service of what might be called "elite femininity." While the domestic workers, Truth and Wilson, addressed the constraints in racializing processes for menial labor, Potter and Keckley emphasized the opportunities they perceived to exist in their work as "beauty," or femininity, entrepreneurs.

Chapter 1, on the 1850 *Narrative of Sojourner Truth*, explores the connection between the critical neglect of the first autobiography published by this well-known former slave and the unlettered Truth's efforts to describe her enslaved labor in ways that contradicted abolitionist genre imperatives. This narrative's publication, along with her public performances from that point onward, marked Truth's initiation into abolitionist publicity and national renown. As a former slave from the North when the abolitionist movement was becoming increasingly identified as a northern phenomenon, this narrative shows how difficult it was to integrate Truth's life story and independent persona into a publicity that depended on the firsthand testimony of fugitive slaves. Far from being the ignorant, "authentic" object of abolitionist narrative, Truth displays the same independence in relating her life story that she displayed in real life. Building on the fact that this text was not her first publicity effort, I discuss the significance of other literary antecedents on this collaboration with her abolitionist amanuensis, Olive Gilbert—a collaboration in which Truth asserts her narrating agency by comparing the honesty and industriousness that she associated with her field work while enslaved (and commemorated in her famous 1851 speech) to the competitive forms of labor she performed once she was free. My account attributes this narrative's exclusion from the black autobiographical tradition (which includes other "as told to" stories) to its conflicts over labor and redresses this oversight with an analysis that recognizes the *literary* origins of Truth's later, well-known working-class persona.

Shifting to the social relations of labor and race in Chapter 2, I employ a contrasting approach to discuss Harriet Wilson's *Our Nig* (1859). *Our Nig* is the story that Wilson (1828–63) related about the abuse and hardships she experienced at the hands of a northern employer. Born free and of mixed racial parentage in New Hampshire, Wilson entered into a form of indentured domestic service at the age of six, when her impoverished parents, no longer able to raise her, abandoned her. Her autobiographical novel speaks to the oppressive conditions that governed the lives of "free" black workers and, like Truth's earlier narrative, questions antislavery contentions about the superiority of "free labor" as well as the trajectories of slave/South–free/North embedded in many popular slave narratives. Critical emphases on the literariness of Wilson's authorship as an African American have, on the whole, I contend, overlooked the way the text spoke to the audience of black workers it invokes in its preface and engaged with problematic discourses in the black community about menial labor. My analysis suggests that an audience of black menial workers, despite its penury, would be the most familiar with Wilson's description of her northern employers' extortion of labor and its related processes of racialization. When Wilson pointed up the ironies in the nation's simultaneous exploitation and disparagement of its free black workers, she depicted the problem many black menial workers faced: the problem of withstanding the attribution of racial inferiority when these workers could not simply abandon labor structures that offered them little choice in the labor they performed. The chapter delineates Wilson's innovation as one that insists on the origins of "nig's" exploitation in the interwoven hierarchies of race and class that mystified productivity, and not simply in taxonomies for racial difference.

In the last two chapters, on hairdresser Eliza Potter and dressmaker Elizabeth Keckley, I move from considering the constraints and exploitations associated with domestic, agricultural, and menial black women's labor to exploring the opportunities that entrepreneurial work offered black women engaged in the "business" of elite femininity. Although understandings about interracial work relations between white and black women rightfully stress the structurally disadvantaged position of black working women, the contribution of *A Hairdresser's Experience in High Life* and *Behind the Scenes* to the African American literary tradition consists, ironically, in their authors' unapologetic refusals to depict themselves as victims of racial and gender domination. On the contrary, in *A Hairdresser's Experience in High Life* (1859), written by New York–born Eliza Potter (1820–?), we have perhaps the most successful and powerful depiction of the capacity of one black woman's entrepreneurial work to refute her racially subaltern status. In this lively, picaresque account of her travels in Europe and the United States prior to settling in Cincinnati, Ohio, Potter represents herself as a willing and successful participant in the nation's western expansion. Elizabeth Keckley (c. 1818–1907), who was born a slave in Virginia, also appealed to her work history as proof of her entrepreneurial femininity in her narrative *Behind the Scenes, or Thirty Years a Slave and Four Years in the White House*. In this autobiography, published in 1868, a few years after the end of the Civil War, Keckley related her own rise to respectability as a dressmaker while still a slave, and the opportunity this status afforded her to buy her freedom. Keckley, who eventually became Mary Todd Lincoln's dressmaker during the Lincoln presidency, represented her work in *Behind the Scenes* as the untold story of the interracial, sentimental bonds she enjoyed with her white, elite, female employers, whom she described as her "friends."

While Keckley and Potter were adamant opponents of slavery, their life stories are not organized along abolitionist lines (even though the first three chapters of *Behind the Scenes* qualify as a "slave narrative"); instead, they emphasize the set of spatial and social work relations that empowered the hairdresser and modiste, both economically and socially. These chapters focus on the dynamics of their authors' claims of contributing to elite white femininity, and how they refuted, like Truth and Wilson before them, but from different venues, perceptions of black women workers' necessary inferiority and incongruity to a modernizing economy. Focusing in this way on black working women's "belabored professions" of precarious independence, I hope to elucidate the life and work stories of these antebellum African American women.

I

CONSTRAINTS

I have . . . come to the immoveable conclusion, that [Americans] have, and do continue to punish us for nothing else, but for enriching them and their country. For I cannot conceive of anything else.

—David Walker, 1829

1 RACE, WORK, AND LITERARY AUTHORITY IN *THE NARRATIVE OF SOJOURNER TRUTH*

I begin this story of African American womanhood, antebellum work, and literary authority with Sojourner Truth, one of the best-known antislavery and women's rights reformers in her time and in our own. Truth's preeminence as a "doer of the word" might appear to contradict my earlier claims about the challenges that "working womanhood" posed to the reform-oriented tradition, but my account historicizes Truth's still-controversial status in contemporary criticism. Up to this day, Truth's complicated relationship with the women's movement before and after the Civil War continues to prove a battleground for feminists arguing over the implications of white feminists' appropriation of Truth's historical liminality. Her most recent biographer, Nell Irvin Painter, contends that she was popular because she was readily perceived as an "exotic" and that Truth remains a dehistoricized "symbol" of our cultural imagination, largely on account of the facility with which her contemporaries could appropriate and instrumentalize the unlettered reformer's speech.[1] Born as the slave Isabella Bomefree in upstate New York in 1797, Truth is most often considered in relation to the remarkable public speaking career she launched midlife when she began participating in the abolitionist movement at age fifty-three, twenty-two years after her emancipation. Truth's legacy has been mired in a critical dynamic that continually recasts her popularity and agency in polarizing terms: either the illiterate Truth was irredeemably susceptible to her interlocutors' agendas, or she was all-powerful.[2] Clearly, this reformer's appeal—then and now—remains to be explained convincingly.

Today's critical problems are due in part to historical difficulties that we have yet to recognize and explore. I believe one key to our questions concerning Truth's popularity resides in reassessing the historical, interpretive frameworks in which the reformer appears to

Sojourner Truth. Frontispiece from The Narrative of Sojourner Truth *(1850). Courtesy of the William L. Clements Library, University of Michigan.*

us. Truth's simultaneously vexed popularity and iconic incongruity do not simply emerge from her amanuenses' and auditors' appropriations of the reformer's words and actions; I would argue that they stem also, and most significantly, from the way Truth addressed herself to her audiences from the very start of her public career through an egalitarian, working-class persona who was misrecognized when viewed primarily as an antislavery activist. Truth's presentation as an abolitionist subject by antislavery and women's rights activists produced unexplored contradictions related to Truth's insistent valuing of her enslaved labor and the moral agency she attributed to that labor. Through this insistence, the reformer refuted prevalent understandings of slaves and workers as necessarily "ignorant" or "unfit" beings incapable of moral reasoning or elevated actions.

From this perspective, Truth's inexplicability, or public incongruity, does not appear related simply to problems of "mediation," but to another set of problems—ones that she shared with former slaves, black workers, *and* white workers: the challenges of speaking the value of antebellum labor and freedom during a period in which both labor and freedom were being commodified (dramatically illustrated in the accounts of former slaves), and in which freedom and democracy became unequivocally identified with, and rendered legitimate only in relation to, capitalist forms of (authorial) self-expression and production. Truth's critical, working-related identifications challenged antebellum reform efforts to assimilate northern workers into an industrializing order and in particular disrupted the links abolitionists had established that predicated black racial legitimacy on literacy and capitalist modes of social mobility. Furthermore, while her biographers have recognized that Truth most often operated in isolation from educated, black abolitionists, not enough has been made of how her working-class style conflicted with black leaders' efforts to "elevate" those they saw below them. This is important because it broadens our interpretive frameworks for analysis: with this piece of the puzzle in place it becomes easier to see that Truth's incongruity as agricultural and domestic worker was not simply a problem of race, but also—perhaps even more importantly—a problem of class. How else are we to interpret Frederick Douglass's description of her as "a genuine specimen of the uncultured negro" and his chagrined recall (fifty years after the meeting he describes) of how Truth "seemed to feel it her duty to trip me up in my speeches and to ridicule my efforts to speak and act like a person of cultivation and refinement. . . . She cared very little for elegance of speech or refinement of manners."[3]

Some of the reasons that we have not fully recognized the historical dynamics underlying this misrecognition lie in our historiographies of Truth, studies in which scholars ground Truth's popularity, for the most part, in the broader archive of self-representation of Truth's speeches and activities, beginning with her 1851 Akron, Ohio, speech before the Woman's Rights Convention. This archive includes the last version of her auto/biography, *The Narrative of Sojourner Truth, A Bondswoman of Olden Time*, which was produced in 1875 by Truth's friend, Frances Titus, but this text draws attention mostly for the fascinating collection of clippings and famous autographs it contains that attests to Truth's widespread reform work after 1850. What remains overlooked today (though included in the 1875 and 1878 versions of the *Narrative*) is a close reading and analysis of the most autobiographical of all the texts we have related to Truth, *The Narrative of Sojourner Truth*, which Truth self-published in 1850 with help from another amanuensis, Olive Gilbert. This focus on her public speaking has had an unintended and somewhat ironic effect in relation to this text, long excluded from discussions of the black autobiographical tradition. Nell Painter confirms, "To this day, the *Narrative* remains outside the canon of ex-slave narratives."[4] By focusing on the *Narrative* as displaced material, I argue that this unlettered woman countered representations of uneducated black workers' inferiority by emphasizing the legitimating properties of what was disparaged as manual and menial labor, the kind performed by the majority of black as well as white workers. This perspective makes the *Narrative* something much more than an antislavery text intent on representing the humanity of African Americans; it shows how a black working woman might draw on literary precedents unrelated to, and sometimes clearly conflicting with, abolition-reform. It also demonstrates how Truth's *Narrative* speaks to black working women's participation in contesting and shaping autobiographical discourses on antebellum labor and black femininity.

Today's emphasis on the vexed history of Truth's public speaking and political engagements has not only rendered Truth's marginal status in the literary tradition tacitly axiomatic; it also bespeaks literary scholars' continuing neglect of alternative forms of African American "linguistic counter-legitimacy" in favor of what are perceived as more "literary" representations of race: those narratives authenticated by the claim "written by him/herself."[5] In other words, I view Truth's invisibility in, and subordination to, an emerging African American abolitionist literary tradition as responsible in part for her modern-day hypervisibility or iconicity as "symbol." This is significant because it sheds light on another form of overlooked mediation: when educated blacks assumed the mantle of "speaking for" the mass of uneducated black workers, including slaves, they often represented them as "unfit" and needing "elevation."[6] Truth's iconoclastic perspective on the role and meanings of her enslaved and free labor —and in particular, the role of this work in establishing her literary and public authority—thus positioned her as politically heterodox to the emerging African American activist tradition, which viewed education and authorship as de facto membership criteria for the capitalizing public sphere.

Truth's 1850 *Narrative of Sojourner Truth* represents an instance of "linguistic counter-legitimacy" that provides new insights into the little-understood contributions that the "unlettered" black (and black women) workers made to the black autobiographical tradition. As such, the narrative should be read as a form of publicity that asserts the value of female slaves' agricultural and domestic labor and that, in so doing, invites us to discern the derivation of antebellum racial logics and meanings from Africans' coerced and subordinate labor for the nation.[7] While activists ranging from white workers to feminists invoked the slave as the ur-figure for oppression during this period of enormous social and economic transformations, Truth, who was opposed to slavery, nevertheless insisted on the value produced by the hardworking slave. Furthermore, in describing this labor as a basis for her public authority, Truth countered the legitimacy norms in which the emerging authority-seeking black autobiographical tradition was itself invested; she breached the decorum of racial uplift–abolition discourse with an egalitarian discourse that shed light on the socially polarizing effects of an industrializing economy.[8] Truth's exclusion from the autobiographical tradition, then, should be recast as the displacement, or untold story, of Truth's unorthodox working persona and "authorship."

The Narrative of Sojourner Truth offers us an authorship model that could best be described as one of "conflicted collaboration," a model that both manifests and obscures the challenges that Truth's emphasis on her labor—in particular, her exploitation in the "free" North—posed to abolitionists whose antislavery positions allied them with the ranks of emerging capitalists.[9] My reading of the narrating dynamics between Truth and her amanuensis in the *Narrative* highlights the discursive and literary origins of the unlettered Truth's appeal for civic recognition and social legitimacy, and suggests the significant role of this auto/biography as an antecedent to the famous 1851 speech that launched Truth's career in public speaking and activism. In the version of the Akron speech that appeared contemporaneously in the *Anti-Slavery Bugle*, Truth spelled out the connection between the agricultural labor she performed while a slave and the rhetorical claims enunciated by the Women's Rights Convention: "I want to say a few words about this matter. I am a woman's rights. . . . I have plowed and reaped and husked and chopped and mowed, and can any man do more than that?" Notwithstanding the controversy surrounding different transcriptions of this speech, one aspect remains constant in all versions of the speech: the analogy that Truth makes between her labor and her entitlement to rights.[10]

When Truth deployed this analogy she spoke the language of yeoman republicanism to subvert the connotations of moral and sexual degradation attached to black women's enslaved field labor.[11] She tapped the vein of independence associated with this rhetoric (something another well-known slave, Harriet Tubman, also did)[12] to challenge received notions of field slaves as necessarily ignorant beings unfit for citizenship. In this way, Truth refuted antislavery and reform rhetorics that portrayed uneducated workers as objects of "restraint and reform," assimilable only when they displayed adherence to middle-class norms of morality.[13] For this reason, I would argue that any assessment of the origins of Truth's iconic incongruity invites us to consider the role that Truth's deliberate efforts to disrupt these discourses played in producing this "exotic" figure, rather than attribute this incongruity solely to the effects of her appropriation of her white feminist transcribers.

Sojourner Truth (Isabella Bomefree at birth, Isabella Van Wagenen prior to her name change in 1843) was born a slave in 1797 in Ulster

County (a formerly Dutch colony), New York, about 100 miles north of New York City. She lived with three different masters prior to her emancipation in 1826.[14] As an Afro-Dutch slave at the turn of the nineteenth century in rural Ulster, where slaves made up 10 percent of the total population, Isabella's experience of slavery was similar to that of slaves around her (30 to 60 percent of white households owned one or two slaves) but very dissimilar to the southern experience of the "typical" mid-nineteenth-century slave. Between the time of her emancipation and 1843, when she became an itinerant preacher traveling in New York and New England, Truth worked most of the time as a domestic worker and occasional farmhand. Despite her intense spirituality and involvement with Methodist evangelism, she was not involved with the abolition movement nor, it appears, very involved as an activist in black schools or self-help societies. As one of her biographers relates, "She wanted to minister especially to blacks, but she often felt that when she tried to, they rebuffed her. . . . Blacks wanted to hear great preachers, Isabella explained, not ignorant ones like herself."[15]

During this time she lived with different employers as well as fellow evangelicals in an intentional community known as "The Kingdom," led by Robert Matthias, a converted Jew. The public breakup of this group in 1834–35 precipitated Isabella's first foray into the nineteenth-century world of penny-press publicity. Having left New York in 1843 to preach throughout Long Island and New England in the ensuing years, Truth (after changing her name) eventually ended up in another intentional community, the Northampton Association (in Northampton, Massachusetts), in 1846. It was there she met a group of abolitionists friendly with William Lloyd Garrison and where she became acquainted with Olive Gilbert (1801–84), the white abolitionist woman who would become her second amanuensis. Gilbert was residing near the Northampton Association during 1845–46 when, at some point, Truth approached her to collaborate on transcribing and publishing her life story. If we are tempted to see Truth as merely a naive instrument of Gilbert's abolitionism, we should remember that at that point Truth had already twice sued in New York courts and won: once for the return of her illegally sold son, and once for libel. The two women collaborated on the *Narrative* between 1846 and 1850, when it was published, during which time Gilbert also lived in Kentucky for two years. The clearly stated goal of publishing the narrative was to raise funds that would enable the homeless and propertyless Truth to buy a home for her old age and to support herself.

When Truth's narrative appeared in 1850 it was neither the first one transcribed by another person nor the first to invoke the slave's work history as a guarantor of narrating legitimacy. Narratives by William Grimes, James Pennington, William Wells Brown, and Frederick Douglass, among others, had all insisted on their protagonists' industriousness as exemplifying the capacity of all blacks (freeborn and formerly enslaved) for participating in the expansion of capitalist production.[16] In these narratives, former slaves like Pennington and Douglass focused on the racism they encountered in the North and the role of this racism in preventing the race (and by extension, the nation) from progressing and prospering. Most often they depicted black men, some of them skilled craftsmen and/or educated, as reduced to performing menial labor, often alongside less-educated whites, suggesting the way that racism impaired the upwardly identified forms of class mobility with which the free labor system was so closely associated. In these stories' retelling of the former slaves' ascendancy into social legitimacy and class mobility, occupational racism prevents the free labor system from enacting the class harmony toward which it was presumably directed.[17]

Ironically, despite evidence that Gilbert conscientiously patterned her relation of slavery after Frederick Douglass's influential 1845 *Narrative of the Life of Frederick Douglass*, it was Truth herself who transformed the genre by asserting the value of all her work as northern slave, domestic worker, and itinerant preacher and by refusing abolitionist mystifications of northern labor and class hierarchies.[18] Consequently, rather than interpreting the circumstances of Truth's autobiographical collaboration with her amanuensis as irrevocably blurring her presence or rendering it "inauthentic," I contend we should read the conflicted textual dynamics of this narrative as an analog for Truth's problematic relation to the hegemonic domains of modern authorship, racial authority, and free labor. Expanding in part on the insights of critics who derive the *Narrative*'s critical incongruity from the conversion narrative it contains, my focus on Truth's labor as slave and worker and as autobiographical collaborator tracks the implications of Truth's intense working-related identifications on the uneasy stability of slave narratives that represented the North's social and economic order as "free."[19]

The Labor of Conflicted Collaboration

This analysis builds on recent work that understands "as told to" narratives as instances of "collaborative" authorship that challenge views of unlettered subjects as the passive objects of narration.[20] This entails revising understandings of Gilbert, a friend Truth met during her participation in the labor-reforming community of the Northampton Association, as having merely instrumentalized Truth's story by shaping it into a traditional antislavery vehicle. According to these understandings, as an antislavery text, Truth's narrative is perceived as having afforded Gilbert, a white bourgeois woman, a public, literary authority charged with disciplining slaveholders and unsocialized slaves alike.[21]

Truth's work history and the labor of her narration in *The Narrative of Sojourner Truth* shed light on the complicated maneuverings that structured Truth and Gilbert's collaboration. Grounding the obscured basis of Truth's textual authority in her own labor—as slave, domestic worker, and as narrator—makes visible the conflicts inhering in this collaboration and permits us to theorize anew about Gilbert's role in the *Narrative* as well as Truth's role in crafting her public authority deliberately in response to this "frame." That is, Truth's representations of her labor at once respond to and influence Gilbert's efforts to "domesticate" the former slave's hypercompetent body. This suggests how we might begin to view Truth's contributions and ideas about her work as central to the text's authenticating force and as a major factor in the conflicts in this collaboration. By attending to the dynamics of her narration and detailing the exchanges and conflicts that take place between Gilbert and Truth in the *Narrative*, we can shed light onto the relation of this labor to the representations of it that Truth was most anxious to assert.[22] In this way we may see how Truth attempted to exploit these conflicts as opportunities for advancing her work-based discourse of civic competence and public legitimacy.

Antecedents

Gilbert's direct citations of Frederick Douglass's 1845 narrative and her insertion of several specifically southern incidents dissonant with the narrative of a northern slave make it obvious that she was patterning Truth's narrative after Douglass's earlier, well-received landmark text.[23] Yet evidence suggests that Truth herself was drawing on other textual precedents. A brief retrospective look into Truth's earlier participation in the northern public sphere reveals the origins and rhetorical force of the former slave's narrating authority. Specifically, Truth's involvement in the 1835 religious scandal surrounding the "Kingdom of Matthias" corroborates Truth's self-publicizing interjection of authority into her collaboration with Gilbert.

The discursive fields of legitimacy, public credibility, and labor sketched out in the 1850 *Narrative* are clearly linked to Truth's earlier public representation of herself, crafted on the basis of her work as a domestic servant in Gilbert Vale's *FANATICISM; ITS SOURCE AND INFLUENCE, Illustrated by the Simple Narrative of Isabella, in the case of Matthias, Mr. and Mrs. B. Folger, Mr. Pierson, Mr. Mills, Catherine, Isabella, &c. &c.—A Reply to W. L. Stone, with descriptive portraits of all the parties, while at Sing-Sing and at Third Street.—Containing the Whole Truth—And Nothing But the Truth* (New York, 1835). This book, produced at Truth's request as a form of quasi-juridical testimony, responded directly to a lawsuit that emerged out of her involvement in the Matthias cult and subsequent "scandal." By and large, recent explorations of the religious cult known as "The Kingdom of Matthias" and its scandal present Truth as innocent of the charges of sexual misconduct and larceny that were leveled against prominent cult members after the death of one of its members. "The Kingdom" was a group of evangelizing merchants and their spouses who fell under the spell of a charismatic leader, Robert Matthias. Truth lived in this community, where she was treated as a spiritual equal (that is, as equal as everyone else subordinate to Matthias) and where she found it congenial enough to remain for three years. The death of one of its members prompted intense public scrutiny into the cult's practices, which included unorthodox sexual arrangements—arrangements for the most part in which Truth did not participate. Despite her innocence in the goings-on, as a former participant Truth became an obvious public scapegoat when other white cult members sought to defend themselves against the unprecedented publicity resulting from this death.[24]

As a counter to the incriminating slanders of former cult members Mr. and Mrs. Folger, *Fanaticism* represents an unprecedented and provocative instance of Truth's early, preabolition desire to innovate a public discourse that would function as a juridical, racially legitimating form of publicity. It features a unique collaboration between Truth and Gilbert Vale, a free-thinking journalist with liberal views on race who worked with the former slave Isabella to buttress her credibility during the scandal. Furthermore, *Fanaticism* consolidates the facts and texts of the short-lived "Kingdom of Matthias" from Truth's perspective—as the title attests—by compiling incidents, gathering evidence, and producing authenticating points of view in a manner resembling the hallmark characteristics of the classic slave narrative. This discursive inheritance, in turn, enables us to sketch out an alternative hermeneutic model for recognizing Truth's tactical and idiosyncratic structuring of narrating authority in the later text, her *Narrative of Sojourner Truth.*

A broad range of continuities exists between the characteristics and concerns that inform Vale's text and the 1850 *Narrative.* In particular, the origins of Vale's text, its collaborative "authorship," and the effects of this dual authorship on its rhetorical production of credibility are of central importance. Vale's opening narration of the details relating to *Fanaticism*'s publication sheds light on Truth's motivations as well as on the foundation of Truth's credible persona in her collaboration with Vale. As Vale explains, Truth (known then as Isabella) approached him on her own initiative after she had identified him as a propitious tool for her purposes on the basis of his editorial comments on the scandal in his newspaper, *Citizen of the World.*[25] Not only does Vale make it clear that Truth chose him to effect her desired defense; he also relates how "Isabella" conceived her defense with a vivid dramatization: "When Isabella was thus informed, that a formidable book was coming out against her and Matthias, by Mrs. Folger, aided by all the Christians, she exclaimed, with much energy, (for she is really very energetic and not very timid,) 'I have got the *truth*, and I know it, and I will *crush* them with the *truth*'" (emphasis in original).[26] Vale's sense of Isabella/Truth's "energy" clearly demonstrates this unlettered woman's acute sense of the mediated and dialogic nature of antebellum publicity: although such publicity could defame her through the auspices of Mr. Stone's book, with the right tools (i.e., another book wielding the "truth") she could not only sustain her credibility but also effect her own form of retribution: "I will *crush* them."

Rather than appearing as the vulnerable and exploited unlettered object of narration, Truth herself instrumentalized the journalist. This dynamic appears confirmed inadvertently by Vale himself in the concluding statement of his introduction. As he remarks, "Thus we do her a service in publishing [her perspective], for she wishes the Truth told: and we gratify ourselves, and render a public service in laying before them the whole truth, which we have taken care to have verified in every possible case."[27] Here, the "service" that Vale provides Truth doubles as his own "public service" to a reading populace (the indeterminate "them"), inscribing the text as impartial and committed to representing "the Whole Truth—And Nothing But the Truth." If this ambivalent rendering of the text's "service" appears to mute the radical implications of publishing a black woman's "word" in direct opposition to the word of a wealthy white couple, our knowledge of Truth's subsequent name change—from Van Wagenen to Truth—registers her "wish[ing] the Truth told" as central to her control over this publicity's production and manipulation. This provisional agency, which marks Truth's "ownership" in this collaborative text, is partially manifested through the titular reference to "the simple narrative of Isabella" and is visually reproduced throughout the volume in its "Narrative of Isabella" page headings.

But it is another related dimension of the text's collaborative form that speaks to the distinctive constitution of Truth's credibility as emerging specifically from her working agency. Expecting a racist audience's disbelief of the "testimony" of a former slave, Vale felt compelled to include a sequence of "white voices" that supported Truth's (and his own) affirmations of her authenticity and credibility. To this end, Vale published a compilation of character references based entirely on Truth's work history. Despite the appearance of this effort as a sign of bad faith on Vale's part, this archive of working "character" proves that Truth herself had solicited them and had them ready, at her disposal, prior to meeting with him. As Vale relates, when he asked for proof of her credibility at their initial interview, she "thrust [them] in my hand."[28] These ten "written characters" were, without exception, letters from Truth's employers (including her former owner) that referred to the adversity Truth had overcome as a slave and that displayed Truth's motivation to erect her own public credibility on the basis of her work history. As Truth's previous masters Dumont and Van Wagenen "certify," reiterating the links between labor and credibility, Isabella "has always been a good and faithful servant . . . perfectly honest. I have always heard her well spoken of by every one that has employed her."[29] Within these "characters" the labor Truth performed as slave is recognized as valuable and productive of social character, not just economic value. In this way, Truth's work history refutes and partly transcends contemporary disparagements of slaves' labor.

This reading of *Fanaticism* allows us to see how Truth's slave (and later, domestic) work forms the bulwark of the meritorious public persona that appears at its center. This persona dramatically "testifies" to Truth's deliberate crafting of her self-representation in accordance with her desire for appearing credible in a public, juridical, and civic domain. And it is precisely this emphasis on a labor-derived credibility that conflicts with the efforts of Truth's second amanuensis, Olive Gilbert.[30] The latter, having Douglass's *Narrative* in mind, unequivocally associated most of Truth's slave labor with a brutalizing regime that refused it any legitimating function and tried hard to deploy this labor as a synecdoche for slavery's dehumanizing properties. Where Douglass spoke of his field labor as a tool for "breaking him,"[31] Truth testified to the self-reliance that this labor displayed, independent of slavery's efforts to effect (in the words of Orlando Patterson) the slave's "social death." Consequently, the link of public credibility and labor that Truth is at such pains to assert in *Fanaticism*—"I have always heard her well spoken of by every one that has employed her"—crucially contends in *The Narrative* with antislavery prerogatives that could not so readily acknowledge how a slave might imagine herself producing value from within slavery's exploitative regime. Furthermore, in light of these antislavery prerogatives, Truth's implication that the "free" North perpetuates slavery's erasure of that value would appear especially discordant. Reframing Truth in the light of *Fanaticism* as a narrator intent on representing the legitimating properties of her labor allows us to discern more readily the parameters and dynamics of the conflicts marking Truth and Gilbert's collaboration. In particular, it reveals Gilbert's battle with this agency through her consistent efforts to contain Truth's hypercompetent working body.

Contending Narrators

Framing the 1850 *Narrative* in light of the 1835 Vale text provides insight into one of the most interesting ironies to emerge from a political analysis of Gilbert's transcription. Customarily perceived as the instrumentalizing white woman, it is Gilbert, not Truth, who appears most closely invested in upholding the prerogatives established by Frederick Douglass. In a manner of speaking, then, it is Truth's, not Gilbert's, motives that are "suspect." It is precisely this suspect status in relation to black and white abolitionist norms that, I contend, gets suppressed and explained as Truth's lack of authoring agency. That is, rather than reading Truth as a subversive presence, critics invoke her unlettered status as a way of translating this subversiveness into Truth's absence as author, as it were.

Reading the 1850 *Narrative* through a model that foregrounds the conflicts marking this "collaborative" venture prompts a closer focus on the labor entailed in representing labor and in turn sketches out where "Truth" abides in this text. Through these means, then, we may reinvoke the narrating and politically subversive presence of Truth in her auto/biographical text. By combing the narrative for the sutures that characterize a dictated text, plotting the text's interlocutory relations, and marking where Truth and Gilbert intervene, we can infer the respective narrating presence of these women. Gilbert's inclusion of "direct" quotes, their logical in/coherence, and a mapping of Gilbert's opinion vis-à-vis Truth's statements shed light on the relative weight of each woman's contributions and the manner in which these contributions "speak" to each other as well. While critics have for the most part been unwilling to cede credibility to Gilbert's reporting of Truth's speech, I believe that working through the internal coherence and frequent contentiousness displayed in these instances of "direct" speech permits us to view them as *approximations* indispensable to pinpointing Truth's often contrary logic. Furthermore, while some may object to Gilbert's reporting of Truth's speech in "standard" English, this representation lessens the inescapable static and subordinating effects attending so many renditions of black speech.[32] These methods allow us to evoke the unlettered Truth's narrating authority, as well as her aims in representing the nexus of labor, credibility, and authority in which she was irrevocably bound as both a slave and as a freedwoman.

One passage in particular, early in the *Narrative*, provides us with a paradigm for the interlocutory relations of work, conflict, and collaboration that permeate the entire text. It pointedly illustrates one of Gilbert and Truth's early contacts as a site in which these women's vastly different views of slavery's work and social relations collide and implode into the narrative. This site of contention paradigmatically addresses the economic value ascribed to slaves by slaveholders, abolitionists, and slaves themselves. It also illustrates how rhetorical struggles over this value refracted the political and social disputes of the growing sectional crisis. Specifically, in this passage, which describes the bad blood that existed between Isabella and her mistress Mrs. Dumont (the wife of Truth's principal master), Gilbert clearly sees the opportunity to disavow the benevolent paternalism that slavery's apologists invoked to justify enslavement. Here the point should be made that Truth does not reject Gilbert's attack on proslavery benevolence per se, but rather the discursive effects that result from the amanuensis's antislavery depiction of the slave.

Gilbert's description of the mistress-slave relation speaks to antislavery beliefs that viewed slave labor as irremediably degraded and inefficient.[33] It reproduces an antislavery logic that potentially exacerbated, rather than ameliorated, slavery's portrayal of the slave as debased. When Gilbert invokes the degraded slave to make the slaveholder's cruelty visible, she paradoxically represents the slave as provoking the slaveholder's cruelty. That is, Gilbert frames Mrs. Dumont's cruelty to Isabella as stemming from the former's unfamiliarity with the inefficient and "down-trodden" slave:[34]

> But Mrs. Dumont, who had been born and educated in a non-slaveholding family, and, like many others, used only to work-people, who, under the most stimulating of human motives, were willing to put forth their every energy, could not have patience with

> the creeping gait, the dull understanding, or see any cause for the listless manners and careless, slovenly habits of the poor downtrodden outcast—entirely forgetting that every high and efficient motive had been removed far from him; and that, had not his very intellect been crushed out of him, the slave would find little ground for aught but hopeless despondency. (18)

When Gilbert represents Mrs. Dumont's cruelty as part of the unfamiliar-northerner-corrupted-by-slavery plot, she obscures the mistress's power over the slave. Her antislavery logic not only effectively conceals the earlier existence of northern slavery, it also reveals itself as radically anti-*slave* since it precludes any recuperation of the value slaves produced. And so, by refuting slaveholders' postulated benevolence, Gilbert, like many abolitionists, also refuted the possibility of cultivating reader sympathy on the basis that the slave might have been hardworking and may have even produced value. At the time of writing (not just in Isabella's past life as slave), Gilbert makes it almost impossible for a former slave to derive any benefit from her own slave labor, regardless of if she might desire to be represented as something more than the "brute" slave that slavery and antislavery imagine her to be.

Unsurprisingly, in this paradigmatic case, Truth covertly intervenes in the paragraph that follows. To counteract this regressive portrayal, Truth does not explicitly disagree with Gilbert's stereotyping; rather, she insists on relating an anecdote that proceeds with alacrity to dispel any idea of Truth resembling the "listless" and "careless" generic slave Gilbert invokes. When she concludes her account of the slave worker's ineptitude, Gilbert refers to her censorship of other details involving Isabella and Mrs. Dumont's relationship—it is partly in relation to this passage that biographer Nell Painter speculates that Mrs. Dumont sexually abused Isabella—but then she explicitly breaches this censorship with an "exception" to this rule *proposed by Truth*. As she proceeds, Gilbert remarks, "One comparatively trifling incident she wishes related, as it made a deep impression on her mind at the time" (18). This comment signals Truth's mediation of Gilbert's description of the slave-mistress relationship, even as it reveals Gilbert's failure to view this intervention as anything but irrelevant—"comparatively trifling"—to her.

At this moment, with respect to Truth's insistence, Gilbert relates a conspiracy by Mrs. Dumont and one of her "free" hired girls to damage Isabella's good standing with her master. This anecdote makes clear that Mr. Dumont's evident appreciation of Isabella's efficiency, and not the postulated inefficiency of the generic "listless" slave, is what provokes the jealous Mrs. Dumont's cruelty to Isabella.[35] Rather than the "creeping gait" and "crushed" intellect to which Gilbert attributes Mrs. Dumont's hostility, Truth's account (and later her speech) insists that Mr. Dumont holds a different view of her labor: "[Mr. Dumont] often shielded [Truth] from the attacks and accusations of others, praising her for her readiness and ability to work, and these praises seemed to foster a spirit of hostility to her, in the minds of Mrs. Dumont and her white servant" (18). Isabella's labor generates conflict between Mr. and Mrs. Dumont on account of its efficiency, not its inefficiency. Mr. Dumont's obvious appreciation of this labor produces the friction between the master and mistress, which the mistress later projects onto the slave herself. As Gilbert/Truth relate, "Her master insisted that she could do as much work as half-a-dozen common people, and do it well, too; whilst her mistress insisted that the first was true, only because it ever came from her hand but half performed" (19). As a result, when Isabella's potatoes suddenly take on a "dingy" appearance one morning (because the hired girl has been dumping ashes onto them), Truth's framing of the conflict ensures that readers suspect foul play rather than the former slave's ineptitude.

Truth's ensuing narration deploys her mistress's wrongful attribution of laziness as a foil for proving her own worth to her amanuensis, Gilbert, and by extension, to her readers. For it is according to Gilbert that we learn that the Dumonts' young daughter, Gertrude, decides to befriend Isabella by watching Isabella's pot while the latter goes out to do the milking. When Gertrude spies Mrs. Dumont's servant dumping ashes into the pot, she loudly vindicates Isabella: "[Gertrude] repeated her story to every new comer, till the fraud was made as public as the censure of Isabella had been" (20). At this point, Gilbert's conclusion also reflects this vindication; her comment on Isabella's restored standing emphasizes the publicity value that this exposure affords the master to reaffirm his judgment of Isabella's worth, as if Gilbert too had never entertained any doubt regarding it: "It was a fine triumph for Isabella and her master, and she became even more ambitious to please him; and he stimulated her ambition by his commendation, and by boasting of her to his friends, telling them that '*that* wench' [pointing to Isabel] 'is better to me than a *man*—for she will do a good family's washing in the night, and be ready in the morning to go into the field, where she will do as much at raking and binding as my best hands' "(20, emphasis in original). The evident ventriloquizing of the master's speech marks Truth's contribution to an anecdote that so obviously contradicts Gilbert's degrading representation of the slave. In response to that unflattering representation, this story insists on the exceptional value that Isabella produces. Furthermore, Truth's description suggests that she concurred with her master's opinion of her labor. In this way, the anecdote prefigures the supra-gendered contention in the famous Akron speech that was closely contemporaneous with the *Narrative*: "I have plowed and reaped and husked and chopped and mowed, and can any man do more than that?" (118). Rather than degrading her, Truth's labor value in this anecdote (like that in the speech) confirms the role Truth sought for it as a form of public credit that she sees herself as earning. She, in turn, deploys this public credit to represent herself as the civically entitled individual she endeavors to portray herself to be, *even while a slave*.

In subsequent exchanges, Truth and Gilbert continually spar over the value that Truth attributes to her working body and its related credibility. Rather than acknowledging how Truth's anecdote contradicts her troping of the ignorant slave, Gilbert converts the hardworking slave into an anachronistic subject presumably rejected by the now-narrating Truth, who is thus viewed as a formerly "colonized" subject. Gilbert attempts to contain the effects of Truth's hypercompetent laboring body, as well as the former slave's assertions of her work ethic, by obscuring the work meanings to which Truth referred and projecting them onto Truth's presumably ignorant and credulous relationship with the master.

In this vein, Gilbert contends with Mr. Dumont's exceptionally good treatment of Isabella by portraying his many kindnesses as a form of bribery that keeps Isabella firmly in his thrall, rather than as something stemming from his appreciation of her work. Alluding to Isabella's "larger share of the confidence of her master, and many small favors that were [by her fellow slaves] unattainable," Gilbert claims that Isabella "at this time . . . looked upon her master as a *God*; and believed that he knew of and could see her at all times, even as God himself" (21). Confirming the temporal distance from the narration suggested in "at this time," Gilbert spells out what she sees as Isabella's past (mis)understanding of her domination: "She then firmly believed that slavery was right and honorable. Yet she *now* sees very clearly the false position they were all in, both masters and slaves; and she looks back, with utter astonishment, at the absurdity of the claims so arrogantly set up by the masters, over beings designed by God to be as free as kings; and at the perfect stupidity of the slave, in admitting for one moment the validity of these claims" (21, emphasis in original). That Truth "*now* sees" how she was dominated is offered in the narrative on the basis of Gilbert's claim alone, however. The conspicuous absence of any corroboration by Truth at this juncture could perhaps be attributed to embarrassment over this example of the "perfect stupidity" of the slave. But, immediately following, another instance of Truth's "direct" speech suggests a different interpretation of the slave's behavior, one that views it as motivated by high principles, not "stupidity."

At a moment when Gilbert posits the irony of Truth's intense honesty (because the slaveholder, not the slave benefits from it), Truth—through the auspices of Gilbert—interjects, "Yet Isabella glories in the fact that she was faithful and true to her master; she says, 'It made me true to my God'—meaning, that it helped to form in her a character that loved truth, and hated a lie, and had saved her from the bitter pains and fears that are sure to follow in the wake of insincerity and hypocrisy" (21–22).[36] Gilbert's efforts to trope Isabella as the hard-working and hence, ignorant, slave fail in light of Truth's contravening effort to frame her loyalty as a character-building practice (a legacy from her mother highlighted earlier in the text)—one that refuses the connotations of sycophancy otherwise associated with slavery. Instead, Truth produces herself as embodying a principled stance while a slave, even, and indeed because of, slavery's lack of reciprocity. Even if she had believed at one time that slavery was "right and honorable," as Gilbert assumes (and would not Isabella's mother's grief over the loss of her children have taught her otherwise?), the point here is that the labor and behavior Truth displayed speak well of her regardless.

Truth's out-maneuvering of Gilbert's antislavery objectifications persists in representing her capacity, as a slave, to infuse her work with intentionality and a form of willfulness that tactically resists slavery's presumption of the slave's "will-lessness."[37] While Gilbert intermittently reiterates that Truth, at the time of the telling, "now looks back upon her thoughts and feelings, in her state of ignorance and degradation, as one does on the dark imagery of a fitful dream," the evidence Truth marshals on her behalf speaks otherwise (25). If Gilbert consistently attempts to contain the effects of this slave's apt performance by distinguishing between the Truth who relates her story and the slave who is the object of the narrative, Truth just as insistently resists this troping of herself as ignorant and misguided. This is further dramatized in the concluding segment of the *Narrative*'s slave narrative, wherein the radical implications attending Truth's apt performance of her labor motivate the former slave's self-emancipation one year earlier than dictated by New York statute (1827).

Truth's description of her departure from Dumont contradicts Gilbert's representation of Isabella as the colonized and abject slave subject. After Dumont breaks his promise to Isabella to emancipate her one year early, in 1826, Isabella interprets Dumont's failure to live up to his word as proof of her value to him. Because of this it becomes clear to the reader that Isabella's efficiency and productivity (not her dependence on Dumont) conflict with the slaveholder's emancipating prerogative. Gilbert's account in this case hesitatingly acknowledges these paradoxical effects of Isabella's working agency: "She plead [*sic*] that she had worked all the time, and done many things she was not wholly able to do, but her master remained inflexible. Her very faithfulness *probably* operated against her now, and he found it less easy than he thought to give up the profits of his faithful Bell, who had so long done him efficient service" (26, emphasis added). If Gilbert conveys some uncertainty regarding the usually kind Dumont's breaking of his promise with her "probably," Truth's subsequent fully cited speech dispenses with any doubt. In what follows, Truth recognizes the conflict of interest that emancipating hard-working slaves posed to slaveholders:

> "Ah!" [Isabella] says, with emphasis that cannot be written, "the slaveholders are TERRIBLE for promising to give you this or that, if you will do thus and so; and when the time of fulfillment comes, and one claims the promise, they, forsooth, recollect nothing of the kind; and . . . at best, the slave is accused of not having performed *his* part or condition of the contract. . . . Just think! How *could* we bear it? Why here was Charles Brodhead promised his slave Ned, that when harvesting was over, he might go and see his wife. . . . So Ned worked early and late, and as soon as the harvest was all in, he claimed the promised boon. His master said, he had merely told him he 'would *see* if he could go, when the harvest was over; but now he saw that he *could not* go.'" (26–27)

Here Truth makes it clear that her experience, like those of other slaves, taught her how difficult it was for slaveholders to relinquish the prerogative of slave ownership. From this perspective, then, Truth's enslavement symbolizes her value and productivity, *not* her abject dependence on her master. And so, in a dramatic moment, Truth depicts her labor as justification for her self-emancipation, belying Gilbert's claims about Truth's dependence, and showing Isabella's motivation "to take her freedom into her own hands, and seek her fortune in some other place" (27).

Gilbert and Truth's narrative collaboration culminates in the slave's self-emancipation. By showing herself leaving her master of her own accord, Truth portrays her labor as a character-building expression of thought and tactical agency, and as sufficient motivation for "tak[ing] freedom into her own hands." Ironically, the principled resistance behind this act is not fully evident because Gilbert's subheading, "Her Escape," makes the *Narrative* appear consistent with the fugitive slave genre. But this continuity in genre is only temporary, the effect of Gilbert's downplaying the very unconventional specifics of Isabella's "escape." Because Dumont was kind to Isabella, Gilbert portrays the slave's decision to "escape" to a farm nearby, where Dumont could find her, as "considerate"—in so doing, obscuring the principles that motivate her departure. These principles become evident, however, when Truth describes her response to Dumont's request for her return: "No, I did not *run* away; I walked away by daylight, and all because you had promised me a year of my time" (29).

In so characterizing her departure, Truth refutes the illicit connotations in Gilbert's term "escape," and narrates it instead in terms that mark her behavior as consistent with the principled worker she was as a slave.

The "escape" that Gilbert describes, then, represents a problematic point of multiple intersections where Isabella "crosses over" from slave to free, a point at which, traditionally, the slave narrative's account of a brutalized life inverts itself with a trajectory that relates the complex mobility—geographic, moral, and social—that the "free" North was conventionally understood to offer its subjects.[38] But it is here, when the *Narrative* takes up Truth's work in the North, that the radical implications of the former slave's against-the-grain depiction of her body as a willing working body become most fully manifest.

Labor and Freedom? North

Notwithstanding Gilbert's efforts to contain Truth's heterodox relation of her past, Truth irrefutably undermines the genre imperative to represent the emancipated North-inhabiting slave as, in Robert Stepto's words, "situated in the least oppressive social structure afforded by the world of the narrative."[39] Briefly, toward the end of the *Narrative*, Gilbert tracks Truth's postemancipation work history, and its termination when Truth decides to take up itinerant preaching. This part of the story line, represented as the end of one form of work and the assumption of another, is plotted with an eye to containing the subversion of notions of class mobility posed by Truth's refusal to participate in the North's exploitation of "free" workers. If Truth's traditionally understood incongruity can be imagined as representing black workers' incongruity in the North, the radical implications of this nonconformity are made evident in Truth's boycott of work there. Rather than collude with antislavery's expectations about the North's economic absorption of unsocialized former slaves as freedmen, the *Narrative* describes the North's loss of this competent and productive worker.

The narrative describes the failure of Truth's hard work in New York—where she relocates after her emancipation—to reward her monetarily and the paradoxical origins of this failure in the northern system of "free labor" (not, as was more commonly posited, in northern racism). Though Truth applies herself assiduously to becoming independent and accumulating an income, Gilbert cannot help but comment on, even as she tries to rationalize, the difficulties Isabella encounters in these efforts: "Isabella had herself and two children to provide for; her wages were trifling, for at that time the wages of females were at a small advance from nothing; and she doubtless had to learn the first elements of economy—for what slaves, that were never allowed to make any stipulations or calculations for themselves, ever possessed an adequate idea of the true value of time, or, in fact, of any material thing in the universe?" (54). Recognizing that Isabella received inadequate remuneration, Gilbert forestalls the critique inhering in this recognition by ascribing this failure to the slave's presumed inability to recognize value. But the history of Isabella's "escape," framed more precisely as the slave's repossession of her own valuable time from Dumont, shows Gilbert's explanation to be an improbable one that wrestles with its own terms.

This conflicted explanation, represented as another improbability writ large, appears when Gilbert narrates the details in Truth's work history that testify to the former slave's exploitation, even though Gilbert resists acknowledging this exploitation: "She toiled hard, working early and late, doing a great deal for a little money, and turning her hand to almost any thing that promised good pay. Still, she did not prosper; and somehow, could not contrive to lay by a single dollar for a 'rainy day'" (78). Truth asserts her textual authority in the ensuing narrative when she explains the logical gap made evident in Gilbert's "somehow."

The pressure that Truth's economic burdens impose on her are represented in Truth's ideas on the roots of this persistent poverty. The former slaves's description of her work history affords Truth the opportunity to interject potentially idiosyncratic questions and answers that are clearly marked as her own and that signal a distinct instance of Gilbert "handing over the reins," so to speak. In this way, Gilbert foregrounds Truth's authority in representing what follows. As the amanuensis relates, "She suddenly paused, and taking a retrospective view of what had passed, inquired within herself, why was it that, for all her unwearied labors, she had nothing to show?" This sequence of unconventional questions culminates in an instance of Truth's direct speech that is potentially problematic because of the explanation it offers for Truth's persistent poverty: "After turning it in her mind for some time, she came to the conclusion, that she had been taking part in a great drama, which was, in itself, but one great system of robbery and wrong. 'Yes,' she said, 'the rich rob the poor, and the poor rob one another'" (78). Through her complaint, Truth unequivocally characterizes her exploitation as rooted in an oppressive class system that gainsays the boons perceived as native to the "free" North. Rather than narrating "the least oppressive" world possible, Truth narrates the domination inhering in a system that operates through an unjust and cannibalistic (read: competitive) distribution of work and earnings, as if this exploitation were on a par with slavery's specifically raced and gendered oppression. That is, Truth's emphatic representation of her tactical "making do" as slave-worker produces a mediating, rhetorical space that renders her existence when "free" in the North appear continuous with, and not incongruous to, slavery's domination of workers.[40] Because she refuses antislavery's representation of the abject slave, Truth cannot generically represent the discontinuity presumed to exist between slavery and the North's regimes of labor.

Truth illustrates her understanding of the poor robbing "one another" with an example that reveals how much this former slave's work ethic diverged from the North's ideology of economic individualism. Gilbert relates that Truth, having been given money to hire a poor man to clear the snow on her employer's household steps and sidewalks, "would arise early, and perform the labor herself, putting the money into her own pocket" (79). But rather than resting satisfied with such exemplary industriousness—recalling Poor Richard's popular aphorism "Early to bed, early to rise, makes a man healthy, wealthy, and wise"—Truth's subsequent encounter with the man, who returns to clear the walks, makes her feel responsible to him and guilty for her acts. Instead of affirming the industriousness of her actions, Truth recasts them in a different light: "She would harden her heart against him, and answer [in response to his query]—'I am poor, too, and I need it for mine.' But, in her retrospection, she thought of all the misery she might have been adding to, in her selfish grasping, and it troubled her conscience sorely and this insensibility to the claims of human brotherhood, and the wants of the destitute and the wretched poor, she now saw, as she never had done before, to be unfeeling, selfish, and wicked" (79). Truth uses this story to enunciate a collectivist ethic that posits the "claims of human brotherhood" over her own individual wants and that, in so doing, overtly critiques the competitive and acquisitive individualism that was central to the norms for mobility associated with the North's brand of capitalism.

Gilbert responds to Truth's anticompetitive critique by again resorting to her rhetorical trope of preference: the ignorant slave. Her effort to defer Truth's critique of northern social class relations recurs to another assertion of the former slave's imputed misunderstanding of value: "These reflections and convictions gave rise to a sudden revulsion of feeling in the heart of Isabella, and she began to look upon money and property with great indifference, if not contempt—being at that time unable, probably, to discern any difference between a miserly grasping at and hoarding of money and means, and a true use of the good things of this life for one's own comfort, and the relief of such as she might be enabled to befriend and assist" (79). Here, Gilbert derives Truth's motives from ignorance, specifically the former slave's lack of discernment between "miserly grasping . . . and hoarding" and "a true use of the good things of this life." But in light of Truth's description of her poverty and lack of accumulation, Gilbert's insinuations of "miserly grasping" fail to suppress Truth's condemnation of the North's economic system. Despite Gilbert's invocation of freedmen's stereotyped inability to distinguish between greed and legitimate forms of accumulation, Truth's "contempt" operates forcefully. The relative weakness of Gilbert's interpretation in comparison with Truth's is also evident in the doubt expressed in the clausal "probably." Finally, Gilbert renders her own interpretation superfluous when she describes the biblical basis Truth invokes for her subsequent decision to effectively boycott the North's labor market and take up itinerant preaching. "One thing she was sure of—that the precepts, 'Do unto others as ye would that others should do unto you,' 'Love your neighbor as yourself,' and so forth, were maxims that had been little thought of by herself, or practised by those about her" (79).

Here, the radical implications of Truth's working identifications become palpable and irrepressible. Truth's moral, working alignments effectively invert the traditional moral trajectory of the slave narrative when they paradoxically imply that her labor under slavery's coercive regime functioned *more* morally than when she participated as a "free" economic agent in another oppressive system: that of the North. If her work as an exploited slave enabled her to cultivate a sense of honesty and credibility, by comparison work in the North's competitive and acquisitive "free" system withheld these rewards. Not only does the *Narrative* represent slave labor as possessing a provisional self-actualizing and character-building potential that links this labor to the moral development of the slave—in Isabella's words, "it made me true to my God"—but this moral, working agency also compels Truth's (and her narrative's) outright rejection in the North of the "metaphorics of ascension" on which the success of many of the northern-produced slave narratives was predicated.[41]

Rather than settling down to the task of accumulating an independent income, Isabella assumes an itinerant identity, renames herself Sojourner, and takes up a "mission," which Gilbert describes thus: "Her mission was not merely to travel east, but to 'lecture,' as she designated it: 'testifying of the hope that was in her'—exhorting the people to embrace Jesus, and refrain from sin, the nature and origin of which she explained to them in accordance with her own most curious and original views" (80). Truth clearly employed her itinerancy to "lecture" on religious hope, as described above, but in addition, Gilbert's description of Truth's itinerancy also suggests that Truth saw this activity as explicitly opposed to itinerant labor market practices. When she seeks lodging, Truth makes it clear upon inquiry that "work . . . was not the object of her travels, but that she would willingly work a few days, if any one wanted" (81).

Most significantly, Truth refuses the wages she is offered, at times taking only the small portion that she deems adequate to her needs: "They offered her what seemed in her eyes a great deal of money as a remuneration for her labor, and an expression of their gratitude for her opportune assistance; but she would only receive a little of it; enough, as she says, to enable her to pay tribute to Caesar, if it was demanded of her; and two or three York shillings at a time were all she allowed herself to take" (81–82). Another unnamed "friend" that Gilbert cites remarks on Sojourner's attitude toward money, relating, "She would not receive money for her work, saying she worked for the Lord; and if her wants were supplied, she received it as from the Lord" (93). Even after Truth "settles" down in the labor-reforming collective of Northampton where she would meet Gilbert, the amanuensis's description of their first meeting highlights the woman's unique attitude toward work and wages: "When we first saw her, she was working with a hearty good will; saying she would not be induced to take regular wages" (98).[42] These observations on Truth's rejection of conventional labor market exchanges make it evident that the former slave refused time and again to endorse an economic order she perceived as exploitative rather than as the apex of social value and racial redemption that many abolitionists and racial uplift reformers claimed it to be.

These concluding descriptions of Truth's itinerant preaching and this preaching's supra-market existence exhibit the paradox that radically excluded Truth—as former slave and as the writer of the *Narrative*—from the nationalist and industrializing imperatives to which the slave narrative's generic conventions adhered. The descriptions represent the hard-working slave as one who insists on her willful work in the teeth of slavery's laboring compulsion, yet refuses to assume the fulfilled, entrepreneurial work identity that appeared to be freedpeople's only ideologically correct enactment of freedom. That is, the *Narrative* refuses to represent as one and the same the black slave's propensity to assimilate into the North's capitalizing work order and the freedom that this order was presumed to represent.

Truth's refusal, then, proves that she fails to prosper not because she becomes the stereotypical lazy freedwoman, but because she, as a northern worker, is *not free enough*. And so, in the end, the *Narrative* poses the question, "In what consists Truth's freedom?"—rather than incontrovertibly assuming that freedom. Truth represents herself as obliged, in order to really be "free," to take up itinerant preaching so as not to collude in the social and economic instrumentalization of others. With her self-naming as "Sojourner," Truth signifies the incomplete nature of freedom in the North, troping ironically on norms of social and economic mobility that view itinerancy, and not the inequality and injustice from which this itinerancy springs, as improper and incongruous.

In so doing, Truth responds to black and white abolitionists' admonitions to freedmen and women to endorse northern social and economic integration, including Douglass's earlier cited cautionary tale on becoming "a stranger and a sojourner."[43] If the slave narrative's journey metaphor projects a teleological destination, most commonly Freedom/North, Truth, *already* in the North, appears as such a "stranger." In tracing these outcomes we can see how Douglass's analysis names Truth's problematic reception as one rooted in her willful rejection of hegemonic social and economic mores. Interpreted in this manner, *The Narrative of Sojourner Truth* "testifies," as its subject did before the antebellum nation, to the profound split that existed, not between North and South or slave and free, as commonly imagined, but between "the idealized nation and the capitalist one," confounding the ready conflation of republicanism with capitalism that formed the ideological bedrock of union nationalism.[44]

Furthermore, by demystifying the bourgeois norms of economic legitimacy and ownership that were central to abolitionist and uplift endorsements of participation in the nation's capitalizing, Truth's autobiography illustrates the tragic limits inhering in the emancipatory, market-driven discourse of racial "self-elevation." The narrative pointedly questions the cultivation of racial legitimacy on the basis of rendering economic service, a common sentiment of the time. As expressed in another instance by Frederick Douglass, "When we can build as well as live in houses; when we can *make* as well as *wear* shoes; when we can produce as well as consume wheat, corn, and rye —then we shall become valuable to society."[45] In contrast, Truth and her text admonish, slavery's domination (like the North's) is founded on exploiting the black body's productivity. To insist then on this productivity as providing an a priori liberatory tool for promoting racial equality under freedom is deceptive since it promotes the dignity of African Americans while subjugating them to dominating market forces. In sum, the ideology of economic individualism reenacts an amnesia about the subjugation of American slaves' incomparable productivity and resulting exploitation.

Truth's refusal to participate in the North's labor and capital market, then, is motivated by this other refusal: the refusal to forget these racial and class relations of working domination and exploitation. This refusal appears in her insistence that Gilbert relate her northern work history with the emphasis on her steady work and her failure to "prosper," and on the inequities between rich and poor that she observes while sojourning through the countryside. It appears in her refusal to participate in market relations in any form (including testifying against a paid ministry)—a refusal that ironically deploys the personal credibility she has cultivated through work to justify its boycott and to suggest the ways in which labor's utopian and emancipatory potential is severely compromised, not served, by the market.

By affirming her definition of her work's value over and against labor's market-oriented, commodified form, Truth simultaneously refuses the commodified form of freedom that she associates with "labor's" participation in antebellum capitalizing social and economic mores. Even the collaborative venture into which she enters with Olive Gilbert to produce a book to support her in her old age refuses the commodifying effects of antebellum publication. As we have seen, not only does Truth resist slavery's and antislavery's objectifying discourses, but the *Narrative* represents a form of labor about her labor that Truth personally distributes to interested supporters, without market mediation. As such, it represents an opportunity for Truth not simply to promulgate abolitionist principles—the primary interest of most of the *Narrative*'s contemporary readers—but to translate her labor and credibility into a narrative that speaks her labor as a just means of support.

In this way, Truth's literary collaboration with Gilbert represents an analogous form of itinerancy. That is, the project of speaking her labor to Gilbert and placing it in circulation resists the proprietary relationship fundamental to the authorship form. If, as Mark Rose has written, "the distinguishing characteristic of the modern author is . . . proprietorship," in which "the author is conceived as the originator and therefore the owner of a special kind of commodity, the work," then Truth can be seen as eschewing a proprietary relation to her own labor, knowledge, and credibility in exchange for their noncommodified circulation.[46] Truth's resistance to accumulation, even in the face of necessity, suggests that for the former slave, value inheres in that which circulates, i.e., in that which can be shared with others, rather than that which can be held as private property. In circulating this value, Truth enacts a disseminating pedagogy that employs preaching, telling, and working on behalf of others as a form of self-development different from that underwriting the bourgeois model of mobility. In the end, then, Truth's itinerancy serves as the means through which she can tell a different version of a truly "free" story to anyone who will hear and be inspired by it.

2 THE VIEW FROM BELOW

MENIAL LABOR AND SELF-RELIANCE IN HARRIET WILSON'S *OUR NIG*

Sojourner Truth's efforts to "speak" her labor, as we have seen, focused on legitimating her work as a slave in ways ordinarily denied by both proslavery and antislavery rhetorics. Consequently, it was only as a "sojourner" that Truth was able to testify to this labor's value in the northern landscape of industrial-capitalist exploitation. A few years later, Harriet Wilson would describe instead the literal, social, and racial immobility that she experienced as an indentured servant in another capitalist space: that of northern domesticity. Her 1859 fictionalized autobiography, *Our Nig*, narrates the racial confinement and reification Wilson experienced as a domestic and farm hand in the middle-class-aspiring "home." Describing the interrelatedness of white privilege and black inferiority, Wilson's text refuses, like Truth's, to collude in the devaluations of black labor at work in the nation's simultaneous disparagement and exploitation of black menial workers. And as in Truth's *Narrative*, *Our Nig*'s analysis of work during the nation's transition from rural to wage labor highlights the contradictions underwriting the ideological formation of "free labor": while the term indicated self-ownership, conditions in the North's industrializing economy potentially reduced "free" workers (who were also "free" of property) to the condition of "niggers."[1] Concerned with the paradoxes inhering in this so-called "free" domestic labor and its role in sustaining white middle-class femininity, Wilson's text targets the processes of racialization that beget the "nig" located at the heart of these work relations.

Since Henry Louis Gates's 1983 rediscovery of this text, critical work on *Our Nig* has focused on resituating Harriet Wilson within the antebellum emergence of African American literacy and literary authority, and on explicating the racial dimensions of the text's genre innovations.[2] One attribute in particular, Wilson's introduction of a third-person narrator, distinguishes *Our Nig* from contemporaneous slave narratives. When she fictionalized her autobiography, Wilson broke away from the first-person slave narrative tradition constituting the mainstay of African American antebellum autobiography. Overall, however, Wilson's innovative text tends to be framed almost solely within a particularizing discourse of raced identity and authorship concerned exclusively with Wilson's explicit intent to expose racism in the North during northern abolition's expanding influence in the public sphere.[3]

Consequently, literary analyses of Wilson's text have tended to render *Our Nig* a literarily anomalous text whose audience—notwithstanding the preface's appeal to her "colored brethren"—remains a conundrum to many. To this day, critics are skeptical of this appeal. Claudia Tate, for example, believes that "the 'colored brethren' to whom she appealed 'universally for patronage' were not in an economic position or numerous enough to support her enterprise." And Patricia Wald also believes that the "common penury" of black workers undermines the text's "putative profit motive."[4] In sum, critics have yet to confirm and explore the implications of such an implausible, though explicitly designated, audience.[5]

This conundrum, I would argue, stems from a critical focus on Wilson's exposé of northern racism among white abolitionists that overlooks the interrelated nature of antebellum class and race formation. While Wilson was undoubtedly the victim of racism, her analysis of racialization points beyond this, more importantly, to suggest this text's contentious relation even to *black-led* abolition and uplift efforts.[6] While it is clear that *Our Nig* seeks to expose the hypocrisy of white abolitionists, I believe it also contests black abolitionists' representation of black workers' upward mobility. Since the mass of black workers in the antebellum North were condemned to social, economic, and occupational margins, I suggest that *Our Nig* especially addressed itself to the black audience that it specifies, not simply to the white readers most critics view as this text's primary audience. For an audience of black workers would be most familiar with the racist class injustices *Our Nig* describes, injustices that prevented working blacks from enjoying the upward mobility associated with the tenets of "self-elevation." Specifically, this particular audience would also be the most likely to appreciate how *Our Nig* responds to black spokespersons who, despite their obvious desire to improve the lot of African Americans, unintentionally reinforced prevailing white views of black menial workers' "servility." As Frederick Douglass commented in 1856, "I am yet of the opinion that nothing can be done for the free colored people—remaining in their present employment. These employments—such as waiting at hotels, on steamboats, barbering in large cities, and the like—contribute to no solid character. They require servility, beget dependence, destroy self-reliance, and furnish leisure and temptation to every possible view from smoking cigars to drinking whiskey."[7] Douglass's description of occupationally produced dependence resolutely elides the structural conditions that produce these racially identified occupational schema, and in so doing, collaborates in the culture's demeaning of the value produced by these workers. He equates black workers' ubiquity in the ranks of "unskilled" or low-status service labor with a lack of desire on their part to just get up and leave. In this way, Douglass frames resistance to "servility" exclusively in a fantastic voluntary stepping outside of the occupational hierarchy, rather than in taking aim at the structure of this hierarchy or making visible the unjust appropriations of black workers' productivity that such a structure establishes and sustains.

Douglass's perspective on the dependence-producing nature of menial labor was not unique to him and was widely shared among black leaders, despite the fact that it proved fertile ground for disagreements among activists formulating the social and economic policies for black "elevation" or "uplift." While we may recognize that these disagreements arose in part because black leaders sought to uncouple the culture's equation of race with menial labor, black leaders themselves came to conflate the low status attached to these menial occupations with the character of those who occupied them. At the 1848 Colored Convention in Cleveland, for example, Martin Delany provoked strenuous responses to his melodramatic claim that he would prefer to hear his family had died than to hear that they were domestic servants to white people.[8] Whereas most African American leaders recognized how necessity and occupational discrimination combined to keep black workers in the lowest ranks of occupations, black leaders to some extent bought into prevailing assumptions about black workers' performance of this labor; at some point, they too subscribed to the long-prevalent idea that workers in service or menial employments were "dependent" and "servile."[9] It was to these reformers that the domestic worker who signed herself "One Who Works" directed her disdain in her 1860 letter to the *Weekly Anglo-African*: "We have been taught in childhood that it is honorable to work. . . . [Yet] many a young lady at service is made to feel most keenly the unnatural distinction made between them and those who were blessed with trades. . . . When our reformers will rebuke these distinctions . . . the world will learn that it is no disgrace for either sex to engage in an honorable employment." Why should any type of work be seen as dishonorable or stigmatized when it allowed people to "work for their living"?[10]

I read *Our Nig* as deploying a materialist critique that portrays the mental autonomy and self-reliance of black menial workers for whom leaders felt "nothing [could] be done," workers who had little hope of sustaining themselves outside the North's exploitative labor structure. That is, Wilson's explication of domestic labor's material and psychological debasements pointed to recognition of *class-based* racial domination as a precondition for transforming black workers' subordination into self-sufficient "possibility."[11] As a basis for this pedagogic project, Wilson's reformulation of menial labor contested the disparagement of black workers' symbolic worth promoted by both white and black leaders in their quest for abolition and "elevation."[12]

It is precisely through this little-addressed angle that *Our Nig* speaks volumes to the black workers who, like the protagonist, Frado, were enmeshed in the networks of intimacy, abuse, and exploitation that characterized antebellum northern labor. And so, *Our Nig* participates in uplift's exhortations to self-reliance, even as it defines self-reliance in ways that participate in, yet differ markedly from, the black activist tradition. When Wilson theorized the interrelatedness of labor, white privilege, and black inferiority, she produced a perspective on the North's labor structure that ostensibly complicated black uplift's emphasis on occupational mobility. Which is not to suggest that she opposed such mobility. Rather, *Our Nig* targeted what well-intended efforts to relocate black workers as skilled workers failed to consider: the manner in which race and labor processes inextricably combined to produce the very categories of "skilled," "unskilled," "black," and "free."

Our Nig addresses the failure of uplift discourse to acknowledge labor's racializing potential by presuming that black workers could abandon one "tainted" occupation for another without considering the way particular forms of labor were linked to social debasement. It analyzes black activists' assumptions about black workers' potential mobility that did not address the way race operated as a symbolic bedrock for the North's occupational structure. In dissecting the cultural logic elaborated by "nig's" work within the North's structures for labor, race, and status, Wilson demonstrated that these structures were not ones from which black workers could simply get up and leave. Instead, when Wilson narrates her subjection to, and eventual survival of, racist northern labor practices, she suggests that debasement and dependency are not their necessary outcomes, *even as she was consigned to them* as servant and as writer. Though Wilson's primary purpose in publishing her book was to raise funds for herself and her son, I read her exposé of how class relations produce reified racial bodies as a form of racial pedagogy: when Wilson described her resistance to northern racializing efforts, in the words of Gayatri Spivak, she rewrote her own "conditions of impossibility" as "conditions of possibility."[13] In this regard, then, Wilson confronted the social implications of the menial labor in which she and 87 percent of employed African Americans toiled.[14]

Our Nig consequently sheds new light on the stakes involved in black workers' compelled and disadvantaged integration into the North's economy. It responds to those who interpreted African Americans' absence from skilled occupations as confirming black workers' inferiority even as it addresses the possible survival of compromised black workers within these structures (instead of simply postulating mobility within them). Pedagogically, *Our Nig* formulates a survivalist ethic for self-reliance that calls for black workers to recognize the value of their labor, not simply through the performance of hard-to-find skilled work, but even, or *especially*, while consigned to racially defined occupations. *Our Nig*, then, opens up an alternative trajectory to economic independence for those workers intent on "self-elevation" from inside deeply racist structures for northern labor.

"Nigger Work" as Family Work

Our Nig's assessment of the coercion and social disparagement associated with household manual labor offers new perspectives on the northern family's role in the historical metaphorization of "nigger work." Recent understandings of the nineteenth-century "servant problem" illuminate how white workers' unwillingness to enter into the rigidly hierarchical (and deferential) class forms characterizing domestic labor differentiated them from black workers. Historian David Roediger derives the emergence of the symbolic construct "nigger work" from white workers' compensatory strategies to define "free labor" exclusively in terms of whiteness so as to mitigate the social dependency traditionally associated with wage labor. Thus, "nigger work" was enlisted to name and contain the degrading potential of wage labor: "Not only was *nigger work* synonymous with hard, drudging labor but to *nigger it* meant 'to do hard work,' or 'to slave.' 'White niggers' were white workers in arduous unskilled jobs or in subservient positions."[15] But while we understand white workers' symbolic construction of "servant" to differentiate their unskilled and degraded labor from blackness, *Our Nig* points to the white bourgeois household as another crucial site in producing and reproducing these classed forms of racial inferiority.

From its first person plural possessive pronoun title "our nig," this autobiographical novel comments on the profound irony entailed in a northern household's "dependence" on the various labors of its indentured servant Frado, a mixed-raced child abandoned at age six by her indigent mother. The novel focuses on the period of Frado's indenture, a span of twelve years, in the Bellmont family, during which time she was exploited mercilessly for her work and subjected to various forms of sadistic abuse, physical and psychological, by the two main antagonists, Mrs. Bellmont, the "she-devil" (as Frado's mother, Mag, calls her), and Mary Bellmont, her daughter. From her entry into the household until her departure at age eighteen, Frado's labors as farmhand and domestic servant in the "two-story" white house referred to in the title page serve as sites of simultaneous domination: that of a young black child (unrelated to the family) and of a key worker in the household.[16]

The servant who provided in-house labor, or "service," to whites was commonly linked to preindustrial forms of deferential labor that were closely associated with the slave's presumed dependence. Combining dependence and deference, these labor forms were incontrovertibly linked to blackness. As one white worker exclaimed to a British traveler inquiring after her "master": "I am Mr. ——'s help. I'd have you to know . . . that I am no *sarvant*; none but *negers* are *sarvants*."[17] And so *Our Nig*'s scrutiny of the interrelated racial and class subordinations entailed in domestic labor additionally implicates the white bourgeois family in the counter-definitional strategies that white workers employed to escape social abjection. In the terms of this collaboratively produced racial symbology, "nigger" took on its meaning as the preeminent figure for inferiority and abjection so that white workers could represent themselves as white, and aspiring white bourgeois families could represent themselves as middle-class. In this way, the national realms of productive and reproductive labor operated together to differentiate, define, and dominate the entire nation's black workers (and not simply the southern population of slaves).

Frado's vulnerable and dependent position in the Bellmont household produces the racial inferiority, dependence, and degradation that came to typify antebellum, and later postbellum, rationalizations for the continued exploitation of African American household workers inside and outside the domestic home.[18] Her body, a site on which cultural-psychic and corporeal processes intersect, represents a surface on which the negative effects of domesticity's presumably benevolent disciplines are made dramatically visible.

Bearing the marks of intense racial, intragender, and class violence, Frado's body graphically registers the contradictions inhering in domestic ideology's representation of middle-class authority. If former slaves dramatized the potential of slavery's power structure to corrupt southern slaveholding women (Douglass's Sophia Auld representing perhaps the best-known example), Mrs. Bellmont represents the potentially diabolical enactment of the moral authority that white bourgeois women were expected to exert in the northern home.[19] This description of the northern domestic woman, elaborated from the vantage point of a household worker, vigorously counters those hegemonic cultural narratives that posit white women's "rule" in the private home as benevolent while exposing the coercions to which white "domestic" women—themselves engaged in their own battles for authority—resorted in implementing the culture's obsessive moral disciplining of the nation's children and household workers. These coercions blatantly belie the loving familiarity and emotional bonding assumed to inhere in antebellum households' regimes of discipline, regimes through which white bourgeois females extracted labor and loyalty from their household workers.[20]

Labor as a Technology of Race

> By [age] four you'd do field work; by six you'd be doing small pieces in a tub every washday and bring all the clear water for rinsing the clothes. By eight, you'd be able to mind children, do cooking, and wash. By ten you'd be *trained up*. Really, every girl I know was working-out by ten. No play, 'cause they told you: life was to be hardest on you—always.[21]

How does a "nig" get made? In the northern home, she gets "trained up." *Our Nig* demystifies the social relations structuring antebellum household work by describing the relentless routine of labor and emotional debasement to which Wilson's young protagonist, Frado, is subjected. This routine testifies to the northern home's potent yoking of familial labor and racializing logics, enabling Wilson's reworking of the sentimental heroine plot into one of literal captivity that highlights the overdetermined material and psychological nature of household workers' "training."[22] In *Our Nig*, Wilson focuses on how labor itself is defined through a disciplinary regime that socialized black workers into assuming the affect, consciousness, and subjective identifications associated with the racialized and abject identities of the antebellum "nigger."

Frado's entry into the Bellmont household as a dependent child abandoned by her indigent mother, "Mag," is predicated precisely on the household's potential domestication or "training up" of the child. The crucial role of work in this process is clear in Mrs. Bellmont's stipulations for Frado's incorporation into the family: "'I don't mind the nigger in the child. I should like a dozen better than one,' replied [Mrs. Bellmont]. 'If I could make her do my work in few years,

I would keep her. I have so much trouble with the girls I hire, I am almost persuaded if I have one to *train up* in my way from a child, I shall be able to keep them awhile.'" (26, emphasis added) Closely related as they appear in Mrs. Bellmont's formulation, when Frado enters the household the categories of "nigger" and "child" are not, at that moment, perceived as fully identical with each other. When Mrs. Bellmont states that she does not "mind the nigger in the child," the child's identity is not yet entirely subsumed, or totally objectified into the identity of "nigger." But clearly the potential for such objectification exists, anticipating the future moment when Frado can be called "our nig" rather than a "child," and thus no longer entitled to protection. This defining moment for narrative and family alike underscores the role that a daily, intense regime of work discipline will play in simultaneously generating the story line for *Our Nig* and producing the dependent and loyal servant Mrs. Bellmont so desires. In this way, though Mrs. Bellmont features as the main antagonist in the tale of Frado's sufferings, the degraded connotations associated with the labor Frado is compelled to perform for the entire family pointedly speak to the role of the northern white family's reproductive space—"home"—as an important site for racial reproduction.

Mrs. Bellmont's training up of "nig" largely consists of producing a racial differentiation within the sexual division of labor, one she achieves by consistently delegating the household labor for which she is responsible to Frado. Consequently, Frado performs a wide range of work perceived of as the household's "drudgery" and "toil." Since Mrs. Bellmont is not required to perform this labor herself, it helps establish the unremitting and thankless regimen that compels Frado's labor inside and outside, day and night. An important aspect of this labor's racializing potential is its nature as boundless and boundaryless, i.e., respecting none of the recognized limits associated with a laboring body: in one instance this labor is characterized as "the work of a boy" and in another as "the work of two girls" (90). This work thus places Frado outside the ken of normative embodiments, degendering her and rendering her productivity dehumanizing. In sharp contrast to the rest of the family, which enjoys some apportioning of its members' own labor, Frado's labor knows no such limits. "From early dawn until after all were retired, was she toiling, overworked, disheartened, longing for relief," affirms the narrator (65).

Because of the constant demand for her labor, any deviation from this routine is subject, like Frado herself, to the intense scrutiny of her employer. What little time off she has, to go to school or to religious meetings, has to be contentiously negotiated. The conflicts of interest that this routine enacts ultimately succeed in defining Frado as a necessary, but disparagingly viewed, member of the household. To this end, the various tasks Frado performs, rhetorically generalized by the narrator as "toil," incontrovertibly signal the association of this work with the devalued domestic tasks that were defined partly by, and participated in, the symbolic transformations that took place among antebellum norms for gender and work.[23] If these transitioning norms were perceived as benefiting the white bourgeois woman, the narrative makes it clear that this class privilege came precisely at the expense of the poor domestic worker.

While Frado's labor is clearly intended to relieve Mrs. Bellmont of the bulk of her household responsibilities, it functions primarily, and more importantly, as a site for establishing and mediating power differentials between herself, the Bellmont women, and the family as a whole. Frado's work represents an arena in which racial reproduction is grafted onto intragender class conflict; that is, Frado's work "races" her through her conflict with the dominant white women of the household and continually subjects her to Mrs. Bellmont's relentless iteration of her dependent status. This subjection, in turn, highlights Frado's vulnerability to this abuse, which enables Mrs. Bellmont to reinforce the power she has over Frado: "The same routine followed day after day, with slight variation; adding a little more work, and spicing the toil with 'words that burn,' and frequent blows on her head" (29–30). Ultimately, this relentless labor regime aids Mrs. Bellmont in molding Frado's irrepressible child-body into that of the dependent "nigger," a transformation that amplifies other forms of power that Mrs. Bellmont wields over Frado. As the narrator asserts, "She was under her in every sense of the word" (41).

Not surprisingly, then, Mrs. Bellmont's indiscriminate tongue- and whip-lashings constitute the most significant burden that Frado must mediate in her daily household routines: "She was told she had much more than she deserved. So that manual labor was not in reality her only burden; but such an incessant torrent of scolding and boxing and threatening, was enough to deter one of maturer years from remaining within sound of the strife" (66). Which is to say that while she gets the housework done, Frado's diverse work in the Bellmont household is, above all, directed to fulfilling the connotations of a "nigger."

Frado's work makes her the family's captive and establishes the social relations and familial spaces that produce her visibility as the Bellmonts' "nig." This specific configuration of social, laboring relations results in the Bellmont household's ideological (if not spatial) enactment of the panoptic structures for discipline.[24] Frado is constantly vulnerable to surveillance and abuse, in one instance foregrounded through the single exception to this surveillance that her attic room represents: the "one little spot seldom penetrated by her mistress' watchful eye . . . her room, uninviting and comfortless; but to herself a safe retreat" (87). Frado's spatial fixing heightens her vulnerability to Mrs. Bellmont's household authority and emphasizes the central role of corporeal, menial labor processes in producing the subordinated class relations out of which "nig's" racial inferiority will emerge.

The structuring of labor of the kind that Frado undergoes in the Bellmont household was at the root of the North's symbolic linking of race to degraded and unfit labor, a link that was viewed as "southern" and particular to chattel slavery. From this perspective, Frado's experience parallels her own mother's compelled labor and racialization, which helps explain Wilson's sympathetic understanding of her mother, despite her abandonment. Mag's "fall," as narrated in the opening chapters of *Our Nig*, is not simply a fall from chastity into sexual ruin. It is also a fall into a class system that literally "racializes" her by subjecting her to the optionless condition of the working poor. And so, the experience of compulsion and labor that Mag suffers becomes amplified and extended in her own daughter's inscription as the Bellmonts' "nig" and thereby serves as grounds for identification between mother and daughter.[25]

The "free" northern household's conflation of race and degraded labor is dramatized when Mrs. Bellmont forces Frado to work outdoors in the sun in order to "blacken" her. In this instance, the process and the stakes implied in Mrs. Bellmont's intensely racializing labor regime are made clear; subjected to Mrs. Bellmont's authority, Frado's exposure to work entails a simultaneous exposure to blackness: "The interim of terms was filled up with a variety of duties new and peculiar. At home, no matter how powerful the heat when sent to rake hay or guard the grazing herd, she was never permitted to shield her skin from the sun. She was not many shades darker than Mary now; what a calamity it would be ever to hear the contrast spoken of. Mrs. Bellmont was determined the sun should have full power to darken the shade which nature had first bestowed upon her as best befitting" (39). Frado is compelled to perform all the "variety of duties new and peculiar" that racialize her together with her exposure to the sun. This episode synecdochally represents the whole range of racial effects to which Frado's unshielded exposure to racial and class domination subjects her; in Frantz Fanon's terms, Frado's labor forms the grounds of her "epidermalization," a process whereby blackness is grafted onto the body in the symbolically subordinate and abject form of "nig."[26] When the subordinate Frado is instrumentalized as the Bellmonts' household worker she enters a racializing labor process that constitutively transforms her from a working subject into a patronized racial object.

Through the spaces, practices, and founding conditions governing Frado's incorporation into the Bellmont labor regime, Frado is ruthlessly coerced into and rendered entirely vulnerable to her own racial objectification. While Bridget, the Irish servant referred to when Frado enters the family, chooses to leave the Bellmonts's service, Frado, in contrast, has no choice but to remain in this site of social degradation. This position, in turn, parallels the position of other black women workers who had little choice in the matter of their employment.[27] In this way, we can interpret Frado's youth as representing a state of dependence that parallels the physical and psychic vulnerability of black working women as a group. Themselves "abandoned" by a nation more committed to economic and middle-class expansion than to equality, black women were forced to enter the work force in severely circumscribed positions of occupational vulnerability. Not surprisingly, these positions rendered black women vulnerable to various forms of working domination that were less common (if still prevalent) in the other low-paid occupations to which poor white women had access. This is why I view understandings that conceive of Frado as being "legally free to go" as overlooking the coercive structural dynamics governing black women's "free labor."[28] In this context, Frado's radical dependency and vulnerability to class exploitation *in themselves* mark her as black, suggesting the pernicious ways in which "free" labor could racially immobilize all black workers, nationwide.[29]

Narrating Abjection

Wilson's dramatized third-person/first-person narrator enables a counterreading of sentimental plot and character. Through the overt fictionalizing of a primarily autobiographical form, *Our Nig* offers its readers a psychologically realistic portrayal of how labor processes racialize its protagonist. This fictionalizing device works in part because Frado's immaturity and vulnerable consciousness prevent her, until the plot's climax, from discerning these effects. For example, Frado's initial assessment of her situation displays her naiveté as to her future role and (lack of) status in the household: as night falls on her first day in residence Frado debates whether to remain or "wander away," eventually deciding to stay since she believed "she should, by remaining, be in some relation to white people she was never favored with before" (28). In so tracking the banality of this temporary, but tragic, misrecognition, Wilson illustrates Frado's susceptibility to the Bellmonts' racial objectification of her body. In sum, these narrative innovations provide an opportunity to describe realistically the fluctuating and often self-destructive identifications attending black workers' consignment to the racist working practices on which, paradoxically and unfortunately, their survival was predicated.

Our Nig describes labor practices' psychological creation of black workers, or "niggers." It bears repeating: Frado's status as *labor*, not simply her mulatta identity, designates her a site of "cultural vestibularity," a form of embodiment characterized by coercion and a complete lack of protective emotional or physical boundaries.[30] As the object of narration, Frado demonstrates the simultaneous subjectifying and objectifying characteristics of the modern raced, laboring subject. In this regard, *Our Nig*'s narrating dynamics show how the black worker's labor generates his or her subjectivity as a form of objectification.[31]

The destructiveness of this yoked subject/object–making dynamic are narratively figured in Frado's progressive self-objectification. Effectively, Mrs. Bellmont's regime of verbal and physical abuse means

Frado gradually internalizes the contempt and racist derision with which Mrs. Bellmont and daughter Mary view her. Though initially described as "irrepressible," possessed of a "willful, determined nature," and someone who was "a stranger to fear," the term of her residence in the Bellmont household transforms Frado into a colonized subject who views herself with racial self-loathing (28).

The psychic colonization to which the narrator's alternating use of "Nig" and "Frado" attests focuses on the connection Frado herself makes between her race and her abject status in the family. Frado expresses this abjection as a form of alienation, not only from herself, but from God as well. When she speaks to James about the origins of her abuse in the house, for example, Frado perceives it as originating in God's bias against her race. "Did the same God that made [Mrs. Bellmont] make me?," Frado asks. If so, she responds, "then, I don't like him . . . because he made her white and me black. Why didn't he make us *both* white?" (51). These concerns with race surface again even after her own religious conversion, when as "a believer in a future existence," according to the narrator, she questions her suitability for entering heaven on account of her race: "Her doubt was, *is* there a heaven for the black?" (84).

The annihilating potential of Frado's self-loathing is dramatically manifested in one moment described by a sympathetic family member, James: "I have seen Frado's grief, because she is black, amount to agony. It makes me sick to recall these scenes. . . . In the summer I was walking near the barn, and as I stood I heard sobs. 'Oh! oh!' I heard, 'why was I made? why can't I die? Oh what have I to live for? No one cares for me only to get my work. And I feel sick; who cares for that? Work as long as I can stand, and then fall down and lay there till I can get up. No mother, father, brother or sister to care for me, and then it is, You lazy nigger, lazy nigger—all because I am black! Oh if I could die!'" (74–75). Although it looks like Frado perceives her blackness as somewhat arbitrarily legitimating Mrs. Bellmont abusive labor regime—"all because I am black!"—she cannot as yet imagine resisting her objectification as the Bellmonts' "lazy nigger." In this moment, when Frado's working exploitation appears somewhat clear to her ("No one cares for me only to get my work"), if not to James, who interprets her grief entirely to the simple fact that "she is black," all the abused child can imagine is dying in order to escape the regime. In this regard, Frado's behavior signals her doubt about surviving this cruel treatment.

The most familiar instance of Frado's self-doubt refers to the singular moment when she openly considers, then rejects, the possibility of leaving the Bellmont household prior to the termination of her indenture: "She determined to flee. But where? Who would take her? Mrs. B. had always represented her ugly. Perhaps every one thought her so. Then no one would take her. She was black, no one would love her. She might have to return, and then she would be more in her mistress' power than ever" (108). Here the narrator again suggests Frado's keen awareness of the fact that the social effects of her racial identity are unmerited and unfair. In this example, Wilson foregrounds others' perceptions of her protagonist rather than Frado's own self-loathing as the source of her "ugliness." Yet Frado's subsequent actions appear to affirm these perceptions and her own racial self-doubt. This slipperiness between Wilson's omniscient narrator and Frado-as-protagonist significantly represents the equivocal raced, gendered, and laboring selves that vulnerable black women workers needed to mediate to survive.

Frado's perception of her predicament and her subsequent resolution to "stay contentedly through her period of service" has led many critics to see Mrs. Bellmont as successful in training up the worker she wants to keep for good. This instance of Frado's fear and dependency, which closely resemble those of an abused individual, has led some scholars to interpret Frado's emotional insecurity as complete: "So thoroughly does Frado internalize her indentured status that it is almost impossible to remember, during the course of the narrative, that she is legally free to go."[32]

But we should reframe the question of freedom differently, in the context of the (lack of) choices available to black women, if we consider Frado's internalization as provisional and incomplete, not as "thorough." That is, we may better address directly, and not elide, the ambiguity of Frado's presumed internalization by asking the question to which such an internalization refers: can she really be "free to go?" My rhetorical analysis suggests that the most compelling perspective *Our Nig* offers to workers like Frado engages with the potential for understanding and *with*standing the emotional depredations entailed in menial labor; this analysis does not defer to the "freedom" to opt for different employment because of the constricted nature of that "freedom." From this perspective, *Our Nig* reimagines black workers' relation to resistance by reconceiving it in the context of the structures from which black workers had little hope of escaping: Wilson's description of Frado's abject status opens up an interstitial space within these racist practices to promote a way to withstand them *while still inside them*. And so, Wilson's portrayal of Frado's perceptions bespeaks both abjection and an unspoken resistance to abjection; it reflects the existence of what this text ultimately speaks to: not the total foreclosure of but the possibility of mediating the deleterious psychic effects of northern labor practices.

Instead of imagining an outside to these coercive labor processes, *Our Nig* portrays the potential resistance to racialization and abjection by foregrounding these processes' potential instabilities. Wilson's text tracks the intense psycho-social oppression structuring so-called menial labor—viewing it from both inside and outside—to register the injustice of this oppression. But, more important, she also makes visible the incompleteness of these unjust coercive practices and their inability—in the end—to always predict and enforce the subordinating, racializing boundaries they are charged with producing.

Abjection, Privilege, and Racial Contagion

Our Nig's pedagogic impulse has often been linked to its evangelical conversion narrative; I would argue that *Our Nig*'s most political pedagogy is founded on Wilson's exposé of the diverse spaces and practices of Frado's exploitation as the Bellmonts' servant. Ultimately, this pedagogy makes her exploitation visible by reading it through its effects, that is, by exposing the linked class and racial privilege that menial labor produces. In this manner, *Our Nig*'s description of the contradictions entailed in the production and maintenance of this privilege—especially as it relates to Frado's contributions to this privilege—speaks to its possible subversion.

Wilson's representation of the conflicts related to Frado's labor insists on the servant's symbolic creation of white bourgeois gender privilege, not simply for Mrs. Bellmont, but for Frado's peer, the Bellmont daughter Mary. A considerable part of *Our Nig* demonstrates the "relational privilege"[33] that Mary enjoys as a result of her parasitic relation to Frado. During the family's first discussion about Frado, Jack, one of the sons, dismisses Mary's initial objections by facetiously alluding to the possible status that Frado's residence could offer Mary. "Poh! Miss Mary; if she should stay, it wouldn't be two days before you would be telling the girls about *our* nig, *our* nig!" (25). If Mrs. Bellmont has emphasized the potential subjection of Frado to her "training up" into blackness through labor, "nig's" fulfillment in this role, in related fashion, will presumably boost the white women's status among their peers. This link between status-hungry daughter and mother is suggested in the narrative's depiction of Mrs. Bellmont and daughter Mary as an evil, two-headed monster—and in the ironic parallels between Frado's "training up" from child to "nigger" and Mrs. Bellmont's rearing of her "idol," Mary, into a creature who enjoys the black-labor-derived symbolic privileges of whiteness and bourgeois femininity. If Mrs. Bellmont figures as an anti-mother on account of her creation of a social untouchable, "nig," the daughter that most resembles Mrs. Bellmont, Mary, dramatizes the monstrosity of the racial, gender, and class privilege to which Mrs. Bellmont and Mary so adamantly aspire.[34]

However, this emphasis on the violent and complex conjunctures of race and gender that characterize the Bellmonts' exploitation of Frado also exposes a crucial contradiction: even as Wilson describes how the family benefits from exploiting Frado, she also foregrounds the "costs" the family incurs in its domination of one of the household's members. These costs in turn suggests that the intimate discipline that characterizes the household's exploitation of Frado paradoxically imperils the very racial boundaries that her subjugation is intended to erect.

Mary and Mrs. Bellmont are often described as enacting various defensive efforts to mediate Frado's literal and racial proximity to Mary, inside the house and out, as seen in the mother's anxious and deliberate exposure of Frado to the sun. These efforts themselves testify to the concerns of white northerners and southerners over the social intimacy and racial intermingling that the employment (and/or emancipation) of free black workers would potentially precipitate.[35] In this regard, the family's initial discussion about Frado suggests that Mary—despite Jack's contention about the status she stands to gain—perceives Frado's racial proximity as a threat that can only be contained by the family's intended social subjugation of their servant. Mary's anxiety about this racial threat motivates her appeal to her like-minded mother for support against bringing the child into the house: "I don't want a nigger 'round *me*, do you mother?" (26).

Mary's explicit fear of racial contagion is further exacerbated outside the house, where the spatial structures of Frado's subordination do not obtain. When Frado attends the local school, Mary's implacable hostility to Frado saliently features in the ensuing conflicts. These conflicts all revolve around Mary's efforts to institute a visible hierarchy between herself and Frado outside the confines of the Bellmonts' familial hierarchy. When obliged to walk with Frado to school, Mary, "who was ashamed to be seen 'walking with a nigger,'" forces Frado to walk behind her (31). When Frado is befriended at school, Mary's efforts are again directed at "low[ering] Nig where, according to her views, she belonged," prompting Mary to endeavor physically—in the narrator's voicing of Mary's own words—"'to subdue [nig],' to 'keep her down'" (33).

Like her mother, Mary brands Frado as racially inferior in an effort to sustain her own sense of white racial privilege. This vexed, inextricable structuring of white racial privilege and black labor consistently and invariably marks the domain of conflict Frado and the two Bellmont women inhabit, which in its turn generates the family struggles so graphically depicted in the text. When Mary falls into the river while trying to push in Frado, the Bellmont household erupts into an argument in which Mrs. Bellmont squarely focuses on defining Mary's racial privilege in explicit contrast to Frado's own, notwithstanding evidence that Mary is lying: "Will you sit still, there, and hear that black nigger call Mary a liar? You would have that little nigger trample on Mary, would you? She came home with a lie; it made Mary's story false" (34). Whereas the other family members focus on establishing a truthful sequence of events, Mrs. Bellmont insists on the subordinate relation to white authority and speech that Frado's emphatically iconic status as a "black nigger" supposedly represents. Her seemingly redundant linking of "nigger" to blackness emphasizes the imperative to reaffirm the hierarchical symbolic values attached to black and white, the inversion of which—not the fact that Mary lies—results in "making" Mary's story false.

In this instance, Mrs. Bellmont reproaches her family for failing to shore up relations of racial and class subordination, relations ideologically demanded by the black worker's presence in the white household. For the moment I will defer describing the role of intrafamily conflict in the "costs" entailed in the family's racializing labor; the problem that concerns me here pertains to the hierarchical social relation that the Bellmonts' domination of Frado's labor is imagined, indeed intended, to produce. Wilson's dramatization of this hierarchy complicates, even as it represents, the perceived role of this social, or class, stratification in ensuring the integrity of the family's racial boundaries. In the end, the family conflicts in *Our Nig* related to Frado's "place" in the family suggest that the servant's subordinate role may at times fail to uphold the intended schema of racial stratification that her labor is called on to produce.

Frado herself, along with Wilson's narrator, foregrounds the issue of these boundaries as a potential weak point in Mrs. Bellmont's racializing regime. Most notably, as seen above, Mrs. Bellmont's exposure of Frado to the sun ironically testifies to her anxieties in this regard. Mrs. Bellmont's intended darkening of the light-skinned mulatta (an effort to racially imprint her) aims at forestalling any possible similarity between the black servant and her daughter.

Some of Frado's responses to her intense oppression testify to the subversive opportunities inhering in Mrs. Bellmont's anxieties. In one instance, the family's concern over Mary's and Frado's similar complexions motivates Frado's rhetorical "blackening" of Mary. She jokes about Mary's racial identity after she hears the news of Mary's death. Frado's relish at the relief from Mary's tyranny displays a sinister aspect when she alludes to Mary's earlier fall into the river as a model for Mary's death as another "fall," this time into hell-as-blackness: "She got into the *river* again, Aunt Abby, didn't she; the Jordan is a big one to tumble into, any how. S'posen she goes to hell, she'll be as black as I am. Wouldn't mistress be mad to see her a nigger!" (107). Mrs. Bellmont and Mary's shared anxiety over the danger associated with Frado's blackness isn't simply fodder for Frado's and the narrator's ironic perspectives on the racism of white employers, however. This explication of the dangers that black workers posed to white families shows how *Our Nig* pointedly exposed the ideological contradiction to which these anxieties testify: how northern white bourgeois women could perversely instrumentalize black servants' color as a source of racial and class status for themselves while simultaneously perceiving this color as something degraded and imperiling.

This paradox—wherein racialization simultaneously produced symbolic black degradation *and* white class privilege—framed black workers' and black leaders' perceptions regarding the nation's anxieties over interracial social relations in a postslavery era. Recognizing this anxiety as the basis for statutory and socially institutionalized segregation in the antebellum North, black leaders often highlighted the arbitrary application of these forms of racial prejudice by demonstrating how class domination frequently appeared to mitigate and even suspend whites' fear of interracial relations. In their view, if racial prejudice were indeed the only basis for inequality (rather than, say, class, that failed to explain how color did not always or necessarily signify the racial contamination that this rationale implied. As Frederick Douglass disputed:

> While we are servants, we are never offensive to the whites . . . we have often been dragged . . . from the tables of hotels where colored men were officiating acceptably as waiters. . . . On the very day we were brutally assaulted in New York for riding down Broadway in company with ladies, we saw several white ladies riding with *black servants*. These servants . . . rode not for their own . . . they were there as appendages; they constituted a part of the magnificent equipages. They were there as the fine black horses which they drove were there—to minister to the pride and splendor of their employers. . . . If the feeling which persecutes us were prejudice against color, the colored servant would be as obnoxious as the colored gentleman, for the color is the same in both cases; and being the *same* in both cases, it would produce the *same* result in both cases.[36]

Douglass addressed the cynical yoking of race with subordinate class status that immunized whites from the threat that racial proximity otherwise implied, showing how this class subordination enabled whites to profit symbolically from the proximity of black workers. As servants, black working bodies existed as objectified "appendages," chosen not simply for their labor, but for the ability of this labor to be transformed into and read as part of an employer's privilege—as Douglass paints it, "to minister to the pride and splendor of their employers." In this manner, *Our Nig* predicts the ways in which the social relations of black labor, reinforced by slavery, but most importantly in slavery's absence, could reinforce racial and social boundaries, a use that would be increasingly important in the South after Reconstruction.[37]

Similarly, the Bellmonts' provisional integration of Frado as a socially subordinate "servant" allows them to exploit her and enjoy the status that the presence of black servants bestowed on whites. But Frado's and the narrator's perceptions regarding the Bellmont women's racial anxieties imply that like Douglass's "colored gentleman," at moments the subservient Frado could also prove "obnoxious." That is, these anxieties betray the potential failure of this socially subaltern status to enhance the white family's status while protecting it from racial "admixture." In this way, Wilson revises Douglass's assertion about the presumed innocuousness of blacks-as-servants. For her, the interrelated nature of white privilege and black degradation suggests the potentially unstable character of racializing processes that transformed black bodies into black servants, or "niggers." She insists instead on the possibly subversive implications of black workers' proximity.

Notwithstanding her constant subjection, the anxiety-producing effects of Frado's working body and its status-granting properties in the Bellmont household testify ultimately to this body's racial unruliness. As such a potentially unruly entity, the black worker was not necessarily confined to the class and racial servility that the taxonomy of "servant" and "nigger" intended. By pointing out the instability of a servant's circumscribed status, Wilson also registers the possible subversion of this status. From this perspective, Mrs. Bellmont's relentless racial indoctrination appears incomplete and *un*inevitable, one that does not, despite appearances to the contrary, necessarily assure that Frado will be molded into the "nigger" Mrs. Bellmont so desires to have. Wilson's titular deployment of the Bellmonts' claim to "our nig," then, underscores the irony attached to this symbolic failure: not only does her titular use allow Wilson to contravene the label's dehumanizing attributes, but her irony signals the limits and failure of the term to symbolically domesticate her as it proclaims. "Our nig," she taunts, is what she is *not*.

The potential instability, or failure, of Frado's inscription as "nig" here testify to the ongoing, or performative, nature of this racializing process and the necessity for its constant reinforcement. Wilson thereby denaturalized domestic labor, opening up a space in the northern home through which she reveals subordinated labor's psychic colonization as avoidable. Exposing and exploiting the contradictions that constitute the northern family's maintenance of a "nigger," *Our Nig* dispels this labor's association with immutable servility and degradation. It unearths the diverging forms of "nigger" status that a "trained up" servant might enact to contest her debasement. Wilson thereby formulated her vision of working racial "self-reliance" on the basis of the paradoxical opportunities inhering in black workers' domination, rather than on an (idealized) end to this domination.

Familiar Veilings

Wilson's narrative dramatizes the constraints and opportunities governing black workers' ability to exploit the procedural incompleteness of race and class domination *from within* these subordinating structures. In particular, it is in relation to the whole Bellmont family that Wilson portrays Frado's resistance to the emotional debasements entailed in her racialized "nigger" status. Wilson's staging of race and labor within this family eventually culminates in the knowledge that Frado's exploitation originates in the veiling of her productivity—not, as postulated, in racial inferiority. Significantly, Wilson's description of how Frado's productivity gets suppressed shows the other family members, despite their good intentions, as colluding in Frado's exploitation.

As the narrative reiterates time and time again, Frado's family membership is predicated, above all, on her labor: "It was now certain Frado was to become a permanent member of the family. Her labors were multiplied: she was quite indispensable, although but seven years old" (30). But while her labor integrates her into the household, this membership also assists in mystifying the value of that self-same labor. At the same time, the family members fail to address her vulnerability to Mrs. Bellmont's physical and verbal abuse despite, or because they benefit from, Frado's contributions to the household. More important, however, the familial conditions of Frado's labor promote psychological conflicts that initially keep Frado herself from recognizing her own labor's value. The narrative of Frado's residence in the Bellmont family eventually counters this erasure by reiterating the scope and significance of Frado's work for the family within its mystified context. When Wilson restores this productivity to view, the narrator and then Frado dispel the Bellmont family's erasure of her labor, a move that consequently enables her to resist the family's racializing domestication.

Wilson restores the value of this labor through a third-person narrator that inventories and provides insights on Frado's labor that are not patently evident at first to Frado herself.[38] That is, Wilson's third-person narrator attests to Frado's exploitation, as well as her productivity, in ways that if voiced directly by Frado would make her appear impudent or "saucy." This third-person narration also enables the representation of differing, though not necessarily mutually exclusive, moments of awareness between narrator and protagonist. Because of this narrating gap, I would argue that we are wrong to view Frado's colonization as complete: her recognition of her exploitation is significant precisely because it emerges from within seemingly total domination.

With the possibility of Frado's eventual recognition of her productivity as a menial worker, Wilson pinpoints graphically, as the militant activist David Walker did before her, the economic rationality that underwrites white racist appropriations of black labor. As Walker insisted in 1829, "I have . . . come to the immovable conclusion that they have, and do continue to punish us for nothing else, but for enriching them and their country."[39] The "she-devil" and the whole Bellmont family represent the rewards that the entire nation, despite its own professed good (antislavery) intentions, stands to reap from exploiting its population of black workers, i.e., by "punishing" those that enrich it.

Our Nig's narrator contests Mrs. Bellmont's training up of the antebellum "nigger" by attributing Frado's exploitation to the value of her productivity—to the fact that her labor is worth stealing—rather than to a presumption of Frado's biological inferiority. Notwithstanding the degradation associated with Frado's performance of household "drudgery" and Wilson's description of the unrewarding nature of her "toil," the narrative never fails to keep in view the economic value that this labor represents to the entire Bellmont family; the multitude of tasks for which Frado alone is responsible encompasses almost all the work associated with the household. These tasks include feeding the livestock, shepherding sheep, tending to the fire, housecleaning, "all the washing, ironing, baking and the common *et cetera* of household duties, though [she was] but fourteen" (63). Only occasionally are other Bellmont family members represented as working, and these rare depictions occur strictly in the context of the Bellmont men entering or leaving the house to carry out some nebulous type of outside labor. If Frado represents only a supplementary form of labor on the Bellmont farm, the narrator leaves no doubt that Frado carries the burden alone inside the home: "Nig was the only moving power in the house" (62).

Even though Frado views some of the Bellmonts as friends and supporters of one kind or another, this exposé of the Bellmonts' ruthless exploitation points to the whole family's collusion in the perverse rationality behind Mrs. Bellmont's abuse. This collusion is dramatized when Mr. and Mrs. Bellmont privately argue over Mrs. Bellmont's treatment of Frado. When Mr. Bellmont suggests that Mrs. Bellmont should spare Frado some of her abuse, his wife emphatically denies that she could hurt the girl, precisely on the basis of the girl's output: "You know these niggers are just like black snakes; you *can't* kill them. If she wasn't tough she would have been killed long ago. There was never one of my girls could do half the work" (88–89). This dramatic depiction of how black workers' productivity was marshaled against them unequivocally asserts the perverse, yet totally rational, nature of white oppression.[40] Despite his good intentions, in light of his previous failures to protect Frado, it could even be inferred that Mr. Bellmont offers his advice to prolong her usefulness to them.[41]

Not surprisingly, this productivity motivates Mrs. Bellmont's violence against Frado and justifies continuing the abuse in order to keep Frado in her house. For this reason, Mrs. Bellmont resists her husband's suggestion to ease her harsh disciplinary regime. To do so will hurt them more than any harm Frado might incur through her abuse, she claims: "If you should go on as you would like, it would not be six months before she would be leaving me; and that won't do. Just think how much profit she was to us last summer. We had no work hired out; she did the work of two girls—I'll beat the money out of her, if I can't get her worth any other way" (89–90). Mrs. Bellmont's sinister hyperbole exposes the economic value of her racialized work schema; Frado's black body is so valuable, in fact, that it is possible to extract "worth" simply by beating it. Furthermore, Mrs. Bellmont suggests, to relent would in some way afford Frado the opportunity to abandon them entirely. In this way, Mrs. Bellmont herself foregrounds the perverse utility of her abuse and its role in mystifying the relations of exploitation in which Frado is enthralled.

Our Nig enjoins readers to reinterpret the abuse to which black workers were subject as based in, or justified by, assessments such as Mrs. Bellmont's and the concomitant masking of workers' value, rather than in the postulated racial inferiority of African Americans. Rather than signifying racial degradation, the abuse heaped on black workers signifies nothing more nor less than worker exploitation. The problem foregrounded here, however, is that within the paternalistic context of familial dependence, this exploitation is so covert that persons with less abusive tendencies, like the other Bellmont family members, nonetheless tolerate and benefit from it. Time and time again, the narrator represents the efforts of the various Bellmont family members to help Frado as consisting in "expressions of sympathy," in the "tearful eye" of Mr. Bellmont, or in Aunt Abby "slyly providing her with some dinner [and leaving] her to her grief" (36, 37, 46). With this pattern of ineffectual benevolence, Wilson's narrator invites an ironic reading of the family's ostensibly good intentions. She exposes the way a paternalistic and charitable discourse of domesticity successfully cloaked productivity by familiarizing domination. It is in direct response to these familial contradictions that Wilson's text represents a model for racial self-reliance that speaks to other black workers enmeshed in similar circumstances.

Wilson's foregrounding of the economic benefits that the family derives from Frado's labor engages with the complicated issue of how the familial spaces and dynamics that define Frado as "our nig" allow less willing family members to collude in her exploitation. Perhaps more important for Wilson's purposes here is that these familial social relations also conspire to hinder Frado's own recognition and affirmation of her work's value. Despite Mrs. Bellmont's role as the primary agent of oppression, the same "familial" circumstances that allow the whole family to participate in and benefit from Mrs. Bellmont's mischaracterization of Frado's productivity render Frado's status in the family as ambiguous (as a dependent, is she a member of the family "white and black"?), deferring Frado's own recognition of the significance of her labor to the family. That is, Frado's status as dependent—a judgment shared by both racist and "less racist" family members—ensures the almost complete invisibility of her household contributions, not only to them, but to her.

Wilson's staging of the various Bellmont family conflicts, and in particular the battles over Mrs. Bellmont's mistreatment of Frado, foregrounds the problems that workers might encounter in negotiating this familial ambiguity in their laboring status. These problems are especially important in Frado's case since the vexed family and work life she inhabits clearly intensifies her own internalization of racial inferiority. That is, the paternalistic structure of the household does not simply erase Frado's contributions; it makes it extremely difficult for her to assert her working value without damaging the tenuous relationships she tries to build during her stay. Frado's reliance on family members for the affection of which she is so remorselessly deprived, then, further intensifies her vulnerability to Mrs. Bellmont's racist regime. Moreover, complicating this issue of familial identifications is the fact that at times such identifications could be perceived not simply as a matter of sustaining affection but as increasing the possibilities of mere survival, since family membership presumably entitled Frado to some form of protection.[42] And so, Frado's inclination to identify with the family and to establish some stable emotional ties with the different family members appears not as a desideratum but as a liability that exposes her to further violence.

If being perceived as a member of the family is deemed potentially beneficial—i.e., people intercede for Frado and treat her kindly to compensate for Mrs. Bellmont's treatment—this perception also makes her vulnerable to familial abuses of authority. This becomes patently obvious in one instance when James tells her after a particularly severe beating, "You must try to be a good girl" (50) and in another expression of support he offers that implies how Frado might withstand Mrs. Bellmont's abuse simply by understanding that Mrs. Bellmont's views on race are not shared by the others:

> She has such confidence in me that she will do just as I tell her [states James]; so we found a seat under a shady tree, and there I took the opportunity to combat the notions she seemed to entertain respecting the loneliness of her condition and want of sympathizing friends. I assured her that mother's views were by no means general; that in our part of the country there were thousands . . . who favored the elevation of her race, disapproving of oppression in all its forms; that she was not unpitied, friendless, and utterly despised; that she might hope for better things in the future. Having spoken these words of comfort, I rose with the resolution that if I recovered my health I would take her home with me, whether mother was willing or not. (75–76)

While it remains unclear whether Frado finds consolation in James's statement of pity, James does not address the paradox of the girl's loneliness within the bosom of the family or the failure of family relations indicated by Frado's "want of sympathizing friends." James's assessment of his providing Frado "words of comfort" signals instead the absence of Frado's response to this statement of support, a statement that does not begin to address adequately her role in the household as worker (and not just as "nig"). *Our Nig*'s deliberation on the black domestic worker's painful and problematic status in the white northern family thus offers a domestic analog to the juridical "neither citizens, nor aliens" principle expressed in *Dred Scott*. At times contesting, at times reinforcing this principle, the Bellmont family arrangement generates the paradoxical identifications that Frado experiences during her stay, as well as the dubious benefits offered by her loyal adherence to the family.

Wilson represents these negative familial ambiguities in describing the family's failed "rescues" of Frado. While different family members always intervene after a beating, it is clear that these interventions fail entirely to address the structuring conditions of Frado's vulnerability to Mrs. Bellmont's abuse. In some cases, Mrs. Bellmont even "compensates" for these interventions by causing Frado additional pain; this consequence emphasizes the less-than-innocent effects of the Bellmonts' ineffectualness. Most important, these rescues ultimately appear effective only insofar as they guarantee that Frado may resume her work.

The narrator represents the ironic ineffectiveness of the Bellmonts' interventions on several occasions. Once, after James intercedes to tell his mother that he "would not excuse or palliate Nig's impudence; but she should not be whipped or be punished at all," the narrator relates the terrible consequences that follow: "[Mrs. Bellmont] only smothered her resentment until a convenient opportunity offered. The first time she was left alone with Nig, she gave her a thorough beating, to bring up arrearages" (72). In another instance, after Frado receives a particularly severe beating, the dying James and the family conspire to keep her temporarily away from Mrs. Bellmont so that she may recuperate. But the narrator remarks that this instance of family unity and assistance constitutes only a temporary reprieve and that "a comfortable night's repose following, she was enabled to continue, as usual, her labors" (84). "As usual" simultaneously foregrounds the ineffective nature of the family's interventions and the inescapable routine of Frado's labor. This suffocating climate of intimacy and exploitation, combined with Frado's extreme isolation from the rest of the community, foregrounds the difficulty of mounting any resistance. Consequently, rather than develop her own mode of resistance, the most Frado can hope for from this familial captivity is to prevail on James to take her with him, away from his mother, transferred as domestic worker from one family member to another (52).

Ultimately, the narrator makes clear that Frado's loyalty to the kind Bellmont family members, combined with the family's ineffective support for Frado, only intensifies her vulnerability to Mrs. Bellmont's abuse. Furthermore, this loyalty also prevents Frado from imagining plausible escapes from her damaging environment. Frado's final escape, however, suggests that this impediment to flight in fact eventually propels the final resolution to Frado's dilemma: in the end, the family's failed efforts and the constant setbacks Frado suffers eventually make it clear to her that the task of battling back is one in which she alone has a defining interest and in which she alone can prevail. That is, the difficult circumstances that initially impede Frado's resistance themselves operate pedagogically, eventually motivating Frado to successfully mediate the family's conflicting claims on her affection, loyalty, and labor. In this way, the Bellmont family does not function simply as the context of Frado's wholesale "domestication." Instead, the narrative suggests that the Bellmonts' indecisiveness and complicitous exploitation eventually lead Frado to value emotional and economical independence rather than assimilation "like one of the family."[43] The moment Frado finally realizes that she cannot rely on the Bellmonts for any substantial help is the moment she also realizes that she must depend on herself. And it is precisely in relation to her first substantial resistance to Mrs. Bellmont's abuse that Frado comes to recognize most fully her own value as a worker.

Labor as Resistance

Frado mounts her first successful self-defense against Mrs. Bellmont in the incident at the woodpile. In this dramatic moment, Frado protests her abuse in a manner that finally offers her some relief from Mrs. Bellmont's disciplinary regime. Though some critics do not see this incident as an act of resistance because it is preceded by Mr. Bellmont's covert sanction—"He did not wish to have her saucy or disrespectful, but when she was *sure* she did not deserve a whipping, to avoid it if she could" (104)—Mr. Bellmont does not at all suggest the terms of her eventual resistance. Instead, the effectiveness and significance of Frado's resistance emanate solely from her: when she opts to leverage her work through the threat of withholding it she obliquely refers to and exploits her status as the household's sole worker:

> It was not long before an opportunity offered of profiting by his advice. She was sent for wood, and not returning as soon as Mrs. B. calculated, she followed her, and, snatching from the pile a stick, raised it over her. "Stop!" shouted Frado, "strike me, and I'll never work a mite more for you"; and throwing down what she had gathered, stood like one who feels the stirring of free and independent thoughts. By this unexpected demonstration, her mistress, in amazement, dropped her weapon, desisting from her purpose of chastisement. Frado walked towards the house, her mistress following with the wood she herself was sent after. (105)

For the first time, independently of the narrator, Frado herself successfully and explicitly asserts her work's value. She strategically forestalls the attack at the precise moment she unveils the basis of Mrs. Bellmont's abuse in her need for Frado's work and in her dependence on Frado. This revelation disarms Mrs. Bellmont ("Her mistress, in amazement, dropped her weapon") and represents a psychic watershed for Frado, who subsequently understands not only that she possesses a form of power but that this power derives precisely from leveraging her own labor. "She did not know, before," the narrator concludes following the incident, "that she had a power to ward off assaults" (105).

This episode speaks to Frado's dawning recognition of the value inhering in her labor and the latent power to which that value refers. It is precisely in relation to this emergent recognition that Frado experiences what the narrator describes as "the stirring of free and independent thoughts." More important, however, this recognition simultaneously refuses the inferiority and debasement associated with her labor. In this context, Frado's claim to her labor's value dispels the mystifications that the Bellmont family had promoted in relation to it. When Mrs. Bellmont's dependence on her labor becomes visible, Frado refutes her postulated racially inferior or dependent status and sets the scene for her new, "disalienated" relation to her labor, one that generates anew a desire for economic independence and motivates her eventual departure from the Bellmont household and her subsequent strivings.[44]

The crucial significance of this moment of self-reliant assertiveness is established when Frado's subsequent residence in the Bellmont house quickly winds to a close. Though many have emphasized the fact that Frado decides to stay on after this incident, I would argue that she does so on entirely new terms, terms that make it clear that her work is deemed sufficiently valuable to ensure that she be treated well if she is to work for Mrs. Bellmont. As the narrator describes the situation, "She remembered her victory at the wood-pile. She decided to remain to do as well as she could; to assert her rights when they were trampled on. . . . She had learned how to conquer" (108).[45] Though related by the narrator, this militant formulation is clearly attributed to the protagonist herself and demonstrates the rhetorical possibilities ("to assert her rights") emanating from black productivity. In this dramatic case, as a gain derived from her own labor, Frado's "conquest" legitimates her subversion of a racist nation's unjust social hierarchies.

Frado's new awareness of her work's value subsequently motivates her to strike out on her own at the end of her indenture. This awareness stimulates a new independence in Frado, even prior to her departure, through which she perceives herself as distinct from the family in a new way; this awareness is evident in her relationship with Mrs. Bellmont and the whole family prior to her departure. In contrast to the rest of the family, Frado appears in this part of the narrative to be the only one capable of withstanding Mrs. Bellmont's persisting abusiveness. As the narrator comments ironically, "There seemed no one capable of enduring the oppressions of the house but her" (109). Most important, Frado's newfound emotional independence relates to the rest of the Bellmont family as well. When the kind daughter, Jane, finally offers to take Frado with her despite the latter's previous, intense desire to leave with James, the newly independent Frado refuses: "Jane begged her to follow her so soon as she would be released; but so wearied out was she by her mistress, she felt disposed to flee from any and every one having her similitude of name or feature" (109–10). From this point forward, Frado channels her energy into cultivating her religious feelings and into "striving to enrich her mind" in preparation for her departure. Her desires are transformed from simply surviving her daily work routine to focusing on the day that she will benefit from her work and be responsible for supporting herself. The last thing Frado wants is to remain "dependent," and consequently she unequivocally refuses to enact the debased "nigger" status deployed to keep her at Mrs. Bellmont's side.

The sharpness of Frado's refusal is made particularly manifest at the moment of her imminent departure from the Bellmont house. Here, the narrator provides Frado with an opportunity to respond ironically to Mrs. Bellmont when she asks her to stay past the term of her indenture: "Mrs. B. felt that she could not well spare one who could so well adapt herself to all departments—man, boy, housekeeper, domestic, etc. She begged Mrs. Smith to talk with her, to show her how ungrateful it would appear to leave a home of such comfort—how wicked it was to be ungrateful! But Frado replied that she had had enough of such comforts; she wanted some new ones; and as it was wicked to be ungrateful she would go from temptation" (116). At this juncture, Wilson's irony turns on Frado's own explicit recognition of the speciousness inhering in Mrs. Bellmont's claim to providing her with "comfort." While Mrs. Bellmont's entreaty again affirms Frado's utility—"she could not well spare one who could so well adapt herself to all departments"—Frado's ironic response, "she had had enough of such comforts," confirms her recognition of Mrs. Bellmont's subterfuge for what it is. This instance of "sass" makes it patently clear that Frado feels empowered enough and willing to take her chances in striving to support herself.

Notwithstanding the terrible toll that the unremitting labor regime has taken on Frado's "delicate" health, the narrative's emphasis on labor-derived empowerment figures prominently in the description of Frado's post-Bellmont life. In this brief account, Wilson vividly recounts the ensuing difficulties and uncertainties attending Frado's persistent bid for economic independence. These difficulties closely resemble those her mother experienced at the beginning of the narrative and revolve entirely around her efforts to become independent: "Many times her hands wrought when her body was in pain; but the hope that she might yet help herself, impelled her on" (123). During an illness Frado views the Bellmonts as obligated to take care of her, making it clear that this temporary dependence derives from the family's exploitation of, and thus their debt to, her, and not to her "dependency." "She felt sure they owed her a shelter and attention, when disabled," relates the narrator, and Mrs. Bellmont's physician-brother concurs: "All broken down. . . . It was commenced longer ago than last summer. Take good care of her; she may never get well" (120). In sum, Frado's post-Bellmont efforts testify to the persistence of her self-reliance in the face of the difficulties she experiences in sustaining this independence. Despite her illness, a failed marriage, and the inability to support her son in her post-Bellmont life, the colonized "nig" of the Bellmont family persists in recognizing her labor power's value and in firmly refusing the dependent and inferior status entailed in the relations of domination in which she lives.

Frado's drive for independence, cultivated during her tenure in the Bellmont family, bears significant implications for the multitudes of black workers who, like herself, were consigned to the nether regions of the North's occupational structure. While a slave could escape slavery by leaving the South, there was no escape from the North's structural inequities for those free and emancipated blacks desiring to remain in their native land. This unjust consignment did not merely place black workers in the contradictory position of perpetuating the labor system that exploited them; it also produced contradictions in the very language black leaders mobilized on behalf of black "elevation" during the antebellum era.

The trajectory of social and occupational mobility that was central to the metaphorics of uplift traded African Americans' relative immobility in the North for a postulated assimilation into, and rising up through, the North's expanding capitalist economy. But in contrast to the pattern of the "heroic slave" on which uplift activists modeled the success trajectory of free blacks, Wilson's narrative abrogates the metaphorics of mobility. As Beth Doriani notes, Wilson "does not move 'up' from slavery or oppression—as in the pattern of ascension that Stepto describes for Afro-American narrative—but moves 'within' the oppressive community, struggling for independence and selfhood within the confines of racism."[46] Because Frado's desire for economic independence does not aim for abundant material success, but instead focuses on mere survival, *Our Nig* refuses to enact this trajectory of mobility in either narrative form or content. Instead, it suggests uplift ideology's racially undermining potential, particularly in relation to the mass of black workers who, despite all efforts, really could not get up and leave their structurally disadvantaged occupational position as disparaged, menial workers.[47]

Frado's struggles, in the final analysis, amount to a lesson in racial working self-reliance resolutely framed within Wilson's materialist recognition of the North's racial immobilization of black workers. The production of white racial and class privilege through the racing of domestic workers suggests the entrenched, rather than accidental, nature of this dynamic of race and labor. Because of this racialization's structural nature, Wilson did not opt for the ideals of economic mobility that black leaders saw as central to surmounting Northern whites' racial prejudice. Instead, *Our Nig* counters the mystifications of black productivity that this racialization represents, enabling and demanding black workers' *counteridentification* with their white employers as a way of ameliorating the colonization entailed in their economic subordination. By representing ideologies of racial inferiority as so many alibis that obscure the white theft of black productivity and value, *Our Nig* offers up the grounds on which black workers could resist succumbing to the racializing disparagements of their labor. As Frado's confinement to the ranks of menial labor shows, survival required that black workers cultivate and rely on their emotional independence in their daily, ordinary working relations precisely as a means of surmounting the banal violence in which they were enmeshed.

Ultimately, Wilson's formulation of self-reliance assumes its significance within the context of her novel's foregoing of the conventional happy endings of either marriage or material success. Wilson's conclusion, "And thus, to the present time, may you see her busily employed in preparing her merchandise; then sallying forth to encounter many frowns, but some kind friends and purchasers. Nothing turns her from her steadfast purpose of elevating herself" (130–31), highlights Frado's striving in labor as an end in itself, suggesting how exhortations to self-reliance and self-elevation could be especially pertinent to workers trapped in racializing, menial occupations. To black workers, both male and female, who encountered discrimination as a real and widespread erosion of skill, the pursuit and attainment of economic (and emotional) independence necessitated a will-to-independence they would have necessarily shared with Wilson. In this regard, Frederick Douglass's formulation of agency within the black community appears particularly pertinent: "Every day brings with it renewed evidence of the truthfulness of the sentiment, now, in various quarters, gaining the confidence and sympathy of our oppressed People, THAT OUR ELEVATION AS A RACE, IS ALMOST WHOLLY DEPENDENT UPON OUR OWN EXERTIONS. If we are ever elevated, our elevation will have been accomplished through our own instrumentality."[48] In contrast to the debates among black leaders about the questionable "honor" involved in menial labor, *Our Nig* shows how this labor could function as the object of workers' "own instrumentality." But Frado's experience also suggests the crucial need—before domestic or menial labor could function in this instrumental way—for workers to recognize how the degraded meanings associated with their labor enabled whites to appropriate their productivity. In other words, for black workers to profit, even if only symbolically, from the value of this labor, they had to explicitly recognize how whites themselves profited from it—formulations about the worthlessness of "nigger work" to the contrary.

In one of his most expansive considerations of the problems facing black workers, Frederick Douglass expressed the uplift community's commitment to the acquisition of skilled trades. This commitment manifested Douglass's and the community's adherence to the ideology of economic individualism and their belief in the racially emancipatory potential of skilled labor: "Now, colored men, what do you mean to do, for you must do something? The American Colonization Society tells you to go to Liberia. Mr. Bibb tells you to go to Canada. Others tell you to go to school. We tell you to go to work; and to work you must go or die. Men are not valued in this country, or in any country, for what they *are*; they are valued for what they can *do*."[49] Pragmatic as this sounds, Douglass implies that black workers had to be convinced of the necessity to work: "To work you must go or die." Representing black workers as failing to participate in the ideology of economic individualism—"[Men] are valued . . . for what they can *do*"—obscures the structural conditions governing black workers' domination. By postulating a utopian national free labor norm, Douglass and other black leaders overlooked the manner in which the North's occupational structure itself led to keeping blacks in low-esteemed occupations denoted as "nigger work."[50] In so formulating the case, these leaders colluded with portrayals of black workers as responsible for their own underrepresentation among the skilled trades. *Our Nig* contests this reductive simplification of free labor's potential. In this country, Wilson's tale suggests, black workers are compelled to *do* what they *are*: they are forced to be the nation's "nig's."

The "colored brethren" to whom Wilson appealed in her preface would understand how she disavowed the stereotypical attitudes advanced by both whites and blacks toward black-associated occupations and thereby countered the common, widespread disparagement of these workers' symbolic and economic worth. In other words, *Our Nig* vigorously suggests that black workers in menial positions could actually aspire to racial independence and self-reliance, despite their evident exclusion from norms of occupational mobility. In this way, rather iconoclastically, *Our Nig* refused to reinscribe the exceptionality of the individual whose survival was predicated on the romantic exempting of himself or herself from relevant structures. And so, Wilson's text talked back, not only to white racist abolitionists, but to the whole black community, and in particular to those engaged in uplift who framed the problem of racism in the North as a problem of black workers' failure to move outside the discriminatory occupational structures to which they were consigned. Wilson's narrative thus exposes the contingency of formulations of racially identified "servility" and its opposite, "mobility," revealing the basis of this exploitative binary in a racist mystification of value sustained by northern labor practices.

Our Nig affords us valuable insights into antebellum uplift's tragic blindness to the intricacies of race and labor in the North. This blindness would manifest itself more fully and contradictorily after Reconstruction, according to Kevin Gaines, in a "bourgeois race consciousness patterned after missionary notions of uplift [that] precluded an understanding of class conflict and the exploitation of workers, black or white."[51] This blindness to the racializing propensities of free labor contributed in no small measure to the unfortunate torque inhering in what W. E. B. Du Bois called Booker T. Washington's "dangerous half-truths" at the end of the nineteenth century.[52]

Instead of exhortations to mobility that overlook the vexed structuring of economic opportunity in a racist social order, *Our Nig* derives racial authority and legitimacy from the contributions of the ordinary black worker. It carefully frames black workers' contributions within their relevant unjust orders: familial, regional, and national. When Wilson exposed common erasures of black productivity, she crafted a language of laboring recognition unique to racial uplift—one that linked herself and ordinary black workers to the value they produced within the constrained circumstances in which they lived their everyday lives.

II OPPORTUNITIES

The fact is "black" has never been just there either. It has always been an unstable identity, psychically, culturally, and politically. It, too, is a narrative, a story, a history. Something constructed, told, spoken, not simply found.

—Stuart Hall, 1987

3 ENTERPRISING WOMEN AND THE LABORS OF FEMININITY

ELIZA POTTER, CINCINNATI HAIRDRESSER

When Sojourner Truth and Harriet Wilson appealed to their audiences' recognition of the self-reliant and civically entitling nature of what was viewed as menial labor, they tried to surmount the rhetorical limits, or "constraints," associated with the low status of women's farm and domestic labor. Disparaged as the lowest-ranking of workers, Truth and Wilson countered representations of black working women as servile and degraded. In contrast, Eliza Potter and Elizabeth Keckley took up the burden of promoting black working women's social legitimacy from the vantage point of skilled and entrepreneurial work, as hairdresser and dressmaker, respectively, to wealthy white women. As successful practitioners of their trades, both women profited economically and socially in ways that were important enough to motivate them to publish their work histories, which they did in different regions of the country, nine years apart. Despite their differences—Keckley was a southern-born former slave and Potter was northern-born and free—the women shared a perspective on the opportunities their work afforded them for geographic, social, and economic mobility. In particular, as black women employed in designing dresses and combing the heads of affluent white women, Potter and Keckley sought to make their contributions to white elite femininity visible as contributions that placed them at the center, rather than at the margins, of this domain. This repositioning of themselves as dignified and self-supporting black working women vis-à-vis their bourgeois and elite female clients is of the greatest significance to modern readers interested in the contested terrains of class, race, and gender that these women address in their texts.

Notwithstanding that the majority of black women worked in "menial" occupations during the nineteenth and twentieth centuries, over the past decades historians have shed light on the mostly unrecognized heterogeneity of their occupations and, in particular, the opportunities they exploited in running the small businesses to which many black women—kept out of factory and clerical work—resorted. Today we have a clearer picture of the immense creativity and business acumen with which black women responded to myriad economic injustices and their significant participation in the era's ranks of entrepreneurs. The diversity of business enterprises owned and managed by free colored women (some of whom were former slaves) is nothing short of remarkable: in addition to running plantations and owning commercial farms, black women were merchants, real estate developers, caterers, financiers, dressmakers, milliners, health care workers, boardinghouse owners, retail shops owners, and even slaveowners.[1] Though the majority of African American women entrepreneurs ran gender-based businesses in domestic manufacturing (of soaps and medicines, for example) or in cooking and laundry, black women also worked in "male-defined" fields as morticians, financiers, and shoemakers. Elleanor Eldridge of Rhode Island, for example, made enough money from wallpaper hanging to justify her depiction with a wallpaper brush in the frontispiece of her book of memoirs. One former slave, Clara Brown, headed to Colorado after buying her freedom at age fifty-five to set up a cooking and laundry establishment. Seven years later, she invested $10,000 of her earnings in Colorado gold mines and began to earn large profits from prospectors who shared a half-interest in their claims with her. By the eve of the Civil War, Brown had purchased the freedom of her entire family and thirty other individuals and had invested in two wagon trains of free blacks migrating from Colorado to Fort Leavenworth, Kansas.[2] During the Gold Rush, Mary Ellen Pleasant made a fortune in California operating a wide range of businesses that included boardinghouses and real estate interests in addition to her investments in mines.[3]

Today we still have too little appreciation for those black workers who exploited any and all loopholes in the nation's racialized and class-structured hierarchies to become skilled and entrepreneurial workers. Notwithstanding that they were both antislavery, Eliza Potter's emphasis on her white clients and Elizabeth Keckley's talk of the "bright side" of slavery need to be placed against this long-overlooked, but essential, historical context if they are to be understood. Though reprinted in 1991, Potter's text, *A Hairdresser's Experience in High Life* (1859), remains largely unread. Elizabeth Keckley's text, *Behind the Scenes* (1868), has received much more attention due in large part to the pioneering work of Frances Smith Foster; but as I will discuss below, its mix of slave narrative and political memoir (as well as its publication soon after the end of the Civil War) has made it a difficult text to locate in relation to our critical rubrics for antislavery and late postbellum literature.[4] These women's clear focus on representing the legitimating capacities of their self-supporting labor speak less overtly to those concerns we associate with black women's texts: literacy, sexual vulnerability (as enslaved and free workers), their roles as mothers, and their public contributions to collective efforts on behalf of abolition or racial "elevation." While female reformers emphasized the collective dimensions of their labor for the race, entrepreneurial women staked a claim for their rhetorical autonomy on the economic independence they achieved through self-supporting labor. Whereas black women reformers might have felt their independent status imperiled by prevalent stereotypes of black women serving as white women's "drudges," these women boldly acknowledged their contributions to white women's class and racial privileges, often representing themselves as much more expert in relation to elite femininity than their female employers.

Though they performed what was classified as manual labor at a time when such labor was increasingly stigmatized, the artisanal (or skilled) nature of their trades in the field of "beauty" could be represented as a form of aesthetic labor and offered Potter and Keckley a rhetorical site from which they could participate in and mediate their clients' performances of elite femininity.[5] The lucrative nature of these trades attested to their significance in this regard, but also meant that as economically independent women, the hairdresser and the dressmaker wielded a cultural authority with their clients that we have yet to take into consideration in our accounts of black women's subjectivities. In sum: Potter's and Keckley's work histories as skilled and entrepreneurial laborers invite us to imagine anew how we might integrate black working women's successes into our narratives of their exploitation.

Black Hairdresser and Social Critic

Reprinted in 1991 as part of the Schomburg Library of Nineteenth-Century Black Women Writers, *A Hairdresser's Experience in High Life* has received relatively little critical attention in comparison with other volumes in the series. Originally published in 1859 in Cincinnati, Ohio, for its author, the book is a biting exposé of the city's rich and famous, in particular the elite society women of the "upper tens." It also constitutes our major source of information on Potter, a free-born, peripatetic woman worker. As such, it tells us relatively little about her, a fact reflected in the criticism on *A Hairdresser*, which has viewed the text as unorthodox and as camouflaging its author's racial identity.[6] Since Potter foregrounds her clients and her unabashed enjoyment of her travels through Europe and the United States as a domestic servant, the distinctive racial politics of her text have been identified as having produced the relative invisibility of Potter's race. From this perspective, Potter's invisibility derives from a conscious (and understandable) effort to "pass" for white and to rhetorically evade the white reader's racializing gaze.[7] In sharp contrast to other texts in the black autobiographical tradition, *A Hairdresser's Experience in High Life* forestalls white readers' objectifying gaze by "veil[ing] her identity" and by deploying a "specifically gendered style of masking" that includes the omission of Potter's name from the title page.[8] But this accounting of Potter's racial particularity, I would argue, begs the question of her racial identity and assumes what appears as racially visibile. Furthermore, two reviews published in local papers prove that Potter was known as "colored" and did not pass for white.

A Hairdresser appeared in October of 1859, shortly after abolitionist John Brown's bloody raid on Harpers Ferry, and was initially reviewed in two of Cincinnati's daily newspapers, the *Cincinnati Daily Gazette* and the *Cincinnati Daily Commercial*. (A third review, which did not gloss Potter's racial identity at all, appeared in the *Cincinnati Daily Enquirer* a few days later.) The reviews in the *Gazette* and the *Commercial* offered sharply differing opinions, but both made it clear that the work was not perceived as a controversial abolitionist text or as a polemic demanding racial equality in the bustling border city of Cincinnati. On the surface, the book's racial politics appeared so innocuous that the reviewers did not link Potter's race to the Harpers Ferry raid that featured prominently in the nation's thunderstruck headlines. Instead, the reviewers feuded publicly over what each perceived to be the relative merits of the gossipy volume. The *Gazette*'s headline blared, "Revelations of a Fashionable Hair Dresser: The Upper Ten of Cincinnati, by One who Knows Them" and opened its favorable and generously excerpted review with a flourish: "The fact that no man is a hero to his valet has become a portion of the proverbial philosophy of nearly every spoken tongue, and to the thoughtful mind it is no less apparent that even the fairest of her sex is not a heroine in the eyes of her hairdresser. The most obstinate skeptic must throw down the weapons of his unbelief, when to the voice of reason are joined the revelations of a volume which has just seen the light in this city."[9] In contrast, the *Commercial*'s reviewer deadpanned, "*A Hairdresser's Experience in High Life* . . . This is the title of a book just published by the author and placed on sale at RICKEY, MALLORY & Co.'s." Following a brief description of the book, this reviewer concluded, "However truthful, [it] will make said society neither better or [*sic*] wiser."[10]

After reading his rival's lavish review in the *Gazette*, however, the *Commercial*'s reviewer apparently had second thoughts. In two lengthy stories running over the next three days he took jabs at the *Gazette*, labeling its review a "base" effort to boost circulation: "That such a book should not only be published but elaborately puffed in the columns of a respectable journal, affords a bitter satire on the base uses to which the press may come," he fulminated.[11] Perhaps the motive was to erase any doubt his readers might have about his judgment, or perhaps he was following the dictum "if you can't beat them, join them"; in any event, he then generously excerpted the *Gazette*'s review (and *its* excerpts) in the *Commercial*, providing his readers with a so-called "review" of the reviewer in which he tried belatedly to set the record straight.[12]

Despite their aesthetic differences, what makes these reviews remarkable is that they agreed on the truth value of Potter's text. Even though the *Commercial* reviewer initially considered this "gossipy" book as below his consideration, he did not question the veracity of the exposé and indeed corroborated Potter's claims by describing her as "a colored hairdresser, extensively known and patronised by the ladies of this city."[13] The *Gazette* reviewer, in turn, foregrounded what he called Potter's "acute insight" into the lives of fashionable women.

In other words, aside from their different opinions about the quality of the book, both reviewers shared the assumption that what Potter the hairdresser knew and related about "high life" was true or authentic, even reliable. This fact is hard for us to conceive, given our understandings of racially polarized antebellum public spheres as domains in which black writers' truth claims could never be assumed, understandings that make it difficult to imagine how the "bold" pen of a black working woman criticizing her class and racial superiors—"the fairest of her sex"—was not seen as racially scandalous. How could a black working woman get away with speaking thus about her employers, much less garner the wildly favorable review the *Gazette* gave her?[14] Against the backdrop of these questions, *A Hairdresser*'s frank criticism of white women who were seen as its author's social superiors appears to contravene current understandings of antebellum U.S. racial and class hierarchies. This seeming indifference to race appears even more noteworthy when we remember that *A Hairdresser* appeared simultaneously with news of the Harpers Ferry raid.

I attribute the relatively uncontested "authenticity" of Potter's text to its author's emphasis on her empowerment as a hardworking and in-demand hairdresser. By foregrounding her working agency Potter subordinated overtly racialized concerns and recast the coercions of black women's labor exploitation; to this end she used her independent, entrepreneurial, and very lucrative work as one of the nation's first hairdressers at the moment that the production of white bourgeois femininity was emerging as an income-generating "beauty" industry.[15] Furthermore, this emphasis on women's entrepreneurial labor marks her text's particular contribution to the African American literary tradition, a contribution that consists, ironically, in her unapologetic refusal to depict herself as a victim of racial and sexual domination in the antebellum United States. Though she was staunchly opposed to slavery like most black authors, when Potter related her "experience" she did not organize her life story along abolitionist lines. Instead she told the story of her womanhood in the context of her work for elite white women, a context she depicted as an empowering set of social work relations that authorized her economically, socially, and rhetorically. Rather than portray herself as the "drudge" serving wealthy white patrons (Martin Delany's term for black female domestic servants), Potter innovated a racial logic based on her visibility as hairdresser to her clients and readers that refused to collude in the nation's disparagement of her labor. In so doing, she projected the relevance of this work to readers outside the black community in terms that reached beyond the racialized norms of abolition and sentimental reform.

It is not surprising that Potter's narrating emphasis on her labor remains for the most part untheorized: simply put, the hairdresser's own liberatory representation of her labor as the basis for her rhetorical authority is itself problematic for modern readers. As a black worker, Eliza Potter represents a population we define by its nationally disadvantaged status and lack of social legitimacy. Despite this status, Potter chose to represent this work as empowering, not oppressing, her because she perceived the social value of hairdressing in a rather novel way: as contributing knowledge to society about society. She made this understanding abundantly clear in her opening address to *A Hairdresser*'s readers. As she stated in her "Author's Appeal":

> The physician writes his diary, and doubtless his means of discovering the hidden mysteries of life are great. The clergyman, whose calling inspires the deepest confidence, and into whose ear the tales of sorrow are unreservedly breathed, sends forth his diary to an eager world, and other innumerable chroniclers of fireside life have existed; but the hairdresser will yield rivalship to none in this regard. If domestic bitterness and joy, and all the heart-emotions that exist, cannot be discovered by her, she defies all the rest of the world to find them out. (iii)

Potter's comparison of hairdressing to medicine and the clergy is a striking one on several levels. By drawing on an analogy between the hairdresser and professionally identified men who know about the "hidden mysteries of life" Potter attempted to persuade her readers to view her text as a "chronicle" and as pedagogic—as revealing another "hidden" domain, that of "domestic bitterness and joy, and all the heart-emotions that exist." In this way, the hairdresser borrowed the social authority ascribed to the two professional men and rewrote her work—combing heads—into a form of social labor that displaced the negative connotations of women's manual labor. When Potter likened her work to the doctor's and the minister's, she exploited her participation in an emerging beauty "industry" to posit hairdressing's social relationships as the definitive feature of her occupation instead of the actual practice of dressing hair.[16] She affirmed to her readers that hairdressing did not just produce combed heads and beautiful brides; it also, and more important, transformed the hairdresser into a social expert.

Establishing her authority to speak about "domestic bitterness" in this way led Potter to pose another relevant question for her readers: "Why, then, should not the hair-dresser write, as well as the physician and clergyman?" (iv). Why not, indeed? The case Potter made for her readers holds lessons for readers today. Despite black women workers' hypervisibility as the nation's most disparaged labor force and as cultural symbols of racial degradation, the rhetorical authority enunciated by *A Hairdresser* represents an instance of the little-recognized, yet powerful, potential that labor held for authorizing black women's speech in predominantly white, male, and bourgeois public spheres. For this reason, and because of the questions it raises about Eliza Potter's occupational underwriting of her authorship, this volume yields new understandings of the role that black women's work played in shaping and contesting antebellum racialized and gendered languages for public legitimacy.

With its emphasis on the capacities and opportunities unique to this black woman's antebellum labor, *A Hairdresser's Experience in High Life* diverges dramatically from the typical forms and concerns of the reform-oriented narrative tradition of African American literature. Though Potter's text, framed as an autobiography, certainly accords with the recognized centrality of the genre to the nineteenth-century African American literary tradition, this is its strongest and perhaps sole link. Her text for the most part broke ranks with the cultural aesthetics of antebellum abolition, and Potter did not associate herself with the black community's activism on behalf of racial "elevation." Even if her entrepreneurial success clearly indicated the race's capacity for elevation, as a black woman Potter did not fit into the model that viewed entrepreneurial aspirations chiefly as the province for developing black masculinity.[17]

A Hairdresser's Experience in High Life did not offer its readers the reforming woman or the black activist as its chief protagonist. Instead, the narrator related a picaresque tale organized non-chronologically by the places she had visited. Initially appearing as a domestic worker (principally as a children's nurse) and then later as a hairdresser, Potter conceived of her life story as interesting by virtue of where she had been and what she had seen, and not for any kind of conversion from poor to rich, fallen to saved, dominated to free, or single to married. Her text related her travels as a worker to France, England, and U.S. resorts that included Saratoga Springs in the emergence of its heyday and the southern cities of New Orleans and Natchez, Tennessee. The total effect of this non-chronological account is one that Potter appeared to have anticipated when she begged her readers to "overlook much that you will find a little '*harum scarum*'"—in this context, such an appeal was not an empty self-effacing literary gesture, but one that emphasized the degree to which Potter dictated how readers would interpret and value the "sketch" of her life (11).

For Potter's readers, the "rambling and desultory" nature of the hairdresser's account ensured their interest in her well-traveled life (11). This was because her travels intersected with those of a newly emerging social elite that actively sought to display its wealth in venues such as grand hotels, opera houses, and department stores; hence her travels represented both novel work and novel authorship opportunities.[18] The picaresque journeying of the hairdresser through myriad social spaces at home and abroad opened up a space that enabled Potter to represent herself as an interpreter of fashionable life and, in particular, as a mediator to her socially aspiring Cincinnati clients and readers alike. Though she traded on understandings of travel as a socially privileged practice that endowed travelers with cultural authority, the hairdresser located her expertise not simply in her circulation through locales—like Europe or Saratoga—but in a parallel circulation through a social sphere—"high life"—that spoke to her readers' desires to emulate the lifestyles of Cincinnati's elites. *A Hairdresser*'s generic imperatives thus extended beyond the boundaries of the travel narrative with an ethnographic study of a social class, a study that innovated by depicting rich subjects rather than poor ones and that built on earlier "customs and manners" texts, like that of Frances Trollope, which exploited the foibles of Cincinnatians through a similar critique.[19] As Potter commented somewhat sharply in her opening pages, "No one need go into alleys to hunt up wretchedness; they can find it in perfection among the rich and fashionable of every land and nation" (iv). Consequently, though important experiences unrelated to Potter's witnessing of "high life" do make brief appearances in the text—these include being sent to jail for aiding a fugitive slave and being insulted by a woman who called her an abolitionist when such a term was perceived as disreputable—these experiences appear as background to Potter's central role as the "popular and in demand" hairdresser of Cincinnati's elite women. As such a widely circulating and recognized figure, Potter explicitly rejected the terms that posited black women workers' status as incongruous with a modernizing economy and instead represented herself as an expert mediator of dominant social ideologies—in particular those of femininity—and their links to "domestic bitterness."

It is this aspect, Potter's particular inscription within the field of white femininity, that marks the singularity of her trade and her text. For the geographic mobility and economic independence Potter enjoyed while dressing hair effectively rearticulated norms for black femininity in relation to corresponding norms for white elite femininity. Despite her structurally inferior status as hairdresser to her presumed social "superiors," in her representations of her work Potter appears at an advantage relative to her white female employers, not as their racial subordinate; her experience serves to display the foibles of her "betters." In the capacity of the author-hairdresser who is enjoined to listen to all, Potter exploited hairdressing's structural relations of "anonymous friendship" to inscribe herself not as the gossipy and socially inferior servant but as an expert in her clients' shortcomings as ladies. In this way, Potter's less-than-heroic characterizations of her clients are sustained by a professionalized identity that contradicts our understandings of white femininity as always proving deleterious to black women's public legitimacy.[20]

A Hairdresser's reconfiguration of Eliza Potter's working status into one of professional identity is rooted in the hairdresser's liberatory reading of her wage labor. Potter articulates this reading in the account of her initiation into the labor market: "I was brought up in New York, and went out, at an early age, to earn my living, in the service of people of *ton*. For some years, this occupation was agreeable to me; but at length I wearied of it, and being at liberty to choose my own course, I determined to travel, and to gratify my long-cherished desire to see the world—especially the Western world: so I started as soon as possible toward the setting sun" (11). In sharp contrast to the majority of contemporary texts written by African American authors, Potter posits her liberty at her text's beginning, not as an eventual outcome. Being "at liberty" to exercise her choice in employment and, by virtue of that employment, able to "gratify" her "desires," Potter narratively plots the course of her life along lines of autonomy and independence with which her readers could have identified. It bears repeating that this somewhat clichéd declaration of independence is crucial: without it, the stated desire of a domestic servant "to see the world" and to succeed in doing so would not appear feasible. In the ensuing two chapters covering Potter's travels to France and England as servant to different families, her employment remains framed within the context of "choos[ing] my own course," a course that repeatedly enacts the fulfillment of her "desire to see" the different sights of palaces, homes, and parks in the French and English capitals through which she travels. Though descriptions abound of different European tourist sights, such as the Palace of Versailles, Windsor Palace, and St. Paul's Cathedral, rather than unpacking the social meanings of these sights according to the conventions of middle-class travel narratives, Potter's main emphasis remains on "confront[ing] every difficulty in sight-seeing" and marks her gaze on these sights as hard-won and not merely incidental (27, 23).[21]

This framing of Potter's desire "to see" refuted the conventional devaluation of the servant's gaze simply by representing the usually absent perspective of social inferiors. But more important, deriving the very possibility "to see" from the practices of her independent labor established her work experience as central to her text's rhetorical authority. This description of her gaze as one that undergoes a form of special training while in Europe and continues upon her return to the United States thus underwrites her professional claim to produce not simply gossip, but knowledge. This was a high-stakes endeavor, it almost goes without saying, because when Potter's work and travels placed her among French and English ladies, she traversed terrain that was precarious for a minority subject who could easily be perceived as voyeuristic and threatening. That is, the new significance Potter granted her vision could only be persuasive when framed within her own economic independence and, more paradoxically, when represented as a venue for disinterestedness and as a tool for speaking to the public good.

As the review in the *Gazette* suggests, the hairdresser's social critique of her clients corroborated the anxieties many held about the era's unprecedented expansion of wealth and the accompanying new forms of theatricalized, or artificially produced, femininity. These forms for being a "lady" relied on and perpetuated unreliable appearances that enabled socially aspiring women to be attributed with unmerited status and virtue simply on the basis of what they looked like and their participation in the "upper tens" of society. Potter gave proof of what many suspected: that performances of elite status were often deceptive "illusions" with no basis in reality. As the *Gazette*'s reviewer exclaimed, "Before her graphic narrative, as before the spear of Ithuriel, the illusions that becloud the common fancy, disappear like dew before the orb of day; the aroma of divinity with which, aided by imagination, art, French fabrics and perfumery, we are in the habit of investing the lovely creatures in whose sweet faces all the virtues seem to be reflected, is dissipated to return no more forever."[22] Whereas in the past, before market and commercial revolutions, participation in this social domain was contingent on one's unquestionable social standing, the nation's commercial embrace of norms for social mobility made wealth the only determinant. In this new context of myriad, unreliable appearances, Potter's expert gaze exposed the theatricality of femininity enacted in bourgeois/elite social practices ranging across the nation. When she gazed on the "sweet faces" of elite white women, Potter registered the deleterious effects of these social practices on the very bodies of these women. From the pinching husbands to the internecine rivalries initiated by women's competitions for status, Potter exposed how her daily circulation among her clients' many boudoirs revealed the hidden "costs" of these women's aspirations to social status.[23]

How could a simple hairdresser frame her occupation this way? Skeptics could easily point to the irony in characterizing any effort within the emerging commerce of the midcentury beauty industry as disinterested. Potter did testify to the lucrative nature of her occupation, at times relating to her readers the astonishing amounts of money she earned—like the $200 she made in her first "season" as hairdresser on a Mississippi steamboat—but she deployed this aspect of her employment to insist on the autonomy and social independence it provided her. This ready conflation of material independence with social independence enabled Potter to define her participation in her trade more broadly as concerning the proper molding of elite femininity and not simply the artificial production of beauty. For Potter's entry into this occupation afforded her an ambiguous social status that she could exploit to claim such an expertise over her clients' performances of femininity.

An admonition from the 1850s in *Godey's Lady's Book*—"It is a woman's *business* to be beautiful"—attests to the growing dominance of a new field in the antebellum United States that incorporated the mass participation of women as both consumers and producers of a new commodity, "beauty." Historians have tracked the effects of these transformations in the consumption patterns of middle-class women. But less understood is how this industry produced the lucrative, yet socially ambiguous, status of a whole class of workers: beauty entrepreneurs like dressmakers, hairdressers, and cosmeticians, whose work relations constituted a strange amalgam of intimacy, expertise, and manual labor that was in some ways anomalous to the era's increasingly impersonal and market-mediated social practices. The frequent "face to face" interactions between beauty workers and their clients tended to highlight these workers' exposure to, and expert mediation of, ideologies of femininity. Despite the origins of this entrepreneurial field in the era's commercial transformations, then, beauty workers' traffic in intimacy and femininity endowed them with the authority to mediate between their beauty business and the perceived "business" of their clients to *be* beautiful. As one commentator observed in connection with the novel status fashionable dressmakers enjoyed, dressmakers had become "a power in the land."[24]

The Cincinnati hairdresser also appears to have enjoyed a new form of "power," or authority, originating in her trade's dynamics of intimacy and circulation; when Potter described her important role to various clients, she represented her practice as socially wide-ranging and as disinterested—as such, a trade involved in creating *social* knowledge, not simply knowledge about hair. This "disinterested" application of Potter's trade as beauty expert is concretely manifested in the way she represents her work among her elite clientele. Despite its titular prominence, the specifics of hairdressing—the scissors, combs, curlers, and false hair commonly associated with the trade—do not make much of an appearance in the text. Rather, what becomes apparent is Potter's own critical stance toward the profession and industry responsible for her success. While there are occasional society-column-like descriptions of what Miss L. or Mrs. B. wore at such and such a ball, Potter does not appear invested in hairdressing's contribution to the emerging cult of beauty. Her frustration over her clients illustrates this ironic relation to her profession and its cultural milieu: "I find in these days people are more troubled about their looks than they were when I commenced hair-dressing," she expostulates (196). Though she is proud of the demand for her hairdressing skills, Potter's devaluation of the increased emphasis on "looks" squarely located the source of hairdressing's value in the social expertise it provided her, rather than in the grooming opportunities it afforded.

One twentieth-century historian provides us with a context for understanding how Potter's work relations could be seen as participating in the production of such social expertise or knowledge. According to Burton Bledstein, the commercial boom of the antebellum decades was accompanied by an emerging "culture of professionalism" that was rooted in an expansion of professional fields in the wider culture.[25] Under these circumstances, even a simple hairdresser could claim a professional relation to elite femininity. As he explains, "By pointing to and even describing a potential disaster, the professional often reduced the client to a state of desperation in which the victim would pay generously, cooperate fully, and express undying loyalty to the knowledgeable patron who might save him from a threatening universe. The culture of professionalism tended to cultivate an atmosphere of constant crisis—emergency—in which practitioners created work for themselves and reinforced their authority by intimidating clients."[26]

One did not have to go far during the antebellum period to encounter this "atmosphere of constant crisis." Amid the nation's unparalleled prosperity, the increasing theatricality of status and femininity that was associated with the mercantile ideology of social mobility provoked anxieties that one historian has described as generating a "crisis in confidence."[27] Copious advice literature from this period speaks to these anxieties, in particular to the feared prevalence of "confidence men" and "painted women" who signaled the dangerous erosion of preindustrial interpersonal relations. These anxieties spoke to the inadequacy of existing social forms to represent status and class, while also pointing to the serious problem of deducing intentions from the potentially deceptive appearances of socially mobile strangers: "In this world of strangers, the advice writers feared, appearances were valued more than realities, and surface impressions proved more important than inner virtues."[28]

Potter's critical gaze discerns the contradictions posed by a society that readily equated wealth with virtue and happiness as well as the antagonistic, rather than harmonious, nature of a society that ostensibly viewed competition as an instrument for the promotion of the public good. Rather than harmony and cultural stability, Potter's analysis suggests that the possibility of attaining status on the basis of wealth (instead of virtue) engendered a conflicted and hostile social realm that belied the very claims to status it was presumed to uphold. Deploying her trained gaze, the hairdresser pinpointed the problems in "high life" for her readers. One salient instance of this critical gazing and interpretation occurs in relation to the "magnificent sight" of a Saratoga ballroom during one of Potter's stays at the resort:

> In the hight [*sic*] of the season at Saratoga the ball-room presented a magnificent sight. The wealthiest persons in the country were there congregated, each trying to outvie the other. . . . The proud lady of fashion was there, who, having outlived all her better feelings, was only happy, only really existed amid such scenes; and near her the young metropolitan beauty, brilliant in appearance, but in feeling almost as old and heartless as her companion; while not far off could be seen the belle of some small city, blushing, beautiful, trembling, showing plainly, in her innocent countenance, how unused she was to such scenes of splendor. Among the gentlemen were some celebrated . . . men of high station and ability; others widely known on account of . . . their energy in business; and occasionally one could see in the crowd a few well-dressed, handsome gentlemen, apparently intellectual, exceedingly agreeable in conversation, and polite in manner, yet

> mostly avoided by ladies and gentlemen. These are the fortune-hunters, many of whom every season congregate at Saratoga, staying from the beginning of the season until the end in search of wealth. (72–73)

Potter's roving gaze inventories the opulent display and feelings of a Saratoga ball to expose the conflicts that belie the visual pleasure, harmony, and prosperity implied by this scene. Where wealthy persons are congregated, competition, not collaboration, is the driving force, with "each trying to outvie the other." The beautiful countenances of the women hide the existential poverty in which many of them live, some of them even the potential prey of the fortune-hunters circling in the background.

As a prosperous frontier city seeking to establish a stable social identity for itself, Cincinnati displayed a sense of crisis in relation to its own society. *A Hairdresser's Experience in High Life* capitalized on this sense of crisis, like other contemporary writings, by locating the significance of Potter's work relations and professional gaze in their encounter and familiarity with the critical implications of appearances in a socially mobile society. Confronting the apparent waning of feminine virtue and the growing number of "painted women," the hairdresser was uniquely equipped to discern which of her clients really possessed the all-important "inner virtues." Consequently, Potter's mission evolved into the dissection of appearances and the adjudication of who was a "lady" and who was not. As a rule of thumb, Potter self-assuredly asserts, "Society is made up of varieties; but it is easy for the humblest servant to distinguish the well-born and highly-bred lady, under the plainest garb, from the parvenu woman, whose sudden good luck and well-filled purse dresses her in lace, seats her in a carriage, and places her in circles where she is more endured than courted" (13). This representation of a double-masquerade—that of the "well-born and highly-bred lady, under the plainest garb" versus "the parvenu woman . . . dress[ed] in lace"—defines the exegetical task in which Potter as a beauty expert perceived herself to be engaged. The appearance of the "highly-bred lady" in plain garb is based on a gendered ideal of classlessness that suggests this woman is recognizable as a "lady" no matter what she is wearing and that as such a figure she transcends social conflict.[29] Relatedly, the social aspirations of the "parvenu" woman seeking to project her status through expensive clothes signal her "unladylike" participation in a competition for status and in the production of class difference.

Potter's exposé of "parvenu" women's inauthentic performances of status represented a gendered strategy that upheld the hegemonic view of true femininity as symbolizing cultural harmony and virtue—a view that contrasted sharply with new commercial models for competition and profit. In this regard, Potter's critique of these women and her description of a "lady" resonates with historian Mary Ryan's description of the symbolic power ascribed to antebellum "true" women. As Ryan observes, "The female image seemed to disarm and dissolve the contentious differences in industrial America. She was without a class, without a party, and bespoke differences that could be ascribed to nature rather than politics or economics."[30] When she confronts the overt class pretensions of socially mobile women, Potter is in effect appealing to residual cultural ideologies in which gender and elite status appear as forms of classlessness and virtue.

While Potter's travels and her narratives range across the nation and follow the seasonal migrations of the upper class (for example, residing in Saratoga Springs during the summer and New Orleans in winter), the theme of bourgeois women's masquerade as "ladies" receives its fullest treatment in the book's concluding chapter on Cincinnati. In this chapter, Potter's descriptions of her clients are aimed at convincing her readers of several of her clients' false pretensions to ladyhood, and of the failure of their wealth and status to conceal their obvious lack of merit from her discerning eyes. Rather than behaving as the ladies they appear to be, these women are callous to each other while assiduously indulging their social aspirations at the expense of all else, most especially at the expense of propriety. Potter's narrative displays her ample concern with these improprieties, cataloging the indecorous and cannibalizing tendencies of these women's competition for status.

The unseemly behaviors Potter describes include a vicious instrumentalizing of gossip as a personalized tool for publicity "to blast each other's characters" (76), a cynical manipulation of appearances that includes laying traps for rival women with courting males (75), and slandering women behind their backs while "to their faces they were all kindness and love" (77). Potter did not stint in relating these unladylike behaviors, and she often mobilized her work experience abroad to compare her clients unfavorably with "European ladies." In the case of the former, their greedy aspirations to social status were plainly manifest in their ludicrous performance of sociality:

> European ladies go to parties more for the sake of meeting friends and passing an agreeable evening, than for the sake of what they eat; but I have known our ladies refuse to eat either dinner or supper, so that they might be able to eat the more at night, or as many of them express it, that they might stuff themselves; and often when I have been so tired . . . and would complain of being hungry . . . they would say to me, never mind, you will be there to-night, stuff yourself. . . . Yes, I have seen our ladies and gentlemen standing round the door of the supper room before supper was announced, and actually I have heard the waiter beg for room to carry in the jellies, ice creams, and so forth. (202–3)

Greedy clients who recommend Potter "stuff [her]self" clearly disregard the polite and socializing aspects of the parties they attend. With this image of a feeding frenzy, Potter stripped off the thin veneer of social gentility of those she viewed as undeserving socially mobile people.

The depiction of her clients' shortcomings not only suggests Potter's ironic, distanced relationship with both the profession and the clients who have invested her with the cultural capital with which she trades; more important, it also figures as the occasion for the hairdresser to make herself visible in a unique way. Potter's expressed frustration over her clients' faux pas makes clear her nostalgia for a presumably more civil, or genteel, time as well as her own rejection of her clients' attempts to draw her in: "Affairs in our Queen City are not managed as they used to be," she expostulates to one woman, "for I remember the time when a lady would never for a moment think of speaking disparagingly of another in any way; but now the ladies have got a habit of talking about others to make themselves grand; some will talk to their hair-dresser, and some to their milliner or dressmaker, about Mrs. or Miss This-or-That, and pick her to pieces" (281–82). Far from shrinking into the background in response to this behavior, Potter continually represents herself to her readers as disciplining her clients' inappropriate actions. *A Hairdresser* suggests that it was Potter's visibility to her clients in this disciplinary mode that corroborated most fully the claim she made to being an expert in elite femininity.

In one notable instance, Potter describes how her stated refusal to comb one woman elicited another client's request for an explicit statement on her criteria for ladyhood:

> At last mentioning a certain lady's name, they asked if I combed her, I told them no, I did not, as I combed none but ladies. They then wanted to know what I thought constituted a lady. Laying down my work, I rose to my feet and said, "Ladies, I can not tell you what I think constitutes a lady, and keep my seat. I must get up. I do not think all those are ladies who sit in high places, or those who drive around in fine carriages, but those only are worthy the name who can trace back their generations without stain, honest and respectable, that love and fear God, and treat all creatures as they merit, regardless of nations, stations, or wealth. These are what I say constitute a lady. (279–80)

This example dramatizes the inextricability of Potter's occupational agency and her visibility to her clients and readers precisely in relation to her expertise on what "constitutes a lady." It confutes the received wisdom that attributes the black servant's access to privileged social domains to her hegemonic invisibility. When Potter stands up in this client's boudoir, there is no denying that all eyes are on her, including those of her readers.

This novel legitimation of a black woman's laboring visibility is crucial to understanding the gender politics of Potter's iconoclastic speech. The terms of social authority in which Potter as waged beauty worker made herself and her labor visible underscored her allegiance to waning preindustrial social structures and her endorsement of their indices of merit. Potter's definition of "lady" derives partly from birth—she is one who can "trace back their generations without stain"—but also from behavior—she "treats all creatures as they merit, regardless of nations, stations, or wealth." More important, because this formulation of antebellum ladyhood, rooted in dominant values, was perceived as in crisis, it provided Potter with a site through which she could mediate the supposed incommensurability of black and white femininity. On the basis of this professional formulation of white femininity "in crisis," the "humble," or subordinate, status of the black working woman did not have to be viewed as necessarily, or inevitably, degraded.

In this way, apparently motivated by her stated loyalty to preindustrial elites, Potter's hearty pitching of the work-related attributes she cherished—hairdressing's independence, its mobility and "public" status as a marketable and lucrative occupation—forestalled the possibility of readers perceiving her as flouting sentimental gender mores. Furthermore, Potter's "dressing down" of her clients represented a critique of white bourgeois women firmly grounded in the name of elite white femininity, rather than in an overt rejection of such femininity per se.[31] The recitation of failed ladyhood at the heart of *A Hairdresser* suggests that despite her unsympathetic treatment of her clients and her reiterated narrating independence, Potter's commitment to the professional field of beauty articulated a nostalgic investment in preindustrial gender norms that belied prevailing cynicism over the motivation of workers in this lucrative field. As such, Potter's text could be perceived as confirming, rather than provoking, bourgeois whites' anxieties about their unstable and worrisome gender system.

In this light, the parallel that the *Cincinnati Daily Gazette* reviewer drew between the hairdresser and the valet shows how even as a representative of a new industry the hairdresser could be figured within older frames of social value. Notwithstanding Potter's very modern embodiment as an economically and emotionally independent woman, as a worker embedded within, but also displaced from, social domains dominated by masquerade, she occupied something of an anachronistic role as a preindustrial residuum not (directly) involved in, nor aspiring to, social masquerade.[32] *A Hairdresser* exploited these contradictory rhetorical interstices and permitted Potter to subvert provisionally the racial and class order through her descriptions of her employers' less-than-laudable natures. For this selfsame subversion of the social hierarchy could be perceived simultaneously as representing an investment in the maintenance of a preindustrial and racialized class order.

When grafted onto the servant's anachronistic status, typically interpreted as signifying the black woman's incongruity to a modernizing economy, the hairdresser's personalized services represented an opportunity for Potter to rewrite herself as an apt interpreter of feminine modernity. In this regard, then, Potter's text shows us that black women could "reconstruct womanhood" and mediate the presumed incompatibility of race and femininity with figures that went beyond the race-reforming or middle-class domestic subject. *A Hairdresser's Experience in High Life* speaks to the possibility that gender performances by black women workers could in reality have appeared much more wedded to, even while in tension with, hegemonic frameworks for antebellum womanhood than we have been willing to recognize. Capitalizing on the increasing cultural emphasis on beauty and femininity, this black woman leveraged her conventionally disparaged status as public and manual laborer into a forum for expertise on the effects of the era's social mobility on women. In this way, she rewrote what it meant to "subscribe" to these norms. Potter's status as beauty expert enabled her to professionally perform norms for womanhood without actually having to embody them herself. Professionally it does not "take one to know one," and as a result, as an author/narrator embedded in an independently established professional perspective, Potter evaded the problems commonly associated with marginalized black authors. Just like the doctor she invokes whose treatment of the sick patient is unrelated to his own health, Potter could "treat" the unladylike without herself having to qualify as a "lady." In this way, we may account for the professionally mediated rhetorical legitimacy at the heart of *A Hairdresser*'s representation of its author's raced, gendered, and classed identity. For it is in offering her services to society as a whole, and not simply to her race or to any specific political cause like abolition, that Potter could occupy the culturally unstable social network that provided her with lucrative employment as hairdresser and with rhetorical proto-professional "employment" as social critic.[33]

The Reception of the Hairdresser

Cincinnati newspaper reviews of *A Hairdresser's Experience in High Life* confirm that, on the whole, Potter's text was perceived as attesting to bourgeois whites' own prevailing anxieties about their emerging and worrisomely unstable class system.[34] Furthermore, while two reviews were sympathetic and one was unfavorable, all of these reviews suggest that these anxieties over the era's cultural and social transformations were prevalent and significant enough to displace (even if only temporarily) anxieties concerned with preserving the racial status quo.

"No man is a hero to his valet" is how the *Cincinnati Daily Gazette* reviewer opened his lengthy and largely favorable review of *A Hairdresser*. Rather than reading Potter's critique of her clients as a form of impudence, the ironically imputed disaffiliation between stereotyped servant and employer to which this adage refers instead foregrounds the hidden knowledge the intimate servant/employer social relationship provides to the valet de chambre. From this perspective, Potter's critique, while novel to modern readers attuned only to the racially defensive nature of black writers' social criticism, takes on the appearance of a universal trope. It also underscores the servant's simultaneous marginality and importance in a conservative, and hence powerful, function. Where the social superior appears dominated by change and masquerade, the servant—who as the "valet de *chambre*" could very well be the predecessor of the hairdresser who labors in the "private boudoir"—appears anachronistically as a preindustrial residuum *not* involved in, nor aspiring to, social masquerade.[35] The servant's recognition of his or her employer's unheroic nature, then, is valuable to the community as a whole because it holds out the possibility of continuity and stability amid social change.

The *Gazette*'s review referred to the conservative tenor of Potter's critique even as it exploited *A Hairdresser*'s selling points as a gossipy tome revealing the foibles of the city's elites. Following the reviewer's brief introduction, the article devoted the entirety of two of its leading columns, adjacent to an editorial on John Brown, to thirteen subheaded excerpts from the book, which it claimed constituted the "most sagacious criticism on the society and institutions of our own beloved city."[36] Attributing the critical text to the "bold, if not very polished pen of MRS. POTTER (formerly Mrs. Johnson)," the review characterized Potter's perspective as displaying an "astonishingly acute insight into motives and thoughts, [the] same sturdy independence of opinion" that should convince even the most "obstinate skeptic" what others understand through the "voice of reason": that "even the fairest of her sex is not a heroine in the eyes of her hair-

DAILY GAZETTE.

Office—Gazette Buildings, North-East Corner of Fourth and Vine.

WEDNESDAY, OCTOBER 19, 1859.

☞ City Subscribers, 15 cents per week, payable to carriers. Orders left at our Office, corner of Fourth and Vine, will be promptly attended to.

UNPAID LABOR IN INSURRECTION.

Capital and labor have essentially a common interest. With their relations at all correctly adjusted, there can be no antagonism between the persons representing the one power and the other, in the machinery of political economy. One is necessary to the other. Both are invested in the means of production for a common good. When these two elementary powers, therefore, come in conflict, there is somewhere a serious wrong. The fault may be on one side or the other. It is not necessarily to be found on that of capital alone. The laborer is sometimes unreasonable in his demands, as to price and conditions. He not unfrequently "strikes," bringing about a combination altogether wrong in itself, even if the object sought to be gained may be right. Yet it cannot be denied that there is usually some real grievance on the part of the employer, when the employed are found resorting to violence in order to remedy alleged evils. It takes very much to rouse and combine any considerable body of laboring men, even where their ordinary association is somewhat intimate. The laboring classes have generally proved themselves very forbearing, even

REVELATIONS OF A FASHIONABLE HAIR DRESSER.

The Upper Ten of Cincinnati, by one who Knows Them.

The fact that no man is a hero to his valet has become a portion of the proverbial philosophy of nearly every spoken tongue, and to the thoughtful mind it is no less apparent that even the fairest of her sex is not a heroine in the eyes of her hair-dresser. The most obstinate skeptic must throw down the weapons of his unbelief, when to the voice of reason are joined the revelations of a volume which has just seen the light in this city.

A HAIR-DRESSER'S EXPERIENCE IN HIGH LIFE is the title of a handsome duodecimo, which we are authorized to attribute to the bold, if not very polished, pen of Mrs. POTTER, (formerly Mrs. Johnson,) long and favorably known in the most exclusive circles of the West and Southwest, in which she sets forth her Life Thoughts — the experiences of the hair-dresser, the cosmopolite and the confidante, in her travels through the broad expanse of the Union, and in more than one voyage across the storm-crested Atlantic. Whether she leads the reader in imagination amid the historic associations and imperial pomps of the French capital, amid the labyrinthine mazes of London, or to the scenes of gayety and resorts of fashion in America, the same astonishingly acute insight into motives and thoughts, the same sturdy independence of opinion marks her transcripts of events of which she can truly say *Magna pars fui.* Before her graphic narrative, as before the spear of Ithuriel, the illusions that becloud the common

Cincinnati Daily Gazette *review of* A Hairdresser's Experience in High Life, *October 19, 1859.*

dresser." That is, this reviewer accepted Potter's claims to independence pretty much on her own terms.

The "acuteness" that the review attributes to Potter's insights and opinions, in particular, firmly upholds Potter's claims to penetrating the obvious. The reviewer concurred with Potter's assessment of city society women's deceptive performances of virtue as "illusions that becloud the common fancy." His startling Miltonic parallel, comparing Potter's exposure of these women to the exposure of Satan's seduction of Eve, makes evident on whom he cast his opprobrium. This analogy simultaneously figures Potter's critique as an instrument for the public good and represents the elite women Potter describes as gone to the devil. The review thus roundly endorses Potter's description of this social world and concurs with her description of this domain as an irremediably fallen one, despite its alluring and wonderful appearance.[37]

Potter's judgments, characterized in this review as "important truths," are also described as her "Life Thoughts—the experiences of the hair-dresser, the cosmopolite and the confidante" and appear clearly mobilized in the service of the public welfare and cultural stability, rather than as subversive. This description of Potter's interpretations as contributing to cultural stability, and ultimately to her own legitimation, does not coincide with contemporary descriptions of manual wage laborers. Rather, what this representation of Potter's labor suggests is the manner in which *A Hairdresser*'s combination of independence, frankness, and special work-related training—all tending toward the public good—point to nineteenth-century understandings of the professional as one who "improv[es] his worldly lot as he offer[s] his services to society."[38]

For my purposes, the second, less favorable review that appeared in the *Cincinnati Daily Commercial* displays a marked tendency to resist the legitimating properties of Potter's critique. Yet in its very resistance the competing review (produced by a politically more conservative paper) supports the legitimating potential to which Potter's self-representation as hairdresser testifies. In fact, it is precisely the *Gazette*'s laudatory interpretation of *A Hairdresser's Experience in High Life*, rather than Potter's text itself, with which the *Commercial*'s reviewer takes issue. The *Commercial*'s follow-up review headline, "A

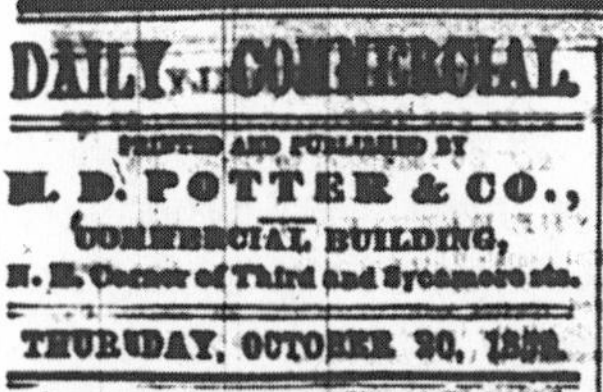

DAILY COMMERCIAL.

PRINTED AND PUBLISHED BY

M. D. POTTER & CO.,

COMMERCIAL BUILDING,

N. E. Corner of Third and Sycamore sts.

THURSDAY, OCTOBER 20, 185[9]

A report of the proceedings of the American Christian Missionary Society in session in this city, will be found in another column. It is very numerously attended, and many distinguished preachers are enrolled among the delegates.

We print in another place a very interesting letter from Kossuth. It gives his impressions concerning the Villa Franca peace, and abounds in important information. There is little in it that is comforting to Austria, and much that must be productive of profound disquietude in the halls of the Kaiser.

The Harper's Ferry Business.

There is no doubt but our dispatches regarding this affair, receive a coloring from the inflamed condition of the public mind in the communities from which they are received, and that nothing of a sensational nature is lost in course of transmission over the wires; but there can be no longer any cause for hesitancy, in declaring that the facts which are clearly apparent, are of the most remarkable nature, and calculated to startle and amaze the whole country. The "Abolitionists" are at the bottom of it sure enough. The developments made in the telegraphic dispatches, which will be found under the appropriate head, are clear as to this point. There appears in the plot as now exposed, all the characteristics of the extreme Abolition faction—its total impracticability, its incendiary want of regard for consequences, its incapability of appreciating circumstances, its intemperate and incoherent zeal, its frantic fanaticism in behalf of a single purpose, and that unattainable, its fullness of courage and emptiness of discretion, sympathy untempered by reason, and devotion to an end without understanding as to the means. The long and loud madness of these people has taken form. It has been crystalized into a plot. It has for the moment abandoned vague declamation, and essayed definite action.—The result is an attempt by a score of men, to Revolutionize the States of Virginia and Maryland. Now who of all the world, but an Abolitionist, does not know that if the Provisional Government of old John Brown had been backed by a disciplined force of ten thousand or fifty thousand men, it would have been speedily crushed out? But Mr. Brown & Co. concluded that twenty men were sufficient. Their measures were characterized by the marvelous secrecy and cunning noticed in the tricks of the patients in insane asylums. They selected that which they considered the tender point of the South, and there collected munitions of war, Sharpe's

A Reviewer Reviewed.

The Gazette of yesterday had the extraordinary good taste to devote two of its leading columns to extracts from what it terms "Revelations of a Fashionable Hair dresser." The book in question—briefly noticed by us yesterday—was written, or procured to be written, by a person fashionably known as a "lady ob color," who has spent her life in combing, frizzling, curling, and otherwise adorning, for a suitable consideration, the female members of "our best society." The book is distinguished by nothing so much as that total lack of taste and delicacy which we should expect to find in a work professing to narrate "a hair-dresser's experience in high life." The innate vulgarity, the prying curiosity, the offensive coarseness of the class to which the author belongs, are fitly and fully illustrated in its pages. To have been, or to have imagined herself to have been, the trusted *confidante* and the intimate toilette companion of a lady, is here made a warrant for writing down and deliberately publishing to the world whatever tales of gossip and scandal may have floated to her ears respecting that lady or her circle of friends. To have been elevated to the high honor of dressing a lady's hair, is here made a license for publicly assuming the office of the arbiter of her character, the critic of her person, and the censor of her morals.

It is the production of this impudent pretender to literary honors, whose sins against grammar and good taste are only excelled by her shameless violation of all the confidences of private life, that the exemplary Gazette introduces to the world, with the following flourish of head lines, and of praise:

REVELATIONS OF A FASHIONABLE HAIR-DRESSER.

THE UPPER TEN OF CINCINNATI, BY ONE WHO KNOWS THEM.

A Hair-Dresser's Experience in High Life

Sets forth her Life Thoughts—the experiences of the hair-dresser, the cosmopolite and the confidante, in her travels through the broad expanse of the Union. The same astonishingly acute insight into motives and thoughts, the same sturdy independence of opinion, marks her transcript of events, of which she can truly say, *Magna pars fui*. Before her graphic narrative, as before the spear of Ithuriel, the illusions that cloud the common fancy disappear like dew before the orb of day; the aroma of divinity with which, aided by imagination, art, French fabrics and perfumery, we are in the habit of investing the lovely creatures in whose sweet faces all the virtues seem to be reflected, is dissipated to return no more forever.

That is—to translate the rhetoric into plain prose—Here is a book which we pronounce a successful effort to dispel all the "illusions" which have heretofore invested the feminine character and the domestic circle; to render public and common all that has hitherto been regarded as private and sacred; to tear the veil from the face of modesty, to profane what is holy, to vulgarize what is virtuous, and to belittle what is noble; in short, to exhibit to the public, by the help of skillful innuendos and downright initials, the virtues, faults, graces, foibles, and other characteristics of the wives and daughters of our most

Cincinnati Daily Commercial *review of* A Hairdresser's Experience in High Life, *in which the writer takes exception to the* Gazette*'s favorable review of the book. October 20, 1859.*

Reviewer Reviewed," confirms this angle on the text and its ensuing publicity.

In its initial review (appearing the same day as the *Gazette*'s), the *Commercial* provided a rather innocuous paragraph briefly noting the title, identity of the author, and the text's place of sale. It was only in its review the following day that the *Commercial* reviewer explicitly castigated what it perceived as the *Gazette*'s shameless bid for readers. Responding to the *Gazette*'s dedication of "two leading columns" to a book he had seen fit to dismiss, the *Commercial*'s reviewer questioned the *Gazette*'s portrayal of Potter's text as useful. Somewhat ironically, as part of this refutation, the *Commercial* reviewer himself generously excerpted the rival review's own excerpts, not only undermining his own critique, but also inadvertently attesting to the appeal of Potter's text.

The *Commercial* termed Potter's text "a vast amount of gossip," even so conceding, as mentioned above, that "however truthful, [it] will make said society neither better or [*sic*] wiser, but will doubtless *sell* the book, and perhaps the purchaser."[39] Despite its skepticism, the *Commercial* review nonetheless registered the very possibility of the public service that Potter claimed. Only in the ensuing debate that engaged both papers' reviewers did the *Commercial* reviewer disavow the possibility to which it had earlier admitted by retracting its initial attribution of "truth." Taking on the *Gazette*'s affirmation of Potter's professionally derived "acute insight," the *Commercial* reviewer focused subsequently on refuting the link Potter made between her occupation and her penetrating gaze. "To have been elevated to the high honor of dressing a lady's hair," he argued, "is here made a license for publicly assuming the office of the arbiter of her character, the critic of her person, and the censor of her morals."

In contrast to the *Gazette*, which accepted Potter's exegetical and femininity-upholding claims, the *Commercial* read Potter's exposé rather literally as "render[ing] public and common all that has hitherto been regarded as private and sacred; [as] tear[ing] the veil from the face of modesty, profan[ing] what is holy, vulgaris[ing] what is virtuous, and belittl[ing] what is noble." In other words, this reviewer displaced the crisis to which Potter's expertise referred; he did not see virtuous femininity as imperiled by social mobility so much as imperiled by a presumptuous hairdresser. He overlooks Potter's self-proclaimed independence from this femininity (this is one explanation, at least, since he does not discredit her independence as an outright lie), pinpoints *A Hairdresser*'s origins in Potter's social aspirations, and labels the author an "imitator of fashion, and a pretender to gentility." That is, even as he refutes it, this reviewer recognizes the claim to public good that Potter makes through her critique of socially aspiring parvenus: "A vulgar and incompetent person undertook publicly to criticise things utterly beyond her capacities, and appears to have assumed that her function of hairdresser to refined ladies entitled her to perform the same office by their characters, *for the benefit not of themselves but the public*" (emphasis added). It should not surprise us that the *Commercial*'s reviewer, true to the name of his paper, would resist recognizing the social crisis in confidence that Potter and many others perceived accompanied the nation's commercial expansion. Consequently, this reviewer can only undermine Potter's claims to providing a public service by displacing the anxieties to which her text refers: it is the hairdresser's social aspirations to authorship, and by extension her vulgarity, not her clients' social pretensions and shortcomings, that he finds worrisome.

The reviewer bases a large part of his critique on his tautologically established opinion of Potter's "vulgarity" and on his frank bemusement over the authority accorded Potter on the basis of her "profession." Ironically, however, this reviewer concedes hairdressers' epistemological privilege, even as he refutes Potter's, by admitting that some hairdressers (including fictional ones!) were competent to the task: "Little Miss MOWCHER, in DAVID COPPERFIELD, whose profession constitutes the only point of comparison to the author of this book, was possessed of wit and of prudence; the present writer appears to possess neither the one nor the other." This critic's refusal of Potter's imputed cultural authority signals the difficulties involved in asserting cultural influence on the basis of manual labors. Instead, the review links Potter to a "crisis" of another kind—a literary one that radically denies the critical and cultural authority of workers.

Declaring Potter to be an "impudent pretender to literary honors, whose sins against grammar and good taste are only excelled by her shameless violation of all the confidences of private life," this reviewer depicts Potter's text as marking a significant breach in literary authority. His points concerning the author's "indifferent knowledge of the correct use of language" and her flawed presentation—"she exhibits no skill in the treatment of motives or the analysis of character"—are central to his critique. But in framing *A Hairdresser's Experience in High Life* as a literary failure, and by disregarding Potter's own disclaimers about her "humble condition" and "harum scarum" narrative, this reviewer again signals, even when he refutes, the text's social potential: "When we find a genuine satirist, who exposes the foibles and the follies of fashionable life with an unsparing hand, we welcome him as a benefactor to society; but when we see an incompetent and vulgar person, who begins by betraying confidence, and ends by vulgarising the proprieties of life, and blazoning private relations to the world, we are forced to take note of it as an impertinence and an imposition." Here it is clear that this reviewer rejects *A Hairdresser* on the basis of Potter's postulated literary incompetence and her failure to qualify as a "genuine satirist"—rather than on the basis of the information she provides. For the *Commercial*'s reviewer, literary and cultural authority are irrevocably linked to bourgeois male gender privilege, and it is Potter's trespass against this privilege against which he fulminates.

Ultimately, Potter's literary trespass provokes a comment from this reviewer that is as revealing as it is ironic, specifically in relation to the critic's refusal to address the social crisis Potter's text points to: "The sole reason of the censure we felt bound to record, may be found in the fact that whenever we see an elaborate endeavor in any quarter to impose upon the public, we are accustomed to expose it to the best of our ability. In the present case, it is probable that the wretched performance in question would have escaped a portion of its deserts, but for the attempt, publicly made, to give it the *entrée* to respectable society." While the critic gives no credence to the problems Potter diagnoses pertaining to social mobility, he casts *A Hairdresser* itself as a parvenu whose "wretched performance" is aimed at attaining unmerited respectability. In this way, the *Commercial*'s reviewer calls Potter's bluff as it were, representing her textual embodiment as social critic as a form of social mobility as egregious as any described within her text. In this backhanded way, he confirms the "problem" represented by the social mobility of the undeserving at the heart of *A Hairdresser*, even though he perceives the threat in terms of a transgression of literary professionalism.

To different degrees, then, both reviews affirm the relevance of Potter's text to its cultural milieu, recognizing, even as they disagree, the potential social authority that Potter wields as hairdresser. We see in this antebellum debate over the meanings of social mobility, femininity, and labor how a black worker might make herself visible as an expert in the field without always having to resort to racially evasive measures (without having to "veil" herself), or without having to commodify herself for the benefit of her white readers' consumption. As hairdresser-turned-author, Potter exploits and straddles the ambivalence that her occupation represents to the social order.[40] In this case, hairdressing opens a rhetorical interstice through which Potter represents her investment in the maintenance of a preindustrial and racialized class order, even if that order would deny her the very authority she claims it yields her.

This is just one of the paradoxes related to Eliza Potter's claims to social authority. Another has to do with how the status of a lowly esteemed servant, valet de chambre, or hairdresser might have provided black workers the opportunity to mediate publicly and to figure in the nation's transformation from preindustrial to modern. If Potter's status as a beauty worker located her in a preindustrial "face to face" social relationship that offered her clients and readers some intimacy and stability in the face of momentous change, it was also as a harbinger of gendered modernity, or as a successful participant in an emergent industry, that she was able to position herself as an expert in femininity. Such were the instabilities in the cultural domain of womanhood that Potter could be both premodern and modern in powerful and unrecognized ways. For the remainder of this chapter I will take up another paradoxical aspect of the era's cultural instabilities: how they offered and withheld the democratic potential that underwrites Potter's representation of a "poor working woman." While it is clear that the economic independence Potter's work affords her as beauty expert is crucial to her rhetorical and social independence (as narrator and as employee), *A Hairdresser's Experience in High Life* also brings into view some of the limitations inhering in the cultural status of a working woman, white or black. While her work history "authorizes" her in a manner novel for a "humble" hairdresser, the text testifies to another anxiety: Potter's own concern about the erosion in social status that she and other workers experienced during the antebellum commercial transformations.

The Perils of Working Entitlement

The unstable cultural field of hegemonic femininity that Potter exploited to create her liberated, rather than racially disadvantaged, narrating persona produced other effects evident in *A Hairdresser's Experience in High Life*. Though Potter's liberatory reading of her labor testifies to its legitimating potential, *A Hairdresser* makes clear the contradiction that labor itself—even in its liberatory form—could not provide entrance to the world of democratic equality. The anxieties Potter expresses about her status as a "working woman" register the complex negotiations that enabled a freeborn black woman to transform the dynamics of her visibility as black author into a rhetoric that also testified to the precarious status of the writer as *woman worker*.

Alongside the crisis in confidence Potter discerns among her clients and readers, *A Hairdresser* testifies to Potter's own crisis in confidence: one cohering around the emerging stigma associated with labor that enabled female manual workers to become independent from their families. This "crisis" provides insight into the text's ambivalent and often conflicted engagement with discourses of gendered labor, displaying the relish with which Potter described the sociality of her work for elite white women while also speaking to the potential problems this independent status and work-derived entitlement afford her. Though Potter's successful and "in-demand" status prevents her from being confused with the dominant "factory girl" model for the female manual worker, she frequently equivocates between describing herself as "working woman" and "lady." In particular, her defensiveness about her own well-appointed wardrobe suggests that as a self-identified woman worker Potter had to negotiate the subaltern cultural status of the white woman worker as well as that of black women in general.

Specifically, *A Hairdresser* displays Potter's concern about the lack of status accorded to economically and emotionally autonomous women workers. Though Potter frames her work in relation to the republican virtue associated with the dignity of labor, her text rehearses the concerns and contradictions expressed by other women workers who sought to defend the paid (and most often, manual) work that was perceived as imperiling their legitimacy as gendered subjects. Women workers in the antebellum period not only contended with the economically exploitative relations of paid women's work; they also contended with the social stigma associated with working for pay during the emerging dominance of the domestic, middle-class "true woman."[41] In this light, Potter's oft-postulated "liberty," her "desire to see," and her ability to "choose [her] own course," combined with the relative obscurity to which she consigns her familial ties, exemplify both the utopian and the problematic potential of her labor. That is, the terms in which Potter constructs herself as a worker render her unable to simultaneously construct herself as wife and mother (two identities she did in fact possess) in the tradition of abolitionist reform.

Potter exploits the utopian potential of her itinerant labor and contains its problematic potential by framing her account as part travel narrative. As informed traveler at home and abroad, Potter could have been seen as participating in a tradition associated with black male writers like William Wells Brown or Frederick Douglass. More important, readers could possibly associate Potter's freedom of mobility with their own and view her liberty as consonant with, and not necessarily breaching, the bounds of female propriety. For example, while working in New Orleans, Potter recalls, "I determined, what I had not seen . . . I would see now: so I went to the highest circles, then to the lowest; to the free people, and to the slave people; and everywhere it was proper for a woman to go" (184). More pointedly, Potter invokes the propriety of all her actions in a variety of contexts when she describes her frustration over a client's misbehavior: "Often have I labored under such animadversions," she expostulated, "and expect to till I die; but one thing I am assured of, I can defy any individual, North, South, East or West, to say I ever did or said anything but was ladylike and courteous" (201). In relation to her clients and as an expert in femininity, Potter again appears at an advantage. But if we see the hairdresser containing the deleterious effects of her working mobility and autonomy in these instances, elsewhere we can see how the rewards of her labor could put her at ironic odds with the social hierarchies she ostensibly upholds.

Potter's extensive and fashionable dress is the working entitlement that manifests the greatest instability in terms of class and gender meanings. Perhaps concerns about this dress escaped her clients, since Potter's access as beauty expert to the boudoirs of elite women potentially dictated that she dress "high," if not exactly like them. But Potter's encounter with railroad executives for the purpose of reimbursing her for losses in a train fire, and later the friendly advice of a fellow worker, make it clear that, in general, Potter's dress appeared above her station as a "working woman." At these moments, Potter's fashionable dress sense appears linked to the transgressive affinities of working women who enacted their empowerment as wage earners by wearing clothes that were perceived to subvert class hierarchies. Like the factory women who refuted middle-class women's efforts to represent factory girls' newfound buying power simply as a sign of their classed impropriety, Potter as hairdresser worked to forestall the suspect nature of this entitlement by representing her wardrobe as a badge of her earning power, rather than as a sign of anything else.[42]

During one trip to Saratoga, Potter lost much of her wardrobe in a train fire that forced her to lobby the railroad's executives for reimbursement. In order to assess the value of her loss, Potter produced a list of wardrobe items that proved the $200 the railroad offered was grossly inadequate. This list "perfectly astonished" the men, and their incredulity became the grounds for Potter's challenge to their understanding of a worker's wardrobe. In response to their "wide-open eyes" and "catched-up breath," Potter reasserted the value of the items that these men could not believe her to possess: "Mr. F. was aghast at the idea of my paying thirty-five dollars for a moiré antique dress, and said his wife never had a dress cost so much. I laughed, and told him I had a dress which cost me fifty dollars, and a mantle to suit which cost me fifty more. . . . When Mr. F. came, on the list, to a velvet basquine trimmed with deep fringe, he seemed to think it was an impossibility; [Another] seemed quite horrified at the very idea of my having ten silk dresses with me; but it afforded me a good deal of pleasure to let them know I had as many more at home" (100–101). Describing with relish the "pleasure" she derived from these men's bafflement, Potter clearly exploited the opportunity to link her buying power to her labor. As she commented, "I was never more amused in my life, than at seeing the different railroad gentlemen pick up my list, look at and shrink from it, as if it were an impossibility for a working woman to have such a wardrobe" (101). In the end, then, Potter recast her wardrobe to the railroad men and to her readers not simply as a sign of her buying power, but also as a sign of her labor power.[43]

The problem here is that the links Potter establishes so painstakingly between her labor power and her wardrobe are not at all universally accepted or stable. For in a social domain in which class and work hierarchies insist on the inferiority of "working women's" status as manual labor, earnings are not sufficient to entitle one to certain modes of consumption. That is, no matter how much money Potter makes as an entrepreneurial hairdresser, as a worker her wardrobe threatens established social hierarchies. This is clear in the advice that a gentleman friend offers her one Sunday coming back from church. "Iangy, you dress too fine," he tells her, before going on to relate his own loss of a patron after the patron took note of the "finer house" that he possessed. Potter responds, "I told him I worked for my patrons for their money, and when I earned and got it, I did not ask them how I should spend it, or anything else connected with it, what I should eat, drink or wear, or how I should dispose of my money. It remains a mystery to me, to this day, why he spoke to me in that manner" (282). Here, Potter recasts the social relations of her work as earning relations, that is, as relations of economic entitlement rather than as the hierarchical relation suggested by her friend's outraged patron. She works not to perform any kind of social service as an inferior to her employer but "for their money." Following this logic, how she spends that money should not be seen as transgressive. But Potter's confession—"It remains a mystery to me, to this day, why he spoke to me in that manner"—refers us to the "mystery" that underscores this problematic conjunction of labor and fashion. For Potter's earning power as beauty expert pits her, as "working woman," against the very social hierarchies of elite femininity and class she has otherwise made it clear she upholds.

Forging Gender, Race, and Labor into "Working Ladyhood"

A Hairdresser dramatizes Potter's ambivalent working status as economically entitled yet socially disadvantaged, exposing how the era's contradictory democratic discourses ostensibly valorized labor while reorganizing new forms of social hierarchy along lines of class, gender, and race. Though the *Gazette*'s review indicates that Potter succeeded in representing her manual labor as a form of social labor that produced elite femininity, *A Hairdresser* also indexes Potter's tenuous status as a "working woman" (rather than as a former slave, or as a black woman); that is, the text also displays the disjuncture between a public rhetoric that asserted the republican value inhering in manual labor and, as historian Stuart Blumin describes, the "actual economic, social, and cultural circumstances surrounding manual work." Blumin continues, "Inequalities were increasing rapidly in the egalitarian republic . . . the values and attitudes of antebellum Americans—their 'culture,' broadly understood—may have mitigated or further reinforced what thus far looks very much like a hardening of class boundaries along the manual-nonmanual fault line."[44] This hardening of class boundaries was increasingly evident in the social stigma attached to (even skilled) manual labor—a stigma that, *A Hairdresser* suggests, even economic independence itself could not mitigate. While Potter clearly did not view herself as economically exploited, she does represent her "dignity" as "aroused" by the culture-wide disparagement of manual labor that violated biblical and republican injunctions to respect those who earned their wages "by the sweat of their brow" (170). *A Hairdresser*'s emphasis on its protagonist's entrepreneurial skilled work thus manifests and contends with the social divide in which the mental/manual labor binary took on critical power for defining the social symbolic, notwithstanding workers' complaints to the contrary.[45]

When Potter informs her readers that she writes this text at her home in Cincinnati, "under my own vine and fig tree," however, she emphasizes the opportunities her independent productive labor provided her, not its limitations (18). Her formulation of entrepreneurial black femininity should be understood, then, within the larger context of independence that was made possible by women's economically successful labor—something we should note was more the exception (like Potter herself) than the rule. Such an interpretive strategy calls for adjusting our discursive models for antebellum black femininity so that modern readers may recognize the paucity of discourses (then and now) that adequately address the opportunities and limitations inhering in black women's public, paid labor.

As Madame C. J. Walker's ambiguous status in the early twentieth century suggests (Walker was Potter's famous successor in the field of African American femininity), black women's entrepreneurial business success did not map neatly onto black middle-class and patriarchy-inflected trajectories for social mobility. For this reason, Potter's text provides evidence of a little-recognized fact: women workers in the black community were not only worried about their status as *black* women in relation to the culture's racial biases; they also shared anxieties with white working women about their class positions as women *workers*. More important, they did not share these anxieties from the position of failing to live up to the middle-class patriarchal norms for femininity, but from the position of feeling entitled to, and deriving enjoyment from, the benefits—like economic and emotional independence—that their non-domestic, non-reform-oriented public labor potentially afforded them.

We may view *A Hairdresser* as speaking to the contradictions associated with black women's labor even as we recognize that it bridges the conceptually overlapping, yet incompatible, domains of femininity and labor with which the black hairdresser contended. As an entrepreneurial beauty professional producing a form of social labor founded on customarily disparaged manual labor, Potter's rhetorical mediation of the "lady" and the "working woman" occupies an unstable middle ground that appears, on the one hand, distanced from dominant gender models for middle-class femininity (black and white) and yet is emphatically *not* the disparaged, often figuratively raced form of the impoverished white woman worker, a figure we see dramatized in Harriet Wilson's depiction of her "white" mother's fall into race and labor.[46] Potter also innovated, I would argue, by producing a model for race, independent labor, and gender that anticipated the norm for the independent "working lady" that twentieth-century white women factory workers would articulate as part of their efforts to render their status as workers compatible with their status as women.[47]

In this way, *A Hairdresser's Experience in High Life* makes visible the utopian possibilities that nineteenth-century black women workers saw in their labor even as it testifies to the instabilities inhering in these possibilities. While Potter the beauty professional was able to transcend the postulated incommensurability of black women and femininity, her text manifests the risks of representing herself through the ambivalent figure of the "working woman." If Potter manages to break through the problem of "degraded" black femininity on the basis of her entrepreneurial labor, that same labor repositions her squarely within the assumed "degradation" of the working woman. Consequently, *A Hairdresser* shows how even a successful representation of manual labor potentially eroded a female worker's status and, indeed, could potentially work against her rise in status, no matter how independent she might be. In this way we can see how Potter's apparently unique text shared, even as it pointed beyond, the opportunities and constraints with which other black working women authors contended—authors such as Truth, Wilson, and Keckley, who each represented their labor simultaneously as the grounds of their exploitation and their empowerment.

4 BEHIND THE SCENES OF BLACK LABOR

ELIZABETH KECKLEY AND THE SCANDAL OF PUBLICITY

As an enterprising, working woman, dressmaker Elizabeth Keckley, like her contemporary Eliza Potter, represented the utopian possibilities of work in her autobiography. She described the rewards of the "labor of a lifetime" in her 1868 autobiography, *Behind the Scenes, or, Thirty Years a Slave and Four Years in the White House*. Born into slavery in 1818, Keckley worked industriously enough as a slave to buy her freedom at age thirty-one and find herself, at the time that she became employed by Mary Lincoln in 1861, one of Washington, D.C.'s preeminent dressmakers. One local journalist noted about Keckley's dressmaking establishment, "Stately carriages stand before her door, whose haughty owners sit before Lizzie docile as lambs while she tells them what to wear."[1] Keckley's upward mobility from out of slavery and into the dressing rooms of Washington, D.C.'s elite women indicates her remarkable work ethic and ambition to us today, as it did to those who knew her. Eulogizing her in 1907, the Reverend Dr. Francis Grimké described Keckley as "a woman of remarkable energy and push . . . a woman who thoroughly respected herself."[2] Self-made and self-sufficient, Keckley exemplified black working women's potential for overcoming and succeeding against enormous odds.

Working at her trade, first as a hired-out slave in St. Louis and later as a freewoman in Washington, D.C., the exceptionally skilled Keckley occupied an unstable and ambiguous position that distinguished her from the destitute and consumptive seamstress of the penny press and the black washerwoman who did white folks' "drudgery." In this regard, like Potter, Keckley forged a new space for black femininity that improbably straddled what I have described as the overlapping but incompatible domains of antebellum womanhood and labor. She viewed her work history, as did Potter, as a source of cultural legitimacy and authority. But though she was economically independent from a young age and managed to support her impecunious slaveowner's large family, Keckley apparently did not accumulate the amount of property we know Potter to have acquired; Keckley has an aura of gentility and propriety that distinguishes her from the more conspicuously dressed and opinionated Potter. Well-connected, successful, and independent, Keckley took a different tack from her contemporary in describing her relationships with her clients. She does not, for the most part, express the admonitory and disciplining tone of the hairdresser who confidently told clients that she knew a lady when she saw one; instead, her autobiography displays a collaborative aspect that points to her southern, enslaved history and to how she saw her work as contributing productively to, and participating in, her clients' elite womanhood. Whereas Potter viewed the cash nexus of wage labor as absolving her of preindustrial deference—"I worked for my patrons for their money, and when I earned it and got it, I did not ask them how I should spend it"—Keckley expressed the entitlement she obtained from her labor precisely in the interracial sentimental affiliations and intimacy she experienced with her clients. To this end, she concluded her autobiography by emphasizing what she had made clear throughout: "I have experienced many ups and downs, but am still stout of heart. The labor of a lifetime has brought me nothing in a pecuniary way. I have worked hard, but fortune, fickle dame, has not smiled upon me. If poverty did not weigh me down as it does, I would not now be toiling by day with my needle, and writing by night. . . . Though poor in worldly goods, I am rich in friendships, and friends are a recompense for all the woes of the darkest pages of life. For sweet friendship's sake, I can bear more burdens that I have borne."[3]

Work, for Keckley, was not simply about the material conditions of production, but more importantly about the emotions of respect and attachment that emerged from her creation and circulation of social value. Fastidiously interweaving her skilled dressmaking work as a slave and freedwoman with the meanings and affectivity this work generated, Keckley insisted on the potential for working intimacy and loyalty between white and black women. In *Behind the Scenes*, Keckley depicts the social relations of dressmaking as a crucial site for mediating the nation's postbellum anxieties over the role ex-slaves and free blacks were to play in a changing economy and society. During this period of political upheaval, white Americans acrimoniously debated the terms for transforming the newly emancipated black population into a free labor force while ensuring their participation in the South's revitalization.[4] Although southerners who sought to reassert their authority over their former slaves promoted stereotypes of freedmen as lazy and unwilling to work, Keckley spoke to the productive possibilities of black laborers. Working as a highly regarded dressmaker in Washington, D.C., Keckley won the affection and respect of women ranging from Varina Davis, wife of senator and future Confederate president Jefferson Davis, to Mary Todd Lincoln, wife of President Lincoln; her life story thus dramatized the possibilities of racial reconciliation and national progress attainable through the successful social and economic integration of freed blacks.

Yet although *Behind the Scenes* invited readings of its protagonist as representing freedmen's capacity and inclination to work, the focus of this narrative was rather extraordinary. In tracing Keckley's upward mobility, *Behind the Scenes* culminates with a lengthy description of the former slave's long-term work relationship with Mary Todd Lincoln. Having worked closely with Mary Lincoln from 1861 through the president's assassination and his widow's subsequent relocation to Illinois, Keckley made this employment and her familiarity with the Lincolns the main focus of *Behind the Scenes*. Ostensibly, Keckley publicized her labor in the Lincoln White House in an effort to intervene in the enormous public outcry that erupted in the national media over the "Old Clothes Scandal." This scandal became public in October 1867 after the former First Lady tried to raise funds for herself through the sale of her celebrated wardrobe. Although Mary Lincoln had been the object of unprecedented media scrutiny throughout the length of her husband's term in the White House, the furor generated by her misguided efforts to solicit funds from Republican politicians was particularly fierce. In response, Keckley, who had acted as Mrs. Lincoln's agent in New York during the events leading up to the scandal, felt compelled to publish her account of events in part to clear her own name but principally to defend Lincoln from what she viewed as gross misunderstandings about her employer's motives.[5]

Keckley insisted from the start of *Behind the Scenes* that the description of her role as Mrs. Lincoln's respected "modiste" and "friend" (according to the title page), was intended to champion not herself but her much-maligned former employer. "[I] have been her confidante," Keckley asserts in her preface, "and if evil charges are laid at her door, they also must be laid at mine, since I have been a party to all her movements." The chivalric dressmaker continued, "To defend myself, I must defend the lady I have served." *Behind the Scenes* invokes Keckley's loyal service as a means to correct the public's misperceptions of the First Lady, rather than as self-serving publicity. For this reason, Keckley admonishes her readers, "For an act may be wrong judged purely by itself, but when the motive that prompted the act is understood, it is construed differently" (xiii, xiv).

Despite Keckley's motives, the story of this groundbreaking African American text—one that seeks to elucidate black female working potential in the volatile postemancipation era—is a vexed one. Tragically, Keckley's deferential intervention on behalf of Mrs. Lincoln was interpreted as its opposite, as a betrayal.[6] *Behind the Scenes* did generate public sympathy for the family of the nation's "martyred president," but the public did not view the dressmaker's representation of White House family life as either just or fair. In shocked reviews, critics made it known that they rejected Keckley's assurance that her intimate labor in the Lincoln White House authorized her to speak publicly about the family. So great was the controversy that a particularly virulent and quasi-pornographic parody entitled *Behind the Seams: By a Nigger Woman Who Took in Work from Mrs. Lincoln and Mrs. Davis* appeared, taking advantage of the forum Keckley's publicity provided to indulge in pernicious race-baiting.[7]

Why did the public turn on her? How could a book in which a former slave claimed that she would choose "eternal slavery, rather than be regarded with distrust" be seen as anything but deferential, or, as some 1970s critics termed it, "accommodationist"? Perhaps most significantly, critics then and now have been unable to pinpoint why Keckley entirely failed to predict the outcome of her book. Lincoln historians read *Behind the Scenes* as a prototype for today's political "kiss and tell," while Frances Smith Foster argues for the racist motives of contemporary critics, but the disparity between Keckley's solicitous and defensive representation of herself and the outrage she provoked remains largely unexplained.[8]

Part of the continuing interpretive problem regarding the reception of Keckley's text has to do with the somewhat anomalous relation of *Behind the Scenes* to a critical African American tradition centered on slave narratives and abolitionist-related texts. While we can locate Keckley's text in relation to the postbellum genre in which the "school for slavery" equips the slave to overcome the hardships of postemancipation reality—a genre of which Booker T. Washington's *Up from Slavery* (1901) is the most noted example—it is not clear how Keckley's self-representation relates to the popular autobiographical tradition of the antebellum slave narrative, best exemplified by Frederick Douglass's *Narrative of the Life of Frederick Douglass* (1845) and Harriet Jacobs's *Incidents in the Life of a Slave Girl* (1861). *Behind the Scenes* diverges rather dramatically from the concerns expressed in these "classic" narratives, which depict a quest for literacy and the obstacles slavery mounted for black women. Although it is clear that Keckley shared many of Harriet Jacobs's experiences as a slave woman—sexual violation, fears for her slave child, and so forth—in her narrative she subordinates these overtly gendered concerns to the details of her work history. As a transitional, postbellum text that combines slave narrative and political memoir, *Behind the Scenes* moves away from the concerns of the slave narrative and focuses mainly on demonstrating how a slave woman might recast the coercions of slave labor so as to produce herself as an empowered agent, rather than solely as a victim of bondage.

When we place this text next to others written by and about black working women striving for economic independence, we can begin to interpret the complexity of the historical and textual scenes of Keckley's labor, even given the problematic nature of this self-representation.[9] Keckley's literary reformulation of black female agency along the lines of labor emphasizes, above all, the dignity of her labor in *all* its aspects: slave, free, interracial, and profoundly gendered. Because of this emphasis, her formulation conflicts with critical theoretical claims about the oppositional relationship of black identity to work and the black community's particular resistance to the degendering often associated with women's labor in the marketplace. From another quarter, Lincoln historians view *Behind the Scenes* as a delegitimated form of political publicity, the significance of which they have long grappled with. In some late-twentieth-century biographies of Mary Lincoln, scholars have dealt harshly with Keckley, reading her text simply as a maliciously intended exposure of the vulnerable and erratic Lincoln.[10] Framed within these ambivalent rhetorical contexts for black female labor, Keckley's attempt to "speak" her labor not only generated devastating critiques from whites and was perceived as a cautionary tale by African Americans, but it also continues to be contested and easily misinterpreted today.[11]

For Keckley, dressmaking represented an opportunity to link herself to a domain of labor that was perceived as skilled and commercially valued. The status- and gender-inflected patterns of consumption associated with an expanding capitalist economy afforded antebellum women of all races the possibility of lucrative careers as artisan-identified milliners and dressmakers.[12] But more important, as a skilled dressmaker, Keckley could participate in fashioning her clients' aspirations to elite femininity, thus establishing the social relations of this work as a way of inserting herself into a network of femininity and class taste that refuted conventional understandings of the "degraded" slave woman. In large part, then, the scandal that greeted Keckley's text arose from her reviewers' refusal to grant her the status associated with being a modiste and their concomitant reinscription of her as "an angry negro servant," the most generic and commonly invoked type of black menial female worker.[13]

In this sense, it is ironic that many modern readers have resisted the connection Keckley goes to such lengths to establish between the social relations of her work and her "virtue." In doing so, these readers rehearse some of the same problematic assumptions about publicity and servants voiced by reviewers in 1868 who saw Keckley as committing "an offense of the same grade as the opening of people's letters, [and] the listening at keyholes." That is, ironically, modern readers' filtering of *Behind the Scenes* exclusively through the lens of the "success" story obscures Keckley's effort to rewrite herself as a market agent who helps to produce social value and her gender identity through the auspices of white female clients and discourses of bourgeois femininity.[14] It is this intimate relationship between black and white, laboring and elite, public and private, that makes Elizabeth Keckley's contribution to national debates on postbellum race relations so remarkable and potentially explosive.

Rather than viewing Keckley's deferential rhetoric as disingenuous or hypocritical, as do critics partial to Mary Lincoln, we might see the gap between *Behind the Scenes*'s avowed intentions and its reception as testifying to the conflict that exists between Keckley's represented labor and the symbolic, or cultural, weight of this representation. That is, Keckley's sentimental relocation of the "external" or "public" marketplace in which she is irrevocably embedded *within* the work relations of "private" white womanhood, intimacy, and loyalty produces rhetorical incompatibilities that destabilize postbellum discourses on labor, race, and femininity. Though Keckley's innovative yoking of slave narrative and political memoir was directed to representing her occupational integrity, her status, and the social obligations that characterized her work, this same innovation produces rhetorical effects that we have yet to account for. Specifically, the norms for black female labor elaborated in *Behind the Scenes* conflict with both common sense assumptions about privacy and the invisibility of the labor that produces the interrelated racial and class privilege at the core of white sentimental subjectivity. In this way, text and reception show how symbolic conflict erupts when dominated, "domestic," and even "loyal" black labor is literally and figuratively emancipated, moving out of its subordinate role "behind the scenes" to take the nation's center stage.

Thirty Years a Slave . . .

Behind the Scenes is divided into two sections that frame Keckley's life. A short slave narrative, which is less frequently analyzed (in particular, by Lincoln historians), is followed by the longer, infamous memoir describing her experiences as an emancipated dressmaker to elite white women in the nation's capital. Although Keckley's three chapters on her life as a slave constitute only a small portion of *Behind the Scenes*'s fifteen chapters, their rhetorical configuration of bondage, work, and freedom are clearly central to the text's laboring logics. In these chapters, Keckley portrays the inhumanity of slavery, particularly its severing of family ties and the injustice of its racialized division of labor. Along with her description of the sale of her father away from her family, the "loan" of her person to a poor relative, and her sexual vulnerability, Keckley tersely narrates the injustices of what she terms the "dark side" of slavery.

What makes Keckley's slave narrative so distinctive, however, is her explicit refusal to represent slave life as unremittingly dark. As Keckley states in her preface, "If I have portrayed the dark side of slavery, I also have painted the bright side. The good that I have said of human servitude should be thrown into the scales with the evil that I have said of it. I have kind, true-hearted friends in the South as well as in the North, and I would not wound those Southern friends by sweeping condemnation, simply because I was once a slave" (xi–xii). Keckley's claims to balanced reporting are underwritten by the "good" she reveals "of human servitude." Before we marvel at such a statement, we might observe how this imperative for fair representation is expressed as an obligation of friendship. For Keckley, the preservation of her "kind, true-hearted friends" supersedes her slave status—"simply because I was once a slave"—a fact that motivates her deliberate writing against the grain of those earlier slave narratives that express only "sweeping condemnation."[15]

But what exactly constitutes the "bright" side that Keckley claims to represent? As the slave narrative proceeds, it appears increasingly clear that Keckley's friends are few and far between. What we find instead is the narration of various scenes of labor that reveal the lessons that slavery, that "hardy school" (in Keckley's words), teaches her. That is, Keckley's descriptions of her slave labor invoke slavery's paternalistic ideology in order to trade on the pedagogical potential that supposedly inhered in this labor's social relations, thereby portraying the "bright" side that slavery offers without eclipsing its "dark" side. Recalling the performance of her "first duty"—attending to her mistress's baby—Keckley describes the child as her "earliest and fondest pet," remarking on the fact that as a four-year-old she herself was hardly old enough to assume such a responsibility. In this regard, she insists, "True, I was but a child myself—only four years old —but then I had been raised in a hardy school—had been taught to rely upon myself, and to prepare myself to render assistance to others. . . . Notwithstanding all the wrongs that slavery heaped upon me, I can bless it for one thing—youth's important lesson of self-reliance" (20).

Describing her labor as a child such as caring for other children and performing various kinds of work, Keckley presents readers with a picture of the self-reliant slave girl who displays "principles of character" (19). And it is here that Keckley's pedagogic claims evince an irony pertaining to their roots in slavery's paternalism. Although it could be argued that "self-reliance" on the part of a slave constitutes an accession to slavery's subordination, what *Behind the Scenes* illustrates is the way in which the slave's "principles of character" can, in fact, shed light on her otherwise obscured productivity. Keckley's description of her early work suggests that one of slavery's crucial "lessons" was that the slave's work was necessary and therefore valuable, notwithstanding slaveholders' protestations to the contrary.

This subversive self-knowledge is manifest in Keckley's repeated resistance to the devaluation of her labor. As she complains, "I grew strong and healthy, and, notwithstanding I knit socks and attended to various kinds of work, I was repeatedly told, when even fourteen years old that I would never be worth my salt" (21). In another instance, Keckley emphasizes the particular importance of her labor to the family: "With my needle I kept bread in the mouths of seventeen persons for two years and five months. While I was working so hard that others might live in comparative comfort, and move in those circles of society to which their birth gave them entrance, the thought often occurred to me whether I was really worth my salt or not; and then perhaps the lips curled in a bitter sneer. It may seem strange that I should place so much emphasis upon words thoughtlessly, idly spoken; but then we do many strange things in life, and cannot always explain the motives that actuate us" (45–46).

Keckley's investment in countering her master's assessment is evident in her pointed marshalling of contrasts: the lone needle providing many loaves for many mouths over many months. Furthermore, her confession about not understanding *why* she responds as she does suggests that she resents the taunt as an insult because it mystifies the *social*, not simply economic, value of her labor. That is, not only is the denial of her worth a mystification of the economic payoff her labor provides, but it also obscures how her work is instrumental to the family's participation in the pleasures of its social and class position. Keckley resents the dismissal of her contribution to her master's position in slaveholding's class structure as much as, if not more than, the literal material underestimation of her work that being called not "worth her salt" represents. With this anecdote, Keckley does not simply link slavery's traffic in laboring bodies to its traffic in esteem and social status; she demonstrates how her role in the creation of status justifies her view of herself as a member-participant in the paternalistic slaveholding "family." As she wrote in a letter to her mother while working temporarily in another household in 1838: "Give my love to all the family, both white and black" (41).[16]

In this manner, Keckley's dramatic, synecdochal representation of her work through the image of the lone needle and its production of economic and social value invokes another irony related to the necessity of her labor within a paternalistic framework. The depiction of her sewing does not merely dramatize the utility of the slave's labor for the market but also that of the slave woman herself. By foregrounding the contribution her needle makes toward the family's social status, Keckley sheds light on the way in which the slave woman's simultaneous embeddedness in the family and her displacement therefrom renders visible her typically obscured domestic labor and the social value or status it generates. Through the auspices of her labor's necessity and its marketability, Keckley perceives her female productivity as a means for generating this social value, not for simply generating profits and/or slave children. As a result, she is able to make her domestic labor discursively visible and evade being cast as the "unproductive" female worker or the slave woman exploited for her reproductive labor. Through this paradoxical appeal to slavery's paternalistic ideology of reciprocal obligations, Keckley is able to represent her self-understanding and her worth as a social agent—a female one at that—in this system of obligations.[17]

Through this formulation, Keckley expresses the contradictory logic that she espouses for surviving her oppression; in her analysis, a woman can resist the dehumanization embedded in slavery's codes of coercion and devaluation by producing social value as a form of alternative "surplus value" that she might be said to accumulate. Even while Keckley recognizes the slave's work as a primary site for social control, she foregrounds what is not obvious: the way in which a coerced labor performance could provide a form of self-production that countered mechanisms of racial and gender inferiority and dependence. After all, those "principles of character" such as self-reliance to which Keckley lays claim are not the primary "goal" of slavery's social relations, even if slaveholders benefit from them. Understandably, the principled character of conscientious slaves appears as a compromised form of resistance because it translates into profits for slaveholders and the perpetuation of slavery's coercions. But in Keckley's schema of value, this is of less importance than acting in accordance with one's conscience or, more precisely, acting in accordance with the value one produces. Through this willful reinterpretation of paternalism, Keckley claims credit, and hence considers herself valuable, on the basis of the social privilege her work as a slave woman affords others.

The centrality of this dynamic of reciprocating status, wherein Keckley sees herself as bestowing and thus in some measure participating in her master's social status, is amplified in the last part of the slave narrative, which details her success as hired-out laborer. While her work in the past supported a family of seventeen by providing them with the leisure and money necessary for maintaining their social position, Keckley's hired-out work, specifically as a dressmaker, involves her even more directly in maintaining the community's system of social status, in particular among elite white women. As dressmaker, or modiste, to southern and later northern bourgeois women, Keckley relies for her success on her adept interpretation of the dress codes that inscribe her female clients' social status. As a result of these intricate class relations, Keckley's investment in her clients' elite femininity and their investment in the circulation of status are rendered synonymous.

Keckley's value as dressmaker increases with her ability to make clothing that mediates her clients' class values, including those of feminine propriety, economic standing, and racial privilege. Keckley eagerly testifies to this competence and to the proper alignment of her identifications when she asserts that "in a short time I had acquired something of a reputation as a seamstress and dress-maker. The best ladies . . . were my patrons, and when my reputation was once established I never lacked for orders" (45). As this statement and the ensuing account of her clients' financing of her bid for freedom illustrate, the specificity of Keckley's lucrative occupation was fundamental to her identification with the class and gender stratification articulated by southern whites.[18]

Keckley's identifications with white elite femininity bear significant weight in the last portion of the slave narrative, which describes how she exploited the widened network of sociality and esteem she inhabited in order to obtain her freedom. As she indicates, the possibility of buying her freedom is made available to her precisely through the social credit she has earned while working as a hired-out slave. It is here that we see clearly how for Keckley, "friends" and clients are one and the same.

The story of Keckley's bid for freedom speaks to her status in the community at large and especially among her female clients. Unable to accumulate the $1,200 necessary to purchase herself and her son because her owners' family "claimed so much of [her] attention," Keckley plans a fund-raising trip to the North. Prior to her departure, she has no problems collecting the signatures of a number of gentlemen as "collateral" against her return until one of these men offers instead to subsidize her escape in the form of an IOU to her mistress. Rather than take advantage of this remarkable offer, Keckley is aghast. As she tells her readers, "I was . . . sick at heart, for I could not accept the signature of this man when he had no faith in my pledges. No; slavery, eternal slavery rather than be regarded with distrust by those whose respect I esteemed" (52–53). With this dramatic statement Keckley makes the stakes clear. To acknowledge this white man's well-intentioned expression of personal regard would involve betraying one of the bases of that regard and, indeed, jeopardizing all she had worked so hard to earn: the esteem and appreciation of her clients, the good intentions of her mistress, and above all, the self-respect that her labor had produced. In this context, freedom had no meaning for Keckley.

In the midst of this quandary, the "credit" that Keckley had established with her clients operates in a powerful way. Even as Keckley is despairing over her situation, the aptly named Mrs. LeBourgois comes to the rescue. Bursting in on Keckley, Mrs. LeBourgois tells her that she would not permit Keckley to go north "to beg for what we should give you." Instead, she emphasizes, "You have many friends in St. Louis, and I am going to raise the twelve hundred dollars required among them" (54). What follows in the few remaining pages of the slave narrative is the story of Mrs. LeBourgois's collection of funds from those "friends" whom Keckley denotes as her "lady patrons of St. Louis" (63). This relation, in turn, is placed alongside the legal documents pertinent to Keckley's manumission. Despite Mrs. LeBourgois's intent to "give" her the money, Keckley "consents" to accept the money "only as a loan," in this way quite literally externalizing her social credit via a formal instrument of monetary credit in anticipation of eventually purchasing herself with her own earnings. Through this materialization of her clients' trust and respect, Keckley is able to renounce her slave status while capitalizing on, instead of jeopardizing, the social "credit history" she has compiled as a slave. Keckley thus concludes the first part of her narrative with a story of freedom intimately linked to a story of interracial trust and confidence fashioned out of, and stitched together by, the labor of her own two hands.

. . . and Four Years in the White House

Although almost all the scandalized critics of Keckley's text ignored the slave narrative that precedes the longer memoir, the lessons contained in that narrative are ironically the ones that set Keckley up for trouble with her northern readers in 1868. For it is on the basis of these lessons that Keckley framed the memoir as the story of the physical and social intimacies that characterized her seamstress work for the nation's southern and northern "First Families," the families of Jefferson Davis and Abraham Lincoln. When she narrates the various scenes that she views, Keckley describes her position of privileged witness as derived entirely from her competent, deferential, and trust-inspiring performance of labor. As such an authorized working spectator, Keckley emphasizes the "inside" knowledge she has of these families as opposed to the "eavesdropping" or "listening at keyholes" form of illicit access commonly associated with the public speech of servants.[19]

For Keckley, the spatial proximity and social intimacy she shared with her elite clients in the nation's capital emerges quite literally out of her enslaved work history. For example, Keckley is able to reside in Washington without paying the requisite fee after a client intervenes, and she is initially employed by Varina Davis "on the recommendation of one of my patrons and her intimate friend" (65–66). Later Mrs. Lincoln remarks to another friend, prior to meeting Keckley, that her name "is familiar to me. She used to work for some of my lady friends in St. Louis, and they spoke well of her" (80). Thus, when Keckley and Mary Lincoln meet to discuss the dressmaker's employment they not only meet as employer and employee, but also as two women with "friends" in common. In this way, Keckley perceives her employment, from the start, as both economic and social.

This simultaneously social and economic relation to her elite clients means that Keckley enjoys physical and rhetorical access to the quotidian knowledge that circulates among her clients' bodies. That is, the intimacy Keckley enjoys not only marks her as an "insider" to her readers but also, more importantly, provides Keckley with a rhetorical space for making her work visible to her readers and for revealing the moral and social value that she claims to generate through her work. This social and physical intimacy creates a forum—in the etymological sense of a public marketplace where exchange takes place—in which the formerly trafficked slave derives status from her own working "traffic," qua intimacy, with the bodies of political elites.[20] Consequently, the physical access she obtains to her employers' politically renowned bodies, as well as the spaces they inhabit and the social interactions taking place in those spaces, not only characterizes the conditions of production for Keckley as dressmaker but the rewards of that production as well.

Keckley's descriptions of the Jefferson Davises provide many examples of how this spatial and social interpenetration of lives works for her. She frames her relationship with the Davis family in terms of her willingness to accommodate herself to their schedule, including often working long into the night to complete important tasks. In turn, this intense contact generates the trust the Davises display in her, the observations of the family that this trusting relationship permits her, and the unique knowledge Keckley obtains concerning Jefferson Davis's prominent role in the secession movement. This inextricability of contact and knowledge emerges in Keckley's story about staying late one Christmas Eve to finish a dressing gown commissioned by Varina Davis for her husband. An unexpected encounter with Mr. Davis, who finds her working late in the family's quarters, enables Keckley to witness firsthand the toll that the nation's growing crisis inflicts on the South's leader-to-be: "Wearily the hours dragged on, but there was no rest for my busy fingers. I persevered in my task, notwithstanding my head was aching . . . I looked at the clock, and the hands pointed to quarter to twelve. I was arranging the cords on the gown when the Senator came in; he looked somewhat careworn, and his step seemed to be a little nervous. He leaned against the door, and expressed his admiration of the Christmas tree, but there was no smile on his face" (68). Keckley takes this opportunity to assert the integrity of the Davis's family relations, in spite of the senator's evident burdens as a southern leader, and to represent the figure who would soon be in the eye of the storm as "a thoughtful, considerate man in the domestic circle." Perhaps more important, she uses this anecdote to participate vicariously in the Davises' war excitement through the auspices of the robe that she was producing at the moment of the scene: "As the clock struck twelve I finished the gown, little dreaming of the future that was before it. It was worn, I have not the shadow of a doubt, by Mr. Davis during the stormy years that he was the President of the Confederate States" (69). If her sewing while a slave helped to provide her slaveowners' class privilege, here the object she produces—the dressing gown—itself participates rather literally in an enormously important national event. Through the clothing she creates, then, Keckley suggests that she herself participates, in a manner of speaking, in these events as well.[21]

Keckley's observations of the Davis family also include political insights, among those some that Varina Davis shares with the dressmaker about the political crisis preceding the outbreak of civil war. Mrs. Davis's open discussion of the political machinations underway in the South and in Washington, D.C., as well as her offer to take Keckley south with her as an employee, clearly signal the trust she has for the former slave. While Keckley is surprised by Mrs. Davis's frankness, she interprets it as a sign of confidentiality: "I was bewildered with what I heard. I had served Mrs. Davis faithfully, and she had learned to place the greatest confidence in me" (72). As a working spectator, Keckley portrays the confidentiality of her work as providing physical access to her employers' bodies—physical access that she, in turn, translates into a form of social access to their trust, confidence, and knowledge.

The kind of physical closeness that Keckley conveys in her one-to-one encounter with Jefferson Davis is central to her representation of the social intimacy she shares not only with the Davises but perhaps more importantly with the Lincolns. In the accounts of her labor for the First Family, Keckley constantly stages the links between her labor and her special relationship with the Lincolns through the intense and repeated use of work verbs and working scenes. While "fitting," "basting," and "arranging" Mrs. Lincoln's dresses, or "combing her hair," Keckley witnesses the mischief of the Lincoln boys, the loving relationship of Mary and Abraham, and the stresses that political life impose on the family during its tenure in the White House. Furthermore, in response to Mrs. Lincoln's solicitations, Keckley represents herself as offering advice on various fronts, from the propriety of transforming state dinners into state receptions to the significance of Mr. Lincoln's proceeding into dinner accompanied by other women. She also proffers her opinion on the chances of Lincoln's reelection in 1864 and claims responsibility for laying out the body of Willie Lincoln after the boy's death (95–97, 144–45, 147–51).

The manner in which Keckley's role as skilled dressmaker translates into a "diversified" source of miscellaneous labor for the whole Lincoln family attests in part to the lack of specificity, or boundaries, that marks the deeply racial and gendered aspects of her labor. Historians have noted white workers' resistance to the overly familial tendencies inhering in paid domestic labor and these workers' dislike of "service" occupations, particularly that of "servant" itself.[22] But Keckley, subverting this equation of familial service with low status, exploits Mary Lincoln's exploitation of her racial and gendered economic susceptibility. Whereas a skilled white modiste might perceive efforts to extract so-called unskilled, familiar labor as undermining her status, Keckley views such efforts as enhancing it. Rather than interpreting the Lincoln family's ready access to the various forms of her labor power as a sign of her social inferiority, Keckley represents it as a marker of social affinity, a move that again displays the former slave's investment in a paternalistic model of work relations. In this manner, Keckley's racial deference to the family—in the sense of being ever at their disposal—bridges the gap between social inferiority and interdependence to assume a sentimental aspect involving the loyal and devoted personal (black) servant. Within this raced and gendered dynamic of loyal subordination, Keckley's work itself operates as a *social* site in which non-kin employer and employee can bond through affect.

This conjunction of intimately gendered labor and sentiment in *Behind the Scenes* culminates in Keckley's status as sole witness to Mary Lincoln's grief in the wake of her husband's assassination. Keckley pointedly relates the various efforts made to locate her immediately following the assassination for the purpose of consoling the distressed widow. In so doing, she stresses her unique role as Mary

Lincoln's only working contact in the days that followed: "[Mrs. Lincoln] denied admittance to almost every one, and I was her only companion, except her children, in the days of her great sorrow" (193). The significance of this sole witnessing should not be underestimated, because Keckley clearly experienced it as a privileged token of trust and value. Representing herself as that lone companion, Keckley insists on her status as a privileged member of the nation. Witnessing Mrs. Lincoln's grief provided Keckley with a singular form of knowledge in the sense that viewing this most authentic expression of grief was conceivably the most intimate way of knowing the personal, emotional effects of Lincoln's assassination.

When Keckley describes this episode of intimate labor she recasts the idea of emotional labor not as exploiting black women, but almost as its opposite: as admitting them into a form of recognized participation in political affect. While part of the critique about extracting emotional labor from domestic workers has centered on the instrumentality involved in portraying them as "one of the family," Keckley instead foregrounds her privilege in the structure of fictive kinship that the whole nation bears in relation to the country's "First Family."[23] To have been Mary Lincoln's only trusted, paid companion during this highly charged and nationally significant moment is produced as proof that Keckley—revisiting the central claim of her slave narrative—is more than "worth her salt" to her employer. The episode works to flag the unique, multifaceted role she played as dressmaker, confidante, and valued companion. Furthermore, in Keckley's opinion, it was on the basis of these many competencies, rather than on the Lincolns' opportunistic deployment of her labor power, that she became involved in assisting the misguided widow with the business transactions that became known as the "Old Clothes Scandal."

Ostensibly, Keckley's narration in *Behind the Scenes* of the secret history pertaining to this scandal was largely responsible for her book's controversial reception in April 1868. The scandal erupted in October of the previous year after the impoverished Lincoln tried to extort funds from Republican politicians and, when this failed, clumsily attempted to sell her extravagant wardrobe. (The phrase "old clothes" suggests how such a gesture was perceived.) When Lincoln tried to call in political chits by publishing her fund requests to Republicans in the Democratic paper the *New York World*, she precipitated a humiliating resurrection of past political animosities. In short order, Lincoln was made the subject of vicious attacks by way of the same publicity machine she herself was attempting to manipulate.[24]

Despite the forthright disavowals of impropriety that appear in *Behind the Scenes*'s preface and throughout the text, Keckley's book was accused of promoting a crisis in bourgeois norms of privacy. After Mary Lincoln's name was dragged through the mud for months, hardly anyone involved in the episode was perceived as innocent, but the dressmaker was deemed by critics the most guilty. As a reviewer in the *New York Citizen* admonished, "We in no wise attempt to apologize for anything that Mrs. Lincoln may have said or done, but we do protest against this atrocious invasion of her privacy, and we hope the press will speak in earnest condemnation of this indecent attempt to entrap the reading public into listening to the vile slanders of an angry negro servant. The violation of privacy is the besetting sin of a portion of the American press, but no newspaper of a higher grade than the *Police Gazette* has ever been guilty of anything so outrageous as the gossip of this woman Keckley."

The remarkable stream of invective hurled by this reviewer fashioned a rhetorical alliance between the sinning "American press," the "reading public," a Democratic paper, and a Republican widow held in low esteem for the sole purpose of repelling an attack mounted single-handedly by "an angry negro servant." The review invoked the vindictive discourse of the fired, disgruntled employee, not only misrepresenting the facts of the case but also repudiating the links Keckley established between her labor and the knowledge it imparted, thereby stripping her of her professional identity. Completely disavowing the dressmaker's legitimate physical proximity to the Lincolns, the reviewer perceived Keckley's publicity as derived solely through illicit forms of access. Her behavior constituted, as the review claimed, "an offence of the same grade as opening others people's letters, the listening at keyholes, or the mean system of espionage which unearths family secrets with a view to black mailing the unfortunate victims. . . . Nothing is sacred to this traitorous eavesdropper."[25] Although Keckley emphasized the social value of her working publicity, the work she went to such pains to publicize was perceived as entirely peripheral and, indeed, invisible in light of the potential entrapment and public danger that this "negro waiting-maid" posed. To render

Keckley's knowledge illicit, the labor in relation to which it was produced had to be disappeared.

Despite the *Citizen*'s attack on Keckley, the self-justification in her preface and elsewhere in her text (where she describes her efforts to defend the First Lady from unflattering publicity) proves that the dressmaker was well aware of the risk of impropriety entailed in discussing White House life. In comparison with the "exaggerations," the "evil report," and the "curiosity" that characterized the media's hostile stance to the Lincoln family, Keckley explicitly invoked her work relations as enabling her to judge the discretion involved in, and the necessity of, revealing the "secrets of the domestic circle." But "discretion," ironically, is relevant only when it points to something unsaid that is valued in relation to something understood, not simply silence. If Keckley can be accused of being indiscreet, her position was that she was less so than others and that her indiscretion was intended to contain, or compensate for, the malicious publicity surrounding the disgraced former First Lady.

A good example of the dynamic of knowing and withholding is the letter from Mary Lincoln that Keckley inserts into her chapter on the "secret history" of the Old Clothes Scandal. Keckley alludes specifically to this dynamic by explicitly suppressing portions of Lincoln's letter. As Keckley explains, the letter describes one of Mrs. Lincoln's trips relating to the sale of her wardrobe: "Mrs. Lincoln wrote me the incidents of the journey, and the letter describes the story more graphically than I could hope to do. I suppress many passages, as they are of too confidential a nature to be given to the public" (296). The four passages marked out in the letter (and similarly omitted passages in the controversial appendix) reiterate Keckley's suppression of the "confidential" while also reminding readers, with the obvious gaps they produce, that Keckley, as editor, is "performing" her discretion openly. As Keckley discloses in her preface, "The veil of mystery must be drawn aside; the origin of a fact must be brought to light with the naked fact itself. If I have betrayed confidence in anything I have published, it has been to place Mrs. Lincoln in a better light before the world" (xiv). Keckley's use of metaphorical unveiling in the name of improving Mrs. Lincoln's public image is significant in more ways than one. Her expressed desire to place Mrs. Lincoln in a "better light before the world" reveals Keckley's assumption of public authority and credibility, while also suggesting the grounds for the reviewers' accusation of trespassing on Mary Lincoln's status as private, domestic subject: as becomes evident, Keckley's insistence on publicly figuring her work and the products of her labor as generating social value renders the privacy of the people for whom she works and the spaces in which she works untenable.

Servants, as adjuncts to domestic femininity, were commonly understood to inhabit a realm of ideological invisibility.[26] In this context, Keckley's notion of her work as socially tangible and as authorizing the publicity of her worth belies the norms of invisibility that structured the meanings and values of subordinate, domestic labor.[27] That is, Keckley's drive to render her work rhetorically visible unintentionally exposes Mary Lincoln to public scrutiny, divested of the veil of privileged propriety that the social relations of domestic labor were called on to produce. This "exposure" of the elite female body, then, was not the result of a malevolent motive on Keckley's part, but an effect that testified to the conflicting imperatives underwriting working visibility and domestic privacy (or invisibility). In other words, this was predominantly a structural and not a personal problem.

The fact that, despite her intentions, Keckley "outs" Mrs. Lincoln in an unbecoming way sheds light on the incommensurability of Keckley's goals and her methods, and signals a series of conflicts that point to the limits of this rhetorical drive toward working visibility. In particular, Keckley's invocation of her employer's trust and her work-related credibility exhibits a structural problem concerning her relation to the representation of her own labor. The scenes of work, intimacy, trust, and rhetorical authority that Keckley goes to such lengths to describe in her text show that she mistakenly assumed that because all her employers vouched for her she could vouch for herself. Ironically, it is on the basis of this assumption that modern readers are justified in denoting *Behind the Scenes* as autobiography, despite the many descriptions of Keckley's text as mere gossip.

As I have argued, for Keckley the bond between employer and employee represents a paternalistic reciprocity of status and obligations. In terms of publicity, this reciprocity works so that Keckley's clients simultaneously publicize their class status, Keckley's skill, and her investment in these structures of status. But what appeared as relations of social reciprocity, especially as pertaining to "publicity relations," mask relations of subordination; that is, the subordinate socioeconomic status of workers and servants makes it impossible for them, and especially for "domestic" workers, to narrate the social, economic, and political value of their work themselves. To base her credibility on these working relations of multiple subordination—in relation to capital, to class status, and to publicity—leaves Keckley open to charges of insubordination and of marshalling her rhetoric against her employers—whatever her actual intentions might be.

These charges point to Keckley's failure to recognize how her subordinate status as servant meant that her work-related attributes could only be narrated by her employer, not by herself. The story of Keckley's quick and skilled production of a dress for Mrs. Robert E. Lee exemplifies how this particular dynamic of client patronage and promotion for the most part benefited Keckley and helped her succeed in Washington, D.C.: "The dress was done in time, and it gave complete satisfaction. Mrs. Lee attracted great attention at the dinner-party, and her elegant dress proved a good card for me. I received numerous orders, and was relieved from all pecuniary embarrassments" (78). This example of sartorial publicity thematically describes the basis of Keckley's success in the "great attention" her dress provides Mrs. Lee, but it also narrates the ambiguity inhering in Keckley's subordinate status in relation to this publicity and her potential misunderstanding of this public circulation of status. When she figuratively represents the "elegant dress" as a "good card" for herself—referring to the social custom of presenting cartes de visite—Keckley interprets the dress as unequivocally speaking for itself and testifying to her skill. With this assumption Keckley potentially overlooks the necessary mediation of Mrs. Lee, for whom the dress in actuality proves a "good card." That is, Keckley's skill is never unmediated and is only appreciated here by being "publicized" by Mrs. Lee as she circulates herself, the dress, and Keckley's skill in a social context that is not open to Keckley herself. Although one might view *Behind the Scenes* as an autobiographical "good card" that succeeds in bypassing the mediation of Keckley's employers, the text's reception then and now suggests that Keckley's subordinate position vis-à-vis her clients provided her with more "credit" than was or is extended to her by her reading audience.

The vexed public relations concerning Keckley's skill foreground the contradictions inhering in her defense of her employer through publicity, as well as the infringement of the employer's mediation that occurs when Keckley vouches for herself. These contradictions signal the structural limits that inhere in workers' speech, even, paradoxically, speech that purports to highlight and trade on the status of the socially superior employer. For as soon as the worker's body appears "on stage," the status and racial privilege that she customarily produces "behind the scenes" is dispelled. This is evident even as we see how Keckley, speaking as the domestic-servant-as-agent, tries hard to perform her intense gendered and class identifications with Mary Lincoln for the reading public. Unfortunately, Keckley's emphasis on Lincoln's need for her labor succeeds too well, setting up the dressmaker in a unique, autonomous position, not simply in regard to her labor, but in relation to the employer she represents. In the scenarios detailing Mary Lincoln's erratic machinations to obtain money, Keckley focuses on how Lincoln engaged her to act as broker and mediator between herself and the designated clothes sellers. And here the problem this publicity produces becomes very apparent: the portrayal of Keckley's competence comes at the expense of that of Mary Lincoln.

The dense textuality of the so-called "secret history" of the Old Clothes Scandal—its palimpsestic layering of newspaper clippings, "press releases," and letters between Mary Lincoln, Keckley, the designated sellers, Frederick Douglass, Henry Garnet, and others, interspersed with accounts of Keckley's meetings with prominent businessmen on behalf of Mrs. Lincoln (56–62)—testifies to Keckley's business acumen in a manner analogous to the slave narrative's display of the authenticating, credit-producing documents pertaining to Keckley's manumission. But the documents in this case, however, suggest that Keckley might have been deemed more credible if she had retained the slave narrative tradition of having others—specifically, white people with social authority—vouch for her character in lieu of promoting herself. Instead, the inclusion in Keckley's autonomously framed narrative of multiple texts relating to the scandal only makes sense in relation to the credibility she claims as Mary Lincoln's trustworthy confidante. And in this light, despite Keckley's intentions, Mary Lincoln's poor judgment relating to her handling of her widowhood, her public image, and the attempt to sell her "old" clothes stands in sharp contrast to Keckley's own judgment.[28] In other words, Keckley does not "upstage" Mary Lincoln so much as she reveals her foibles.

Keckley's expressions of devotion to her employer in *Behind the Scenes* and the text's exposure of Mary Lincoln thus dramatize the contradictions produced by women's work relationships that assume the propriety and the benefits of paternalistic, racialized personal attachments. Although Keckley understood the necessity of making her work visible as a precondition for publicizing her social and economic value to Mary Lincoln, her subordinate and instrumental relation to Lincoln meant that silence rather than speech—no matter how complementary—constituted the only valued, or even recognizable, form of loyalty.[29] Notwithstanding the framing of Keckley's speech as a product of racial and gender deference, the cultural terms and class prerogatives within which this deference is understood clash incontrovertibly with the dressmaker's insistence on being viewed as "worth her salt." This suggests that the very concept of a domestic worker's autobiography is problematic in rhetorical contexts that disavow the social, public aspect of this so-called "private" and invisible labor. Keckley's efforts to exploit cultural understandings of racial loyalty or devotion as a way of rendering her productivity visible consequently overstep the boundaries that the obscured production of white racial and class privilege erects. By failing to attend to the structurally subordinating conditions of the black female worker's speech, Keckley's positive valuation of the interracial trust and confidence she enjoys with her clients and/or "friends" provokes only incredulity, denial, and condemnation rather than the respect and esteem she envisions.[30]

Ironically, Keckley's deference backfired where hairdresser Eliza Potter's sharp criticism of her clients had not. Having established her independence from her clients as wage laborer appears to have worked to Potter's advantage, since it could be viewed as adhering to racial and class hierarchies; in this way the clear distinction she establishes between her economic and social affiliations served her well. Though Potter's story contains many potentially "impudent" observations about her clients, she benefited from the distinction she maintains between herself and them, however negative the implications of her criticism might appear to be. "I often wished that they had better sense," Potter declared, "though, after all, I did not care much what they did, so they paid me my wages."[31] In contrast, deferential as she was, Keckley's blurring of these distinctions—between worker and employer, labor and sociality—made her much more threatening because she was liable to be interpreted as aspiring to participate in (rather than adjudicate, like Potter) national ideals of femininity, ideals that in the postemancipation era remained structured strictly along class and racial lines. Furthermore, while Potter represented herself as offering a public good in the form of discerning what constitutes a "lady" in the abstract, Keckley's personal devotion to an erratic First Lady potentially superseded the public benefit that might be derived by showing Mary Lincoln "in a better light."

The sharply different receptions to texts by two enterprising women working in the field of "beauty" offer us a unique opportunity to compare the relative risks and rewards these texts yielded. In addition to the difference in their authors' rhetorical positions vis-à-vis their clients, another important factor in the different receptions of *Behind the Scenes* and *A Hairdresser's Experience in High Life* in the local press may have had to do with the opinions these authors expressed relative to those of their reading public. Despite her "bold pen," Potter's perspective on the machinations of socially climbing clients corroborated the public's concerns over the dangerous theatricality of femininity, and this allowed Potter to successfully exploit her ambiguous social status as beauty worker. But Keckley's account of Mary Lincoln's "innocent motives" challenged the public's perceptions of the former First Lady's improprieties. Keckley challenged the public not only as one who asserted that, deplorable as these improprieties had been, the ends justified the means (that is, as the widow of the assassinated president, Mary Lincoln deserved the public's support and had to resort to desperate measures only because that support was withheld) but also as a black woman who identified with Mary Lincoln over and above a white public that should have been more sympathetic to her. In other words, while the gist of Potter's book agreed with her audience that her clients should behave better, Keckley's told her audience that *they* had it all wrong (and that they should have known better).

This last dynamic produces the sharpest irony of all: Keckley's book did generate public sympathy for the much-maligned widow not because of what Keckley had said but simply because she had said anything at all. That is, the public did not suddenly sympathize with Lincoln because they believed Keckley's exoneration to be credible; it sympathized with the president's widow as a way of reasserting the white class privilege it shared with Mary Lincoln over and above a black woman's arrogation of public authority. For this reason, contemporary critics who assume Keckley maligned Mary Lincoln because they were of different races not only overlook these women's shared (southern) cultural background; they do not see the forest for the trees. The cultural imperative here is to discipline a black employee (however well regarded) whose speech act assumes that the white public has erred vis-à-vis any white individual—whether such an assertion is true or not. Once the black female employee becomes the object of the public's gaze and makes obvious her employer's "debt" to her, any wrongdoing this employer has done diminishes in importance to the imperative to stand with her against the servant. As the *New York Citizen*'s review admonished in its diatribe against "this woman Keckley": "We in no wise attempt to apologize for anything that Mrs. Lincoln may have said or done, but we do protest against this atrocious invasion of her privacy."

For black working women, in particular, the intimate relations obtaining between paid domestic work and bourgeois white femininity may have offered a tenuous possibility for entering into a domestic "marketplace" that would facilitate reciprocal exchanges of esteem, trust, and propriety between black and white women. But as outlined above, interracial working interdependence was premised on racial, class, and gender asymmetries that offered too precarious a basis on which to promote black working women's social legitimacy. Consequently, notwithstanding the nation's need for its black working women, these texts show that the recognition and public legitimacy to which their authors aspired could not be assumed: as long as the nation benefited, economically and socially, from expropriating the social value they produced, black working women had to rely on the goodwill of individuals (and readers, if they were authors) for recognition. The more these workers enriched the nation economically and symbolically (by providing a foil for whiteness, for example, or by constructing elite femininity), the greater the nation's incentive to exploit them. Black leaders' drive for respectability after the war betrayed tremendous blindness to this dynamic—one that made it clear that neither black wealth nor education would be adequate to the task of abolishing racial injustices in a nation that had profited so much, and for so long, from black inequality.

Yet despite all this, we would be remiss in continuing to overlook what Elizabeth Keckley went to such great pains to describe: how her interracial working interdependence produced social bonds that she was loath to forego. As the record shows, her devotion to Mary Todd Lincoln did not end when the boom came down on her after the publication of *Behind the Scenes*. While employed in 1892–93 as a highly respected teacher of "domestic art" at Wilberforce University in Ohio, Keckley was known for her past association with the famous First Lady. There, she possessed a "large trunk" that contained "pieces of goods that she had saved from the various dresses that she made for Mrs. Lincoln." These remnants bespeaking Keckley's loyalty and expertise were, in turn, "passed on" by Keckley "to her favorite pupils."[32] By circulating these swatches, Keckley kept alive the memory of her relationship with Mrs. Lincoln for herself and her students, thereby including a younger generation in the dissemination of her life story of respect and value.

CODA

MOVING BEYOND ANTEBELLUM REFORM

AFRICAN AMERICAN WORKING WOMEN AND THEIR TRADITIONS

It is the great want of the day. . . . Socially, morally, mentally, and religiously, [woman] is written about; but not as a working, every-day reality, in any other capacity than that pertaining to home life.

Virginia Penny, The Employments of Women: A Cyclopaedia of Woman's Work, *1863.*

When Elizabeth Keckley publicized her work as a former slave and freedwoman to claim the value she produced, she depicted the difficult post–Civil War dilemma in which she and other African American workers were bound. If there were any hope that Reconstruction offered the African American population an opportunity to speak for itself and address anxieties over black contributions to the nation's well-being, Keckley's text dramatized how representations of freedmen as productive and as deserving of social respect and even equality would remain problematic. In this way, *Behind the Scenes* illustrates how on the national stage the terms invoked for racial progress could simultaneously be employed as tools for racial subordination and why as the "prototype" of later black success stories, *Behind the Scenes* actually *differs* from its most famous variation, *Up from Slavery*.[1] Viewed in relation to *Behind the Scenes*, Booker T. Washington's later framing of black labor within the structurally subordinate terms for which he is so (in)famous does not appear as merely an opportunistic surrender to the nation's racial and class discourses but, rather, a response to the rhetorical difficulties of representing black productivity. As he reassured his (mostly) white audience in his 1895 Atlanta Exposition speech, interracial working interdependence did not necessarily threaten the racial status quo: "In all things that are purely social we can be as separate as the fingers, yet one as the hand in all things essential to mutual progress."[2]

Given the assortment of formidable obstacles facing black working women, it is not surprising that these texts reveal African American women's diversity as working subjects. As part of their depiction of working womanhood, these texts testify to a wide and at times ambivalent range of work meanings. Whereas Wilson saw her work's contribution to her white employers' class privilege as a site of exploitation, Keckley experienced her labor as affording her a vicarious participation in her clients' political privilege. While Sojourner Truth saw her waged work as complicit with the competitive aspects of the North's "free labor," Eliza Potter tried to carve out a space in that system that allowed her to enjoy the abundant fruits of her wages, without assenting to a symbolic order that disadvantaged her as a working woman. In this way, these women and their texts speak to the emergence of multiple black feminist traditions in the nineteenth century, earlier than suggested by twentieth-century studies that focus on blueswomen and migrants.[3]

While the majority of the period's historical and literary record documents the emergence of a black "middle class" comprised of school teachers and clubwomen, of professional men (including authors) and reformers, this archive of "working womanhood" speaks to the myriad symbolic resources ordinary black workers used when they sought to meet the challenges of their exploitation through overlooked forms of self-reliance and economic independence as skilled and unskilled farm and domestic labor. Ordinary black working women who were not schoolteachers or clubwomen and who were excluded from industrial or clerical work were adamant about the contributions they made to the nation and to their (racial and gender) communities. These texts show that whether as wage workers or as aspiring entrepreneurs, black women were willing to participate in, refute, and reshape black communities' discourses about womanhood, labor, race, and respectability—long before the twentieth-century migrations with which these conflicts have traditionally been associated.

Methodologically, the range of work and class meanings in this archive preempts easy assumptions about how these women identify themselves relative to their occupations. Consequently, it would be counterproductive to ground analyses of these texts in traditionally discrete categories of identity such as "working class" or "middle class." The complex and nuanced processes of these women's subject-formation suggest we develop theoretical models that speak to overdetermined and multiple identities located at the intersection of discourses about race, gender, citizenship, and labor. In addition, the possibilities and limitations of the labor discourses at the heart of these texts shed light on the potentially regressive political character of antebellum negotiations for racial "elevation." This exploration furthermore calls for us to revise our focus on the New South as the seedbed of black activism.[4] This mapping of discursive possibilities shows that long before the postbellum period, African American workers in the North met the challenges of speaking the positive or emancipatory value of their labor in their quest for legitimacy. These women's discursive legacy points to the *national* rather than regional or exclusively slavery-identified injustices that hampered black workers' efforts to make visible their contributions and to authorize themselves as citizen-subjects. This means that we should attend to the possibilities that other kinds of discourses, beyond those affiliated with reform, allowed African American writers to claim social and civic authority from a wide range of backgrounds and statuses. Such an approach may not offer the neat consolidation of racial identity embedded in our received notions of "black reform" or "protest," but recognizing heterogeneity does offer us a broader, more historical sense of the multiple traditions African Americans shaped and participated in as they quested for racial justice and equality.

More specifically, highlighting the national dimension of labor's representational dynamics locates these texts in a broader perspective that identifies the contributions these black working women, like other working women, made to national, and not simply racial, languages for labor. Despite their exclusion from most industrial labor, black women farm workers, domestic workers, and skilled workers alike saw their labor, disparaged as it was, as entitling them to the social and civic rights for which white workers (male and female) clamored. And even if white male wage laborers had been politically enfranchised at the expense of black men's disenfranchisement, black working women still viewed wage labor as affording them a social and economic independence to which they felt entitled as women.

Since a working woman's independence could jeopardize her respectability in a patriarchy-grounded community, any effort to recuperate the moral value of women's labor had to address "the want of respect for labor, and a want of respect for woman" that feminist labor reformer Caroline Dall identified as at "the bottom of all [working women's] difficulties, low wages included."[5] As black women preachers before them had shown, Truth, Wilson, Potter, and Keckley were living proof of how "respectable" earning a living could be; they corroborated what "One Who Works" had pinpointed in her letter to the *Weekly Anglo-African* in 1860, that "it is no disgrace for either sex to engage in an honorable employment." Yoking the concept of honor to black female employment was probably one of the most difficult of all rhetorical tasks to perform for the nation's most exploited population, especially in an era when the nation's restructuring of race, class, and gender hierarchies belied its own promise of democratization. As "One Who Works" reminded readers, if the culture touted the virtue of earning one's wages "by the sweat of the brow," the increasing stigmatization of manual labor meant that the managerial and leisured classes in black communities, as in the nation as a whole, looked down on working people.

As black working women with different statuses and from different backgrounds, these authors mediated the nation's contradictory discourses about gender and labor to forge versatile models of black "working womanhood," models that built on the efforts of women preachers before them and that looked ahead to twentieth-century factory women's efforts to make their womanhood compatible with their work through the norm of the "working lady." These women appropriated the sense of calling displayed earlier by women preachers and adopted it to a universalistic language claiming all workers' citizenship.[6] In this way, black working women shaped gender discourses that emphasized women's capacity for independence as a social good (rather than simply a religious good) by linking necessity to economic entitlement and then by translating that entitlement into a form of citizenship that delegitimated the nation's exploitation of its working women. While predominantly middle-class white suffragists in this period argued for opening the doors of the professions to bourgeois women (so that a woman would not imperil her respectability by performing white-collar labor), these black working women made the case for national recognition of the contributions to womanhood that were made by women who, it was presumed, had little if anything to offer. "I am a self-made woman," Sojourner Truth was reported to have remarked, a comment about self-fashioning that points beyond the mythical virtues of economic success to the social and symbolic value black women had contributed to the nation, as an argument not for the status quo but for recognition, civic entitlement, and justice.

NOTES

INTRODUCTION

1 Nellie McKay, "The Narrative Self: Race, Politics, and Culture in Black American Women's Autobiography," in *Women, Autobiography, Theory*, ed. Sidonie Smith and Julia Watson (Madison: University of Wisconsin Press, 1998), 96–107.

2 The June 21, 1851, transcription of the speech appeared in the *Anti-Slavery Bugle* and is reprinted in Margaret Washington's edition of *The Narrative of Sojourner Truth* (New York: Vintage Books, 1993), 118. This is the version of the speech that has recently superseded the well-known transcription by Francis Gage. The latter was written much later and contains many discrepancies, not the least of which is the southern "darky" dialect.

3 Karen Sayer, *Women of the Fields: Representations of Rural Women in the Nineteenth Century* (Manchester: Manchester University Press, 1995); Joan Jensen, *Loosening the Bonds: Mid-Atlantic Farm Women, 1750–1850* (New Haven: Yale University Press, 1986); Jonathan Glickstein, *Concepts of Free Labor in Antebellum America* (New Haven: Yale University Press, 1991).

4 Thomas Jefferson, "On Manufactures," in *Notes on the State of Virginia*, ed. William Peden (New York: Norton, 1954), 165. Timothy Sweet offers insight into the contradictions of republican husbandry, which was the sole ideological province of the "freeman" (one who owned land): "One of the most easily overlooked facts about agriculture even today is its class structure. In the pretechnological era, farming often required a good deal of wage labor, supplied by landless men and women." "American Pastoralism and the Marketplace: Eighteenth-century Ideologies of Farming," *Early American Literature* 29.1 (1994): 59–66, quotation 59.

5 David Roediger, *Wages of Whiteness: Race and the Making of the American Working Class* (New York: Verso, 1991), 144–45.

6 According to historian Ira Berlin, under slavery, slave men "monopolized almost all the skilled positions within the agricultural sector, [consequently, the] field force [was] disproportionately female, with young women assigned to the most arduous tasks." *Many Thousands Gone: The*

First Two Centuries of Slavery in North America (Cambridge: Harvard University Press, 1998), 168.

7 Frederick Law Olmsted, *Journey in the Seaboard Slave States* (New York, 1856), 387–88.

8 Ibid.

9 Glickstein, *Concepts of Free Labor*, 89. Glickstein continues, "The disjunction between economic realities and antislavery morality in turn signaled some of the inconsistencies or weaknesses in antislavery logic."

10 This emphasis also rendered Truth problematic in the black community. Current debates about Truth's appropriation by white feminists mostly overlook the role that Truth's working-class style played in alienating her from African American reformers and in her relatively isolated activism on behalf of slaves and black and white working women. See Carl Mabee, *Sojourner Truth: Slave, Prophet, Legend* (New York: New York University Press, 1993), 209–10.

11 Rebecca Warren Brown, *Memoir of Mrs. Chloe Spear, a Native of Africa, Who was Enslaved in Childhood, and Died in Boston, January 3, 1815* (Boston, 1832); Francis Harriet Whipple Green, *Memoirs of Elleanor Eldridge* (Providence, R.I., 1839); Hannah Farnham Sawyer Lee, *Memoir of Pierre Toussaint* (Boston, 1854); and Robert Roberts's servants' manual, *The House Servant's Directory, or A Monitor for Private Families* (Boston, 1827). See Ann Fabian, *The Unvarnished Truth: Personal Narratives in Nineteenth-Century America* (Berkeley: University of California Press, 2000), for an account of the widespread publication of personal narratives during this period.

12 Nell Irvin Painter, "Sojourner Truth in Life and Memory: Writing the Biography of an American Exotic," *Gender and History* 2 (Spring 1990), 3–16. Carla Peterson places Truth and other reforming women in the context of the independence they attained as workers. She also describes the unlettered Truth's engagement with print culture as "truly modern." Peterson, *"Doers of the Word": African American Women Speakers and Writers in the North (1830–1880)* (New Brunswick, N.J.: Rutgers University Press, 1995), 16, 25.

13 David Montgomery, *Citizen Worker: The Experience of Workers in the United States with Democracy and the Free Market during the Nineteenth Century* (Cambridge: Cambridge University Press, 1993), 6–8. James O. Horton and Lois E. Horton, *In Hope of Liberty: Culture, Community and Protest among Northern Free Blacks, 1700–1860* (New York: Oxford University Press, 1997), 167–70.

14 Kim Voss, *The Making of American Exceptionalism: The Knights of Labor and Class Formation in the Nineteenth Century* (Ithaca, N.Y.: Cornell University Press, 1993), 82.

15 Josephine L. Baker, in *The Lowell Offering* (1845), ed. Benita Eisler (New York: Harper & Row, 1980), 82.

16 According to one historian, the emergence of "universal womanhood" during the 1840s and 1850s shifted working women's rhetoric away from protest to attracting public sympathy and made for an environment in which "professions of womanly virtue were better suited than declarations of republican rights." Christine Stansell, *City of Women: Sex and Class in New York, 1789–1860* (Urbana: University of Illinois Press, 1987), 147.

17 "Although the number of militants may have been small, their activity still testifies to how volatile relations of class and gender were in the 1830s and 1840s" (ibid., 131). I would add that the discourses on class, gender, *and* race were volatile during this period and that, ironically, it would be the emerging dominance of abolitionist and reform discourses during the 1840s and 1850s that would help to consolidate the hierarchies of labor against which workers contended to assert their value to the nation. My perspective on this is influenced by Anne Norton, *Alternative Americas: A Reading of Antebellum Political Culture* (Chicago: University of Chicago Press, 1986).

18 The phrase was a popular one among working women, white and black, who argued against working women's exploitation and demanded women's access to a broader (and better paying) range of occupations. *Woman's Right to Labor* is the title of reformer Caroline Dall's 1860 book of essays on women and work.

19 In Boston in 1860, 87 percent of black working women were in domestic service, as were 78 percent of immigrant women and 33 percent of native-born women. What made black women domestics stand out, however, was that they were older and were more likely to be married or widowed: 16 percent versus 9 percent for native-born women. As Thomas Dublin notes, despite advances in blacks' legal status in Boston, economic realities remained harshest for black workers: "Blacks clearly constituted a class apart." *Transforming Women's Work: New England Lives in the Industrial Revolution* (Ithaca, N.Y.: Cornell University Press, 1994), 159–60.

20 Amy Schrager Lang's analysis of white women's fiction traces the mutually constituting, yet antagonistic, dynamics of bourgeois and working-class femininity and the role that race played in mediating the incompatibilities

presumed to exist between women's paid (usually manual) labor and recognized womanhood. "To be poor, to struggle 'manfully,' to be ragged and dirty, to have a brown face, to be dangerous—to be all of these things is to be a millgirl, is to be a slave, is to be black." "The Syntax of Class in Elizabeth Stuart Phelps's *The Silent Partner*," in *Rethinking Class: Literary Studies and Social Formations*, ed. Wai Chee Dimock and Michael T. Gilmore (New York: Columbia University Press, 1994), 267–85, quotation 276.

21 Patrick Rael, *Black Identity and Black Protest in the Antebellum North* (Chapel Hill: University of North Carolina Press, 2002), 179–83. Amy Schrager Lang, *The Syntax of Class: Writing Inequality in Nineteenth-Century America* (Princeton, N.J.: Princeton University Press, 2003), 97–98.

22 Brown, *Memoir of Mrs. Chloe Spear*, 52–58.

23 Green, *Memoirs of Elleanor Eldridge*, 99.

24 *The Colored American*, September 15, 1838, November 14, 1840, and August 17, 1839.

25 Judith Sealander, "Antebellum Black Press Images of Women," in *Black Women in United States History*, vol. 4, ed. Darlene Clark Hine (New York: Carlson Publishing Inc., 1990), 1203–15, 1206. According to Sealander, even Phillis Wheatley, the famous slave poet, came in for criticism by *Freedom's Journal* for her poor housekeeping (1210).

26 See Winthrop Jordan, *White over Black: American Attitudes toward the Negro, 1550–1812* (Chapel Hill: University of North Carolina Press, 1967); Kathleen Brown, *Good Wives, Nasty Wenches, and Anxious Patriarchs: Gender, Race, and Power in Colonial Virginia* (Chapel Hill: University of North Carolina Press, 1996); Robyn Wiegman, *American Anatomies: Theorizing Race and Gender* (Durham, N.C.: Duke University Press, 1995); and Jacqueline Jones, *American Work: Four Centuries of Black and White Labor* (New York: Norton, 1998).

27 Brown, *Good Wives, Nasty Wenches, and Anxious Patriarchs*, 126.

28 James Oliver Horton, "Freedom's Yoke: Gender Conventions among Antebellum Free Blacks," *Feminist Studies* 12.1 (Spring 1986): 51–76.

29 "Woman," *The Colored American*, May 11, 1839.

30 Wiegman, *American Anatomies*, 62–78.

31 A short bibliography of works showing how the transforming nation rewrote dominant norms for gendered subjectivity in a capitalizing mode includes Gillian Brown, Domestic *Individualism: Imagining Self in Nineteenth-Century America* (Berkeley: University of California Press, 1990); Stephanie

Coontz, *The Social Origins of Private Life: A History of American Families* (London: Verso, 1988); Nancy Armstrong, *Desire and Domestic Fiction* (New York: Oxford University Press, 1989); and Amy Schrager Lang, "Class and the Strategies of Sympathy," in *The Culture of Sentiment*, ed. Shirley Samuels (New York: Oxford University Press, 1992), 128–42.

32 From 66 percent to 75 percent of African Americans employed in the North worked in unskilled, menial employment. Black "professionals" were largely ministers or teachers but also included lawyers, doctors, and dentists; they constituted less than 2 percent of all black workers. Horton and Horton, *In Hope of Liberty*, 110, 119.

33 "Racism helped create economic conditions that made it impossible for black men to support their families without the supplementary incomes of their wives and contributed to the numbers of black women, without men, called upon to support families on their own." Horton, "Freedom's Yoke," 58.

34 Douglass's call to men to follow trades appears to overlook his own experience: he was forced to abandon his trade when he arrived in New Bedford. Frederick Douglass, "Learn Trades or Starve!," *Frederick Douglass' Paper*, March 4, 1853, reprinted in *Black Workers: A Documentary History from Colonial Times to the Present*, ed. Philip S. Foner and Ronald L. Lewis (Philadelphia: Temple University Press, 1989), 118.

35 Frederick Douglass, "Make your Sons Mechanics and Farmers, not Waiters, Porters, and Barbers," *Frederick Douglass' Paper*, April 8, 1853. In his call for "usefulness" as the criterion for black workers' legitimacy, Douglass anticipated Booker T. Washington's postbellum argument for vocational training: "The individual who can do something that the world wants done will, in the end, make his way regardless of his race." Booker T. Washington, *Up from Slavery* (1901), ed. William L. Andrews (New York: W. W. Norton, 1996), 72. One wonders how this argument could be made during slavery, when the obvious utility of slave labor did not serve to elevate the slave's status.

36 Cited by Philip S. Foner in his introduction to *The Life and Writings of Frederick Douglass* (New York: International Publishers, 1950), 2:36. Douglass advanced this view during his abortive effort to found a "Manual Labor School" in the 1850s (for which he sought the help of Harriet Beecher Stowe), when immigration and growing racial discrimination combined to reduce the possibilities of black workers' acquiring trades.

37 Glickstein, *Concepts of Free Labor*, 97.

38 A large majority of black women worked in domestic service: in Boston in 1860, over 75 percent of black working women were employed in domestic work. Horton and Horton, *In Hope of Liberty*, 114.

39 *North Star*, February 23, 1849, cited in Rael, *Black Identity and Black Protest*, 191.

40 Maria W. Stewart, "Religion and the Pure Principles of Morality, the Sure Foundation on Which We Must Build" (1831), reprinted in *Classic African American Women's Narratives*, ed. William L. Andrews (New York: Oxford University Press, 2003), 12–13. Carla Peterson offers insights on Maria Stewart's anxieties about falling into the ranks of paid labor after she was widowed in *"Doers of the Word,"* 58.

41 Robert Levine cites these proceedings and the controversy in *Martin Delany, Frederick Douglass, and the Politics of Representative Identity* (Chapel Hill: University of North Carolina Press, 1997), 51–52, 252. Curiously, at this earlier date, Douglass did not miss the opportunity himself to reprimand Delany with a defense of menial labor that later disappears: "He thought as far as the speakers intimated that any useful labor was degrading—they were wrong. He would suggest a Resolution so as to suit both parties, which he thought might be done. . . . He said: Let us say what is necessary to be done, is honorable to do—and leave situations in which we are considered degraded, as soon as necessity ceases." The proceedings are reprinted in their entirety in *Pamphlets of Protest: An Anthology of Early African American Protest Literature, 1790–1860*, ed. Richard Newman, Patrick Rael, and Phillip Lapsansky (New York: Routledge, 2001), 178–89.

42 Martin R. Delany, *The Condition, Elevation, Emigration, and Destiny of the Colored People of the United States* (1852; Baltimore: Black Classic Press, 1993), 43.

43 Maria W. Stewart, "Religion and the Pure Principles of Morality," 11.

44 Frederick Cooper, in "Elevating the Race: The Social Thought of Black Leaders, 1827–59," *American Quarterly* 24 (Dec. 1972): 604–25, was among the first to look at the paradoxes inhering in uplift terminology. See also Evelyn Brooks Higgenbotham, *Righteous Discontent* (Cambridge: Harvard University Press, 1993), 185–230; Eddie S. Glaude Jr., *Exodus!: Religion, Race, and Nation in Early Nineteenth-Century America* (Chicago: University of Chicago Press, 2000), 100; Rael, *Black Identity and Black Protest*, 157–208.

45 Glickstein, *Concepts of Free Labor*, is a valuable resource on the cultural matrix and hierarchies of antebellum labor. Also, Stuart M. Blumin, *The Emergence of the Middle Class: Social Experience in the American City, 1760–*

1900 (New York: Cambridge University Press, 1989), yields insights into the discriminations that emerged among occupations—principally through a binary that organized the poles of mental versus manual (what became understood as "white collar" and "blue collar")—during an era in which the labor that was central to the industrializing nation suffered diminishing status. Nicholas Bromell discusses how writers like Emerson and Thoreau negotiated this binary when confronting their own anxieties about performing only "mental" labor. *By the Sweat of The Brow: Literature and Labor in Antebellum America* (Chicago: University of Chicago Press, 1993). For an incisive analysis of labor reformers' efforts to industrialize workers as part of "reform," see Norton, *Alternative Americas*, 64–98.

46 Mabee, *Sojourner Truth*, 209–10.

47 Frederick Douglass, "What I Found at the Northampton Association," in *The History of Florence, Massachusetts, Including a Complete Account of the Northampton Association of Education and Industry*, ed. Charles A. Sheffield (Florence, Mass., 1895), 132.

48 Recent insights into the role of labor languages in black abolition and reform have broadened understandings of the role work discourses played in reform more generally. But, here again, an emphasis on black men's participation in these languages has reproduced black working women's invisibility in the history and texts of the antebellum period. See Todd Vogel, *The Black Press* (New Brunswick, N.J.: Rutgers University Press, 2001), 38.

49 Frances Smith Foster pioneered critical research into men's and women's slave narratives in "'In Respect to Females . . .': Differences in the Portrayals of Women by Male and Female Narrators" (1981), reprinted in her books *Witnessing Slavery: The Development of Ante-Bellum Slave Narratives* (Westport, Conn.: Greenwood Press, 1979) and *Written By Herself: Literary Production by African American Women, 1746–1892* (Bloomington: Indiana University Press, 1993). Relevant titles by other scholars include William L. Andrews, ed., *Sisters of the Spirit: Three Black Women's Autobiographies of the Nineteenth Century* (Bloomington: Indiana University Press, 1986); see Jean Fagan Yellin's historical research and editorial work on Harriet Jacobs, *Incidents in the Life of a Slave Girl* (Cambridge: Harvard University Press, 1987), and Carla Peterson's work on black women speakers and writers, *"Doers of the Word."* Joanne Braxton, *Black Women Writing Autobiography* (Philadelphia: Temple University Press, 1989); Hazel Carby, *Reconstructing Womanhood: The Emergence of the Afro-American Woman Novelist* (New York: Oxford University Press, 1987); Katherine Clay Bassard, *Spiritual Interroga-*

tions (Princeton, N.J.: Princeton University Press, 1999); Claudia Tate, *Domestic Allegories of Political Desire: The Black Heroine's Text at the Turn of the Century* (New York: Oxford University Press, 1992).

50 Jarena Lee, *The Life and Religious Experience of Jarena Lee, a Colored Lady* (Philadelphia, 1836); Zilpha Elaw, *Memoirs of the Life, Religious Experience, Ministerial Travels and Labours of Mrs. Zilpha Elaw, an American Female of Colour* (London, 1846); Mary Prince, *The History of Mary Prince, a West Indian Slave* (London: F. Westley and A. H. Davis, 1831); Nancy Gardener Prince, *A Narrative of the Life and Travels of Mrs. Nancy Prince* (Boston, 1850); and Harriet Jacobs, *Incidents in the Life of a Slave Girl* (Boston, 1861).

51 Stewart, "Religion and the Pure Principles of Morality"; and Lee, *The Life and Religious Experience of Jarena Lee.*

52 Peterson, *"Doers of the Word"*; Carby, *Reconstructing Womanhood*; Armstrong, *Desire and Domestic Fiction*, 76.

53 See Kevin K. Gaines, *Uplifting the Race* (Chapel Hill: University of North Carolina Press, 1996), for a discussion of the gendered politics of postbellum uplift and African American women's energetic participation in social movements for gender and racial equality.

54 "The Anti-Slavery Bazaar at Minerva Hall," *North Star*, January 7, 1848, cited in Rael, *Black Identity and Black Protest*, 155.

55 Andrews, *Classic African American Women's Narratives*, xxv.

56 Carla Peterson, "'Further Liftings of the Veil': Gender, Class, and Labor in Frances E. W. Harper's *Iola Leroy*," in *Listening to Silences: New Essays in Feminist Criticism*, ed. Elaine Hedges and Shelley Fisher Fishkin (New York: Oxford University Press, 1994), 97–112.

57 The housekeeping, sewing, and child-rearing labor Jacobs describes is consistent with her emphasis on domestic motherhood. For example, there are few instances in which Jacobs represents herself as imitating her grandmother's entrepreneurial labor. In a text with many silences, "Linda's" reprint of Flint's runaway ad omits a significant, work-related detail. Norcom's ad in the *American Beacon* of Norfolk, Virginia, stated, "Being a good seamstress, she has been accustomed to dress well, has a variety of very fine clothes, made in the prevailing fashion, and will probably appear, if abroad, tricked out in gay and fashionable finery." The ad is reproduced in Jean Fagan Yellin's edition of *Incidents*, 215.

58 I should say, from what we *do not* see: Jacobs's grandmother, Molly Horniblow, had five children of her own. Neither "Linda" nor the historical record provide any insight into the father(s) of these children. For all intents

and purposes, Molly may have had very similar experiences to Harriet's; hence, Jacobs's silence around her grandmother's sexual history—there is no mention of a grandfather, dead or alive—works strategically to heighten readers' sense of her own fear and isolation. Jean Fagan Yellin, *Harriet Jacobs: A Life* (New York: Basic Books, 2004), 6.

59 Hazel Carby makes one of the clearest statements concerning Jacobs's deviation from white women's domestic literature in *Reconstructing Womanhood*, 49.

60 Eliza Potter, *A Hairdresser's Experience in High Life* (1859; New York: Oxford University Press, 1991), 12.

61 Nellie McKay, "The Narrative Self," 100.

62 Jacqueline Jones, *Labor of Love, Labor of Sorrow* (New York: Vintage Books, 1985), 11–79.

63 Paul Gilroy, *The Black Atlantic: Modernity and Double Consciousness* (Cambridge: Harvard University Press, 1993), 40.

64 Historian Sharon Harley has been at the forefront in investigations of the meanings of black women's labor. This essay, however, does posit the development of black women's "working-class" consciousness as always already alienated from the labor that black women perform. "'When Your Work Is Not Who You Are': The Development of a Working-Class Consciousness among Afro-American Women," in *Gender, Class, and Race in the Progressive Era*, ed. Noralee Frankel and Nancy S. Dye (Lexington: University of Kentucky Press, 1991), 42–55.

65 These arguments tend to forestall our recognition of how workers might have interpreted socially disparaging attitudes toward their labor as part of the cause, rather than simply an effect, of their subordinated status in the occupational hierarchy. For example, many workers refuted the mental/manual binary that contributed significantly to the tacit racialization underwriting antebellum concepts of "nigger work" upheld by the whole nation, North and South. In addition to the essay by historian Sharon Harley, see Bonnie Thornton Dill, "'Making Your Job Good Yourself': Domestic Service and the Construction of Personal Dignity," in *Women and the Politics of Empowerment*, ed. Ann Bookman and Sandra Morgen (Philadelphia: Temple University Press, 1988), 33–52; and Mary Romero, *Maid in the U.S.A.* (New York: Routledge, 1992), for the relationship between work and black women's identity.

66 The phrase is Henry Louis Gates Jr.'s, from *Figures in Black* (New York: Oxford University Press, 1987), 3–58.

67 "The attention . . . to the nature of modes of production helps to ground these other aspects of the social formation more adequately at the level of the economic structures. . . . However, we cannot thereby deduce a priori the relations and mechanisms of the political and ideological structures (where such features as racism make a decisive reappearance) exclusively from the level of the economic. The economic level is the *necessary but not sufficient* condition for explaining the operations at other levels of society. . . . We cannot assume an express relation of 'necessary correspondence' between them. . . . It requires us to demonstrate—rather than to assume, a priori—what the nature and degree of 'correspondence' is, in any specific historical case" (emphasis added). Stuart Hall, "Race, Articulation, and Societies Structured in Dominance," in *Black British Cultural Studies: A Reader*, ed. Houston Baker Jr., Manthia Diawara, and Ruth Lindeborg (Chicago: University of Chicago Press, 1996), 43.

68 Carby, *Reconstructing Womanhood*, 17–19.

69 Glickstein, *Concepts of Free Labor*; Sean Wilentz, *Chants Democratic: New York City and the Rise of the American Working Class, 1788–1850* (New York: Oxford University Press, 1984); Stansell, *City of Women*; Roediger, *Wages of Whiteness*.

70 I borrow these terms and this historicizing method from Cornel West. See "Marxist Theory and the Specificity of Afro-American Oppression," in *Marxism and the Interpretation of Culture*, ed. Cary Nelson and Lawrence Grossberg (Urbana: University of Illinois Press, 1988), 24. West's "neo-Gramscian" adaptation of Marxism displays a flexibility and rigor that have guided my own methods of historical inquiry. These are driven by a desire to analyze and transform our historical and social understandings of the cultural role of black women's labor. As West writes, "There is no Marxist theory without some notion of operative though transient structural constraints in particular historical conjunctures, just as there is no Marxist praxis without some notion of conjunctural opportunities."

71 "Making do" is how Michel de Certeau describes the means used to contravene the intended use of a material and/or ideological product that are central to a "network of antidiscipline." Many of my ideas on the opportunities work practices can offer build on his examination of such an opportunity, termed *la perruque*. Explored in *The Practice of Everyday Life*, trans. Steven Rendall (Berkeley: University of California Press, 1984), 24–28.

72 Pierre Bourdieu, "Social Space and the Genesis of 'Classes,'" in *Language*

and Symbolic Power, ed. John B. Thompson, trans. Gino Raymond and Matthew Adamson (Cambridge: Harvard University Press, 1991), 66–67.

73 This represents an alternative rhetorical trajectory from the antebellum insistence on bodily definitions of identity that Karen Sánchez-Eppler describes as characterizing reform discourses intent on disrupting abstract, or disembodied, norms of personhood. *Touching Liberty: Abolitionism, Feminism, and the Politics of the Body* (Berkeley: University of California Press, 1993).

74 Horton and Horton, *In Hope of Liberty*; Gaines, *Uplifting the Race*; Martin Burke, *The Conundrum of Class: Public Discourse on the Social Order in America* (Chicago: University of Chicago Press, 1995); and Blumin, *The Emergence of the Middle Class*.

75 In this schema, "labor" is a verb that refers to a process "which leaves no trace," in comparison with "the work of our hands [that] fabricates the sheer unending variety of things whose sum total constitutes the human artifice." Hannah Arendt proposes this schema in her influential book, *The Human Condition* (Chicago: University of Chicago Press, 1958), 90, 136, to refute the "modern prejudice" that disparages all work.

76 Along with "productive" and "unproductive," terms derived from political economy, another popular binary—"mental" and "manual"—emerged during the period to distinguish between what became known as "white-collar" and "blue-collar" labor. See Bromell, *By the Sweat of the Brow*, and Blumin, *The Emergence of the Middle Class*.

77 These women's appeals to multiple forms of work-derived value thus radically undermine the separation of mind and body inscribed in the humanistic rhetoric of individualist subjectivity that theorist Saidiya Hartman discerns as the problematic legacy of antebellum reform. *Scenes of Subjection: Terror, Slavery, and Self-Making in Nineteenth-Century America* (New York: Oxford University Press, 1997).

CHAPTER 1

1 Recent discussions of the charismatic speaker have attempted to locate Truth within a context of agency structured around her speeches and associated activism. Current debates in particular have focused on the authenticity of Truth's famous 1851 Akron, Ohio, speech—customarily referred to as "Ain't (Ar'n't) I a Woman?"—as transcribed in 1867 by white feminist Francis Gage. Work on this best-known version of the speech has highlighted the biases and embellishments characterizing the transcription.

See Nell Irvin Painter, *Sojourner Truth: A Life, A Symbol* (New York: W. W. Norton, 1997), 121–31. See also Deborah E. McDowell's account of how Truth, figured as an heroic but unsophisticated "other" to literary theory, has been used by white feminists and African American male literary critics to devalue black female critics' contributions to recent critical debates: "Sojourner Truth as a metonym for 'black woman' is useful in this context both to a singular idea of academic feminism . . . and to ongoing controversies within that discourse over the often uneasy relations between theory and politics." "Transferences: Black Feminist Thinking: The 'Practice' of 'Theory,'" in *"The Changing Same": Black Women's Literature, Criticism, and Theory* (Bloomington: Indiana University Press, 1995), 160.

2 Debates regarding this particular speech focus on the minstrel-like southern slave type rendered by Frances Gage's transcription of the speech, a transcription produced several years after the speech and intended to assimilate Truth into the late 1860s suffrage movement through racialist appropriation. Painter's biography provides the fullest account of current revisionist critiques of this speech's transcription. Feminist work that has begun to explore Truth's radical "orality" includes Carla Peterson's *"Doers of the Word": African American Women Speakers and Writers in the North (1830–1880)* (New Brunswick, N.J.: Rutgers University Press, 1995) and Harryette Mullen's "Runaway Tongue: Resistant Orality in *Uncle Tom's Cabin, Our Nig, Incidents in the Life of a Slave Girl*, and *Beloved*," in *The Culture of Sentiment*, ed. Shirley Samuels (New York: Oxford University Press, 1992), 244–64. In 1989, Donna Haraway produced the earliest critique of Gage's transcription when she considered Truth's relevance to poststructuralist definitions of "women," in "Ecce Homo, Ain't (Ar'n't) I a Woman, and Inappropriate/d Others: The Human in a Post-Humanist Landscape," in *Feminists Theorize the Political*, ed. Judith Butler and Joan W. Scott (New York: Routledge, 1992), 87–100. Other feminist considerations of Truth in this light are explored by Denise Riley, "Does a Sex Have a History?," in *"Am I That Name?": Feminism and the Category of "Women" in History* (Minneapolis: University of Minnesota Press, 1988), 1–17, and McDowell, *"The Changing Same"*.

3 Frederick Douglass, "What I Found at the Northampton Association," in *The History of Florence, Massachusetts, Including a Complete Account of the Northampton Association of Education and Industry*, ed. Charles A. Sheffield (Florence, Mass., 1895), 132.

4 Truth's narrative does not appear in William Andrews's authoritative vol-

ume *To Tell A Free Story: The First Century of Afro-American Autobiography, 1760–1865* (Urbana: University of Illinois Press, 1987). More recent editions of nineteenth-century autobiographies are beginning to integrate her, however. See *Classic African American Women's Narratives*, ed. William L. Andrews (New York: Oxford University Press, 2003). Andrews's introduction contains an astute analysis of the conflicts that are evident in the *Narrative* between Gilbert and Truth.

5 The phrase "linguistic counter-legitimacy" is Pierre Bourdieu's, from *The Economy of Linguistic Exchanges* (1982), reprinted in *Language and Symbolic Power*, ed. John B. Thompson, trans. Gino Raymond and Matthew Adamson (Cambridge: Harvard University Press, 1991), 98. Earlier assessments of the *Narrative* did not subscribe to more current exclusionary logics: in 1931, Vernon Loggins stated that the *Narrative* "contain[s] so many quotations attributed to her that she is entitled to a place among the makers of slave narratives." *The Negro Author* (1931; Port Washington, N.Y.: Kennikat Press, 1964), 219.

6 For the historical and rhetorical contexts of black workers' racial "degeneracy" and "unfitness" for freedom, see George Frederickson, *The Black Image in the White Mind* (Middletown, Conn.: Wesleyan University Press, 1971), 235–55.

7 As historian Eric Williams suggests when explaining the origins of slavery in the New World, "The reason was economic, not racial; it had to do not with the color of the laborer, but the cheapness of the labor." *Capitalism and Slavery* (1944; repr., Chapel Hill: University of North Carolina Press, 1994), 19. Stuart Hall's more recent assessment of the mutually constituting properties of labor and race also insists on the interpenetration of these social formations. See "Race, Articulation, and Societies Structured in Dominance," in *Black British Cultural Studies: A Reader*, ed. Houston Baker Jr., Manthia Diawara, and Ruth Lindeborg (Chicago: University of Chicago Press, 1996).

8 Sojourner Truth (with Olive Gilbert), *The Narrative of Sojourner Truth*, ed. Margaret Washington (New York: Vintage Books, 1993). Subsequent page references to this text will appear in parentheses. See Martin J. Burke, *The Conundrum of Class: Public Discourse on the Social Order in America* (Chicago: University of Chicago Press, 1995) and Anne Norton, *Alternative Americas: A Reading of Antebellum Political Culture* (Chicago: University of Chicago Press, 1986) for insights into the reactionary meanings of antebellum reform.

9 Frederick Cooper's 1972 article on racial "self-elevation" succinctly pinpoints the paradoxical implications of this activist discourse. "Elevating the Race: The Social Thought of Black Leaders, 1827–59," *American Quarterly* 24 (Dec. 1972): 604–25. The debate concerning abolitionists' endebtedness to liberal, capitalist values is a wide-ranging one. See John Ashworth, David Brion Davis, and Thomas L. Haskell, *The Antislavery Debate: Capitalism and Abolitionism as a Problem in Historical Interpretation*, edited and introduced by Thomas Bender (Berkeley: University of California Press, 1992) and Jonathan A. Glickstein, "'Poverty is not Slavery': American Abolitionists and the Competitive Labor Market," in *Antislavery Reconsidered: New Perspectives on the Abolitionists*, ed. Lewis Perry and Michael Fellman (Baton Rouge: Louisiana State University Press, 1979), 195–218.

10 The version of this speech that has superseded Francis Gage's appeared June 21, 1851, and is reprinted in *The Narrative of Sojourner Truth*, ed. Margaret Washington (New York: Vintage Books, 1993), 118.

11 Karen Sayer, *Women of the Fields: Representations of Rural Women in the Nineteenth Century* (Manchester: Manchester University Press, 1995); Joan Jensen, *Loosening the Bonds: Mid-Atlantic Farm Women, 1750–1850* (New Haven: Yale University Press, 1986); Jonathan Glickstein, *Concepts of Free Labor in Antebellum America* (New Haven: Yale University Press, 1991).

12 Sarah Bradford, *Harriet Tubman, The Moses of Her People* (1869; New York: Citadel Press, 1994), 22.

13 Anne Norton discusses the ways antebellum reform discourses sought to enlist workers into industrializing work processes in *Alternative Americas*, 64–96, quotation 71. Norton locates William Ellery Channing and Ralph Waldo Emerson among antebellum proponents of this assimilation of workers.

14 Truth obtained her freedom as a hired-out hand (though technically still the slave of Van Wagenen) one year prior to New York State's 1827 emancipation of all slaves born before 1799.

15 Carleton Mabee, *Sojourner Truth: Slave, Prophet, Legend* (New York: New York University Press, 1993), 27.

16 James Pennington, *The Fugitive Blacksmith* (London, 1847); William Grimes, *The Life of William Grimes* (New Haven, 1855); William Wells Brown, *The Narrative of William W. Brown* (Boston, 1847); Frederick Douglass, *The Narrative of Frederick Douglass* (Boston, 1845); Lunsford Lane, *The Narrative of Lunsford Lane* (Boston, 1842); Moses Grandy, *The Narrative of the Life of Moses Grandy* (Boston, 1844).

17 Burke, *The Conundrum of Class*, 76–107.

18 Truth dictated her experiences to Gilbert, who then interposed her own observations and experiences with Truth's material. This method of weaving disparate elements provided Gilbert with the opportunity to quote other abolitionist sources. These included Douglass's assessments of slave-owner-sanctioned festivities as "safety valves" that dispersed slave resistance as well as her own account of a brief sojourn in Kentucky. In this way, Gilbert sought to fashion Truth's narrative after the southern-produced pattern that characterized Douglass's best-selling narrative.

19 See Painter, *Sojourner Truth*, 109–10, and Erlene Stetson and Linda David, *Glorying in Tribulation: The Lifework of Sojourner Truth* (East Lansing: Michigan State University Press, 1994), 47. Stetson and David suggest that because former slaves could not customarily demand political and social equality, the Christian ideals invoked in spiritual autobiographies posed a greater challenge to hegemonic social hierarchies. Still, the spiritual autobiographies of Jarena Lee, Zilpha Elaw, and Julia Foote, while distinct from the slave narrative tradition, have enjoyed a degree of acceptance in the African American autobiographical tradition not accorded to Truth's text.

20 Jean Humez, "Reading the Narrative of Sojourner Truth as a Collaborative Text," *Frontiers* 16.1 (1996): 29–46. DoVeanna S. Fulton, on former slave Louisa Picquet's narrative *The Octoroon* (1860), focuses on developing Harryette Mullen's concept of "resistant orality." "Speak Sister, Speak: Oral Empowerment in *Louisa Picquet: The Octoroon*," *Legacy* 15.1 (1998): 98–103. See also Anne Goldman, *Take My Word: Autobiographical Innovations of Ethnic American Working Women* (Berkeley: University of California Press, 1996).

21 See Painter, *Sojourner Truth*, 103–12, for a description of this relationship.

22 Nicholas Bromell provides insight into the links between writing as labor and writing about labor in his book *By the Sweat of the Brow: Literature and Labor in Antebellum America* (Chicago: University of Chicago Press, 1993).

23 For example, Gilbert cites Douglass's interpretation of slaveholder-sanctioned holidays as "safety valves" in depicting Truth's desire to join her family at Pingster and also intermittently inserts her observations about slave marriages and other matters from her visit to the South.

24 Gilbert Vale, *FANATICISM; ITS SOURCE AND INFLUENCE, Illustrated by the Simple Narrative of Isabella, in the case of Matthias, Mr. and Mrs. B. Folger, Mr. Pierson, Mr. Mills, Catherine, Isabella, &c. &c.—A Reply to W. L. Stone, with descriptive portraits of all the parties, while at Sing-Sing and at Third Street.—*

Containing the Whole Truth—And Nothing But the Truth (New York, 1835). For a history of the cult, and Vale and Truth's collaboration in refuting the scandal-related charges, see Paul E. Johnson and Sean Wilentz, *The Kingdom of Matthias: A Story of Sex and Salvation in 19th-Century America* (New York: Oxford University Press, 1994). One important insight suggested by Johnson and Wilentz's innovative treatment of the historical material concerns the linked developments of the scandal and a sensationalizing penny press. The unprecedented publicity generated by this scandal suggests itself as a catalyst for the inception of the unlettered Truth's publicity-savvy manipulation. See also Painter, *Sojourner Truth*, 48–61, and Mabee, *Sojourner Truth*, 25–42.

25 Vale, *Fanaticism*, 5.

26 Ibid., 116.

27 Ibid., 6.

28 Ibid., 10.

29 Ibid., 11. With the exception of one "certificate" dated September 13, 1828, the letters that Truth publishes all date from October 1834, contemporaneous with the Matthias scandal. The selections mentioned above from her two owners are dated October 13, 1834, Ulster County, and are almost identical, word for word.

30 In this regard, Truth's text suggests interesting links to the contemporary genre of collaborative subaltern "testimonio" that has been characterized as a form of juridical intervention used by populations denied access to conventional legal and civic channels. The most notable example is the Noble Prize–winning testimonio of Guatemalan activist Rigoberta Menchú, *I, Rigoberta Menchú: An Indian Woman in Guatemala*, trans. Ann White (London: Verso, 1984). See John Beverly's insightful analysis of the testifying and dictating narrator dynamics of testimonio in "The Margin at the Center: On *Testimonio*," in *De/Colonizing the Subject: The Politics of Gender in Women's Autobiography* (Minneapolis: University of Minnesota Press, 1992).

31 Douglass speaks his labor most eloquently in relation to the "breaking down" regime marking his tenure at Mr. Covey's. The linkage of Douglass's field labor (the only time he engages with it) to slavery's brutalization, combined with his ambivalent discussion of the slave songs, displays how Douglass's *Narrative* refuses to attribute any form of self-producing value or legitimation to the slave's labor. As discussed below, Douglass also differs from Truth in his representation of free, northern labor when he ob-

scures what Truth takes such pains to expose: the North's exploitation of its workers.

32 See Haraway, "Ecce Homo," 97. This dialect, in Haraway's terms a "counterfeit language," is used in an attempt to reproduce Truth as an "ideal type," namely, "The Slave." The fact that Gilbert did not feel called upon to produce a priori such a typologizing effort may be due to an appreciation of the fact that Truth's history on both sides of slavery's divide could not be readily subsumed to any type.

33 It was just one step from the idea that slavery degraded free labor, which emerged in the 1840s, to the idea that slaves must *necessarily* be degraded labor. This idea represented a corollary (though a paradoxical one at best) of the notion of slavery's "soul-killing" effects—paradoxical in two fraught senses: it forestalled understandings of slavery's basis in a very antirepublican theft of the black body's productivity, and it discouraged the related, rhetorical deployment of this productivity as grounds for abolishing slavery. The classic expression of slave labor's presumed inefficiency is recorded in Frederick Law Olmsted's quasi-scientific newspaper accounts of 1854–55, reprinted in *Journey through the Seaboard Slave States* (New York, 1856). For slavery's ideological effects on formulations of free labor, see Eric Foner, *Free Soil, Free Labor, Free Men* (New York: Oxford University Press, 1970), 58–65.

34 Sophia Auld's metamorphosis from ministering angel to shrew in chapter six of Douglass's 1845 account dramatically illustrates this and may well have influenced Gilbert's portrayal of Mrs. Dumont.

35 Nell Irvin Painter has attributed Sally Dumont's hostility to her possible sexual abuse of Isabella. *Sojourner Truth*, 17.

36 Not surprisingly, Gilbert and Truth's framing of this incident invites comparisons with Frederick Douglass's discussion of slave sycophancy in his 1845 narrative. In one passage, Douglass likens slaves aspiring to be sent to the "Great House Farm" to "office-seekers in the political parties," and in another he deploys slaves' paradoxical identifications with their masters to exemplify slaves' ignorance. His distancing of himself from these slaves, evident in his frequent subject shifts from "we" to "them," represents Douglass as exceptional. In contrast to them, he evinces an ability to withstand slavery's bankrupting of the slave's intelligence. But most important, his judgments concur with Gilbert's refusal to perceive slaves' identifications with their masters as staking a claim to the labor (theirs) from which their master derives his "greatness." Douglass comments ironi-

cally at the end of the third chapter, "They seemed to think that the greatness of their masters was transferable to themselves." *The Narrative of Frederick Douglass* (New York: Penguin, 1986), 28.

37 See Patricia Williams, "On Being the Object of Property," in *The Alchemy of Race and Rights* (Cambridge: Harvard University Press, 1991), 216–39, for an insightful discussion of the mind/intention–robbing attributes of slavery's property norms.

38 Robert Stepto describes the symbology that links freedom, mobility, and the North in *From Behind the Veil: A Study of Afro-American Narrative* (Urbana: University of Illinois Press, 1979), 167. The classic "ascent" narrative launches an enslaved and semi-literate figure on a ritualized journey to a symbolic North; that journey is charted through systems of signs that the questing figure must read in order to gain literary freedom. The ascent narrative conventionally ends with the questing figure situated in the least oppressive social structure afforded by the world of the narrative, and free in the sense that he or she has gained sufficient literacy to assume the mantle of an articulate survivor.

39 Ibid.

40 The phrase "making do," along with its "tactical" context, is Michel de Certeau's, from *The Practice of Everyday Life*, trans. Steven Rendall (Berkeley: University of California Press, 1984), 29.

41 Stepto, *From Behind the Veil*, 167.

42 Reforms instituted at Northampton, Mass., in 1842–46 included communal ownership, through stock, of the means of production (a factory for producing silk) and an egalitarian distribution of wages/subsistence intended to abolish gender inequities in the divisions of labor. All members, male and female, took part in meetings, expressed their views, and voted on policies. See Christopher Clark, *The Communitarian Moment: The Radical Challenge of the Northampton Association* (Ithaca: Cornell University Press, 1995), 120–28.

43 Frederick Douglass, "Learn Trades or Starve!" (1853), reprinted in *The Life and Writings of Frederick Douglass*, ed. Philip S. Foner (New York: International Publishers, 1950), 2:225.

44 This specific formulation of the ideal nation vs. capitalist nation binary is borrowed from Lauren Berlant, *The Queen of America Goes to Washington City: Essays on Sex and Citizenship* (Durham, N.C.: Duke University Press, 1997), 26.

45 Douglass, "Learn Trades or Starve!," 223.

46 Mark Rose, *Authors and Owners: The Invention of Copyright* (Cambridge: Harvard University Press, 1995), 1.

CHAPTER 2

1 In this regard, these women's analyses of the waged worker offer insight into black laboring women's understanding of the ironic Marxian formulation: workers are "free" when they have "nothing else to sell." Karl Marx, *Capital: A Critique of Political Economy* (1867; New York: International Publishers, 1967), 1:167.

2 Henry Louis Gates Jr. rediscovered Wilson's text in 1983 and was the first to inventory *Our Nig*'s authorial innovations. See "Parallel Discursive Universes: Fictions of the Self in Harriet E. Wilson's *Our Nig*," in *Figures in Black* (New York: Oxford University Press, 1987), 125–65. Julia Sterne provides an alternative generic model for framing these innovations. She suggests that the "gothic," not the sentimental, serves as the best generic equivalent in describing *Our Nig*'s scathing critique. "Excavating Genre in *Our Nig*," *American Literature* 67.3 (Sept. 1995): 439–66. For a recent and exciting exploration of Harriet Wilson's life after 1859, see the "Introduction," *Our Nig, or Sketches from the Life of a Free Black*, P. Gabrielle Foreman and Reginald H. Pitts, eds. (New York: Penguin Group, 2005), xxiii–l.

3 In his preface to Wilson's text, Gates describes his preliminary investigation of the text as consisting of a search for proof of her racial identity. *Our Nig: Sketches from the Life of a Free Black* (1859), reprinted with an introduction by Henry Louis Gates Jr. (New York: Vintage Books, 1983), xi–lv. Subsequent page references to this edition will appear in parentheses.

4 Claudia Tate, *Domestic Allegories of Political Desire: The Black Heroine's Text at the Turn of the Century* (New York: Oxford University Press, 1992), 42; Patricia Wald, *Constituting Americans: Cultural Anxiety and Narrative Form* (Durham, N.C.: Duke University Press, 1995), 157. Hazel Carby is among the few scholars who have taken Wilson's appeal to a black audience seriously. See *Reconstructing Womanhood: The Emergence of the Afro-American Woman Novelist* (New York: Oxford University Press, 1987).

5 Eric Gardner's detailed exploration of several copies of the 1859 edition of *Our Nig* led him to suggest that "Wilson was not able to reach a large black readership—a community that would at least support her morally, if not financially." He proposes young (white?) readers as the text's primary audience. Whereas we disagree on the primary audience, he makes some noteworthy observations regarding *Our Nig*'s relationship to abolition, among

them: the fact that abolitionists did not promote the book does not mean that the book was not read. He is right to point us to the possible existence of other audiences, but Gardner's claim that "Wilson was responsible for distributing the book herself—and that the distribution was limited to personal acquaintance with the author or her friends or agents" makes me wonder how Wilson's possible sale of the book to black acquaintances does not constitute reaching her stated audience. Gardner, "'This Attempt of Their Sister': Harriet Wilson's *Our Nig* from Printer to Readers," *New England Quarterly* 66 (1993): 226–46, quotation 240. I speculate that Frado's post-Bellmont work history yields us more clues: when Wilson describes her travels as an itinerant worker through New Hampshire and Massachusetts, she mentions "procur[ing] an agency" (129). This suggests that Wilson was hired as an "agent," but as what kind of an agent? For what kind of a society? Perhaps if the semi-educated Wilson had experience (however brief) as a regional or local agent for a black uplift society, she would have had personal contact with a range of "colored brethren" who might well have constituted the audience she invokes. I advance this possibility on the basis of the discussion of abolitionism's work with working-class blacks in the introduction to *The Black Abolitionist Papers*, vol. 3, ed. C. Peter Ripley et al. (Chapel Hill: University of North Carolina Press, 1991), 35.

6 Wilson's open criticism of racist abolitionists and her description of the racism she experiences in an abolitionized North has been perceived as potentially replicating proslavery anticapitalism critiques. In these critiques, apologists for slavery would favorably contrast slavery's imputed paternalism with capitalists' exploitation of "free labor." See John Ernest, "Economies of Identity: Harriet E. Wilson's *Our Nig*," *PMLA* 109 (1994): 424–37. Southerner George Fitzhugh's 1857 *Cannibals All! Or Slaves without Masters* is perhaps the best example of this anticapitalism/proslavery argument.

7 Cited by Philip S. Foner, ed., in his introduction to *The Life and Writings of Frederick Douglass* (New York: International Publishers, 1950), 2:36. Douglass advanced this view during his abortive effort to found a "Manual Labor School" during the 1850s when growing immigration and racial discrimination combined to erode black workers' opportunities for cultivating work skills.

8 Richard Newman, Patrick Rael, and Phillip Lapsansky, eds., *Pamphlets of Protest: An Anthology of Early African American Protest Literature, 1790–1860* (London: Routledge, 2001), 178–89.

9 To call menial workers dependent and servile was to reiterate a premise of political economy that viewed landless laborers as politically "dependent" on their landholder. "Servility" in this initial sense did not pertain to domestic service; it referred to the landless laborer's serving the landholder's political interests. In reference to this condition Thomas Jefferson commented that "dependence begets servility and venality, and suffocates the germ of virtue." *Notes on the State of Virginia*, cited in R. J. Ellis, *Harriet Wilson's "Our Nig": A Cultural Biography of a "Two-Story" African American Novel* (Amsterdam: Editions Rodopi, 2003), 138. To compensate for the emerging dominance of wage labor, wage workers reformulated dependency and servility to refer more exclusively to those in menial or "service" occupations.

10 *Weekly Anglo-African*, June 30, 1860.

11 My approach takes up Barbara A. White's insights into the economic motives she discerns as central to *Our Nig* and the biographical background of Wilson's protagonists, the Bellmonts. The inextricability of race and class in the economic processes under analysis in the novel furthermore suggests to me the audience of "colored brethren" who would be most familiar with Wilson's experience. White, "*Our Nig* and the She-Devil: New Information about Harriet Wilson and the 'Bellmont' Family," *American Literature* 65.1 (1993): 19–52. While I argue that Wilson's materialist critique foregrounds the economic value she produces, I believe it is going too far to suggest that she views wage labor as "salutary," as Thomas B. Lovell suggests. There is no doubt that Wilson subscribes to the view of wage labor's independence-granting possibilities, but her analysis acutely criticizes this system's racializing and class-dominating properties. See "By Dint of Labor and Economy: Harriet Jacobs, Harriet Wilson, and the Salutary View of Wage Labor," *Arizona Quarterly* 52.3 (Autumn 1996): 1–32.

12 See Frederick Cooper, "Elevating the Race: The Social Thought of Black Leaders, 1827–59," *American Quarterly* 24 (Dec. 1972): 604–25, for a description of uplift terminology and a discussion of its paradoxes. In many ways, these activist efforts often appeared to blame the victims of racial discrimination for their poverty and inassimilability.

13 Gayatri Spivak, "Can the Subaltern Speak?," in *Marxism and the Interpretation of Culture*, ed. Cary Nelson and Lawrence Grossberg (Urbana: University of Illinois Press, 1988), 285.

14 I obtained this figure from Leon Litwack's discussion of northern blacks in *North of Slavery: The Negro in the Free States, 1790–1860* (Chicago: University of Chicago Press, 1961), 155. Litwack states, "As late as 1855, some

87 percent of the gainfully employed Negroes of New York City worked in menial or unskilled jobs, and this appears to represent this economic condition in other northern cities."

15 David Roediger, *Wages of Whiteness: Race and the Making of the American Working Class* (New York: Verso, 1991), 144–45.

16 See Ellis, *Harriet Wilson's "Our Nig,"* for insights into the two types of linked "stories" about race and class that mark the generic innovations at the root of what Ellis calls the uniqueness of *Our Nig*.

17 Roediger, *Wages of Whiteness*, 47.

18 With some exceptions, most of the feminist literature on housework makes the unwaged domestic labor of white married women visible while reinforcing the invisibility of waged domestic workers. Consequently, these analyses perpetuate the invisibility of bourgeois women's class privilege, a privilege that enables them to transfer responsibility for their gendered labor onto poor women of color who lack the means to purchase this "freedom." See Mary Romero's discussion of African American women's skeptical perceptions of 1960s and 1970s "women's liberation," in *Maid in the U.S.A.* (New York: Routledge, 1992), 97–133. For a summary of the field, see also Ellen Malos's introductory essay, "The Politics of Household Labour in the 1990s: Old Debates, New Contexts," in *The Politics of Housework*, ed. Ellen Malos (1980; repr., London: New Clarion Press, 1995), 206–18. Other analyses that have informed my work on domestic worker/employer intragender conflict include Stephanie Coontz, *The Social Origins of Private Life: A History of American Families* (London: Verso, 1988); Teresa McBride, *The Domestic Revolution: The Modernization of Household Service in England and France, 1820–1920* (London: Croom Helm, 1976); Aída Hurtado, *The Color of Privilege* (Ann Arbor: University of Michigan Press, 1996); and Bonnie Thornton Dill, "'Making Your Job Good Yourself': Domestic Service and the Construction of Personal Dignity," in *Women and the Politics of Empowerment*, ed. Ann Bookman and Sandra Morgen (Philadelphia: Temple University Press, 1988), 33–52.

19 Stuart Blumin, *The Emergence of the Middle Class: Social Experience in the American City, 1760–1900* (New York: Cambridge University Press, 1989), 179–91.

20 For an account of the emerging forms of "intimate discipline" deployed by the bourgeois in order to assert their moral authority in the antebellum "home," see Richard Brodhead, "Sparing the Rod: Discipline and Fiction in Antebellum America," *Representations* 21 (Winter 1988): 67–96. One of

the interesting aspects of the "servitude debate" of the period is domestic workers' contestations of bourgeois women's efforts to mystify and assert their class privilege as a form of familial rule over them. See Christine Stansell, *City of Women: Sex and Class in New York, 1789–1860* (Urbana: University of Illinois Press, 1987) and Barbara T. Ryan, "'An Uneasy Relation': Servants' Place in the Nineteenth-Century American Home" (Ph.D. diss., University of North Carolina at Chapel Hill, 1994). See Judith Rollins, *Between Women: Domestics and Their Employers* (Philadelphia: Temple University Press, 1985), for an insightful account of how the relationship between mistress and household worker is perceived as "personal" rather than professional.

21 Former household worker Naomi Yates, cited in *Race, Gender, and Work: A Multicultural Economic History of Women in the United States*, ed. Teresa Amott and Julie Matthaei (Boston: South End Press, 1991), 161. Emphasis added.

22 Nina Baym discusses the plot patterns and narrative techniques characterizing popular antebellum women's novels in *Woman's Fiction: A Guide to Novels by and About Women in America, 1820–1870* (Ithaca: Cornell University Press, 1978), 35–44. My account of the twin forms of domination that a household worker in a bourgeois home is subject to—material and psychological—has been informed by Judith Rollins's anthropological field work. Rollins categorizes the complex nature of household workers' exploitation in *Between Women* and in "Ideology and Servitude," in *At Work in Homes: Household Workers in World Perspective*, ed. Roger Sanjek and Shellee Colen (Washington, D.C.: American Anthropological Association, 1990), 74–88.

23 Coontz, *The Social Origins of Private Life*, 161–209.

24 Michel Foucault, *Discipline and Punish: The Birth of the Prison* (New York: Vintage Books, 1979), 195–208.

25 Mag's compelled labor, in other words, is punishment for transgressing prevailing gender mores, highlighting the protection from class realities that these gender codes were perceived to offer white women. See Amy Schrager Lang, "Class and the Strategies of Sympathy," in *The Culture of Sentiment*, ed. Shirley Samuels (New York: Oxford University Press, 1992), 128–42, for insights into how gender difference served to displace class difference and its antidemocratic connotations.

26 Frantz Fanon, *Black Skin, White Masks* (1952), trans. Charles Lam Markmann (New York: Grove Press, 1967), 11.

27 Though the more recent understandings of waged household labor frame

this labor as a transitional site that helped socialize rural, unskilled workers into the industrial force, the fact is that this lateral mobility was confined strictly to immigrants and native-born whites. In other words, black women's disproportionate presence in household work—as 10 percent of the total population, they were 30 percent of household workers—clearly reflects the differential opportunities and possibilities for mobility that existed between white and black working-class women. See McBride, *The Domestic Revolution*, for the role of household work in labor force modernization and Rollins, "Ideology and Servitude," 74, for black women's representation in the household work force.

28 On this basis, I disagree with Patricia Wald's contention that Frado's captivity is entirely self-imposed, since she considers Wilson "legally free to go." *Constituting Americans*, 164. *Our Nig* suggests that Wilson's/Frado's status in the household was tacitly recognized as that of an indentured servant. In this (not uncommon) case, Wilson would not be legally free to go until she attained her majority at eighteen years of age, which is when she does in fact "choose" to leave and become self-sufficient.

29 My formulation of this dynamic of raced-because-coerced labor signifies on Marx's formulation of the grounding conditions for commodified labor: workers must alienate their labor and sell "it" to a capitalist because they have "nothing else to sell." Karl Marx, *Capital: A Critique of Political Economy* (1867; New York: International Publishers, 1967), 1:167. In this regard, I expand on David Roediger's analysis of the ways in which "whiteness" (after Du Bois's use of the phrase) became troped as a form of "wages" that distinguished white workers from black workers. This differentiation, in turn, was deployed to displace the implications of white workers' suspiciously unfree status in the "free labor" economy. *The Wages of Whiteness*, 58.

30 I borrow this term from Hortense Spillers. See "Mama's Baby, Papa's Maybe: An American Grammar Book," *Diacritics* 17.2 (Summer 1987): 65–80, quotation 67.

31 I derive this insight into the overdetermined corporeal and symbolic logics attending raced labor from Robyn Wiegman. She is concerned with the specificity of U.S. race production: "Indeed, the shift from the socially inscribed mark of visibility attending the spectacle to the self-incorporated vision of the panoptic relation coalesced in the U.S., not in successive stages but as intertwined technologies that worked simultaneously to stage the hierarchical relations of race. . . . The disciplinary power of race, in short, must be read as implicated in both specular and panoptic regimes."

American Anatomies: Theorizing Race and Gender (Durham, N.C.: Duke University Press, 1995), 39.

32 Wald, *Constituting Americans*, 163.

33 See Aída Hurtado's formulation of "relational privilege" for insights into the corrosive effects of racial differentiation and socialization on gender alliances, and especially on relations between white women and women of color. "Relating to Privilege: Seduction and Rejection in the Subordination of White Women and Women of Color," in *Theorizing Feminism: Parallel Trends in the Humanities and the Social Sciences*, ed. Anne C. Hermann and Abigail J. Stewart (Boulder: Westview Press, 1994), 136–55. Hortense Spillers has also discussed the power differentials existing between black and white women and the different "genders" emerging from these structural conditions. See "Mama's Baby, Papa's Maybe."

34 Precisely on account of the foundational role Frado plays in establishing Mrs. Bellmont's bourgeois identity, I disagree with readings of Mrs. Bellmont's seemingly "unnatural" proclivity to violence as a sign of Wilson's adherence to the ideology of bourgeois domesticity. The dynamics of Frado's labor relations suggest that what appears "unnatural" is precisely the naturalness associated with the white bourgeois woman's assumption of racial and class privilege. From this vantage point, Frado's own mother, Mag, in her degraded, unmarried, and economically unstable status, likewise represents the contingency of this bourgeois embodiment.

35 Gillian Brown has shown how Harriet Beecher Stowe's abolitionist arguments also betray this racial anxiety, suggesting that white northerners (including abolitionists) shared white southerners' fears over postemancipation racial mixing. *Domestic Individualism: Imagining Self in Nineteenth-Century America* (Berkeley: University of California Press, 1990), 53–60.

36 Frederick Douglass, "Prejudice Against Color" (1850), reprinted in *The Life and Writings of Frederick Douglass*, ed. Philip S. Foner (New York: International Publishers, 1950), 2:129.

37 Booker T. Washington's novel and potentially emancipatory efforts to rehabilitate black labor during the post-Reconstruction era acquired their conservative and socially subordinating character precisely because he failed to acknowledge these historical, structural conditions governing black labor. See *Up from Slavery* (1901), ed. William L. Andrews (New York: W. W. Norton, 1996).

38 Again, in this I disagree with Wald's reading of Frado's predicament (*Constituting Americans*, 166–68). For an analysis of the potential critique en-

abled by Wilson's "fictionalizing" and third-person narration, see Carla Peterson, *"Doers of the Word": African American Women Speakers and Writers in the North (1830–1880)* (New Brunswick, N.J.: Rutgers University Press, 1995), 146–56.

39 David Walker, *David Walker's Appeal in Four Articles* (1829), *Norton Anthology of African American Literature*, 2nd ed., Henry Louis Gates Jr. and Nellie Y. McKay, eds. (New York: Norton, 2004), 227–38, quotation 236.

40 We may find another example of this rationality at work in Sojourner Truth's 1850 *Narrative*, in particular when Truth decides to leave her last master, Dumont. Truth portrays him as having gone back on his word to emancipate her one year earlier than required by New York State law simply because he recognized she was too valuable a worker to give up voluntarily.

41 Notwithstanding Mr. Bellmont's evident sympathy for Frado, the several instances in which he fails to intervene, or only belatedly intervenes, suggest that he is unwilling to pay the costs associated with challenging Mrs. Bellmont's abuse of the child. When his sister Abby suggests that as a man he should bear the responsibility of standing up to his wife, Mr. Bellmont refuses to do so: "And live in hell meantime" (44).

42 This reading thus inverts Wald's interpretation of *Our Nig* as portraying the juridical inability of the white family to assimilate the black family "member" and instead views this attempted assimilation as mystifying Frado's economic value to the family.

43 Mary Childers's novel of the same name, *Like One of the Family* (New York: Independence Publishers, 1956), echoes Wilson's sharp irony in recognizing the boundaries that obtain between patronized household workers and patronizing employers.

44 While technically speaking (in Marxian terms) Frado's subsequent labor, compelled by necessity, still constitutes an alienated relation, I read this moment of simultaneous race and class recognition as anticipating the formulations of Frantz Fanon: "It is apparent to me that the effective disalienation of the black man entails an immediate recognition of social and economic realities. If there is an inferiority complex, it is the outcome of a double process:—primarily, economic;—subsequently, the internalization—or better, the epidermalization—of this inferiority." *Black Skin, White Masks*, 11–12.

45 Gates's reading of this incident as a subject-initiating moment of "speech" removes the speech act entirely from the material conditions in which it takes place (*Our Nig*, liii). Consequently, there is little recognition of how

what Frado says so demystifies Mrs. Bellmont's abuse that it stops the woman in her tracks.

46 Beth Doriani, "Black Womanhood in Nineteenth-Century America: Subversion and Self-Construction in Two Women's Autobiographies," *American Quarterly* 43.2 (June 1991): 199–222, quotation 217.

47 Here again I'd like to underscore Wilson's conflicted relation to the system of wage labor. Notwithstanding her efforts to support herself through her earnings, these efforts are founded in necessity, rather than in some philosophical adherence to an organic ideology of wage labor, especially since such ideologies play a key role in formulations of economic mobility and individualism. While moral value clearly inheres in Wilson's marketplace efforts, I do not think that Wilson sees the market as necessarily moral per se.

48 Frederick Douglass, "Self-Elevation" (1855), reprinted in *The Life and Writings of Frederick Douglass*, ed. Philip S. Foner (New York: International Publishers, 1950), 2:360.

49 Frederick Douglass, "Learn Trades or Starve!," *Frederick Douglass' Paper*, March 4, 1853, reprinted in *Black Workers: A Documentary History from Colonial Times to the Present*, ed. Philip S. Foner and Ronald L. Lewis (Philadelphia: Temple University Press, 1989), 224.

50 See Eric Foner, *Free Soil, Free Labor, Free Men* (New York: Oxford University Press, 1970), 12–13, for explanations of the links between free labor ideology and social mobility and the basis of these links in a broader commitment to middle-class formation.

51 Kevin K. Gaines, *Uplifting the Race* (Chapel Hill: University of North Carolina Press, 1996), 94.

52 The characterization of Washington's philosophies as "dangerous half-truths" is W. E. B. Du Bois's. I would argue that Wilson is anticipating Du Bois's critique of Washington's formula for elevation. In the postbellum era, Washington promoted black workers in the South through now-infamous descriptions of manual labor that only intensified the misrecognitions pertaining to this labor. In response to Washington's efforts, Du Bois, like Wilson, drew attention to the context of race prejudice within which well-intentioned efforts to promote industriousness take place:

> Each of these propositions is a dangerous half-truth. The supplementary truths must never be lost sight of: first, slavery and race-prejudice are potent if not sufficient causes of the Negro's position; second, indus-

trial and common-school training were necessarily slow. . . . In his failure to realize and impress this . . . Mr. Washington is especially to be criticised. His doctrine has tended to make the whites, North and South, shift the burden of the Negro problem to the Negro's shoulders and stand aside as critical and rather pessimistic spectators; when in fact the burden belongs to the nation, and the hands of none of us are clean if we bend not our energies to righting these great wrongs. [*The Souls of Black Folk* (1903), reprinted in *Three Negro Classics* (Avon Books, 1965), 251.]

CHAPTER 3

1 For a fascinating and extensive account of antebellum black women's enterprises, see Juliet E. K. Walker, *The History of Black Business in America: Capitalism, Race, and Entrepreneurship* (New York: McMillan Library Reference/Twayne Publishers, 1998), 127–49.

2 Ibid., 128.

3 Lynn M. Hudson, *The Making of 'Mammy Pleasant': A Black Entrepreneur in Nineteenth-Century San Francisco* (Urbana: University of Illinois Press, 2003), 2.

4 Frances Smith Foster's annotated edition of *Behind the Scenes* is particularly helpful (Chicago: Lakeside Press, 1998). Also, see Foster's chapter on Keckley, "Romance and Scandal in a Postbellum Slave Narrative," in her book *Written by Herself: Literary Production by African American Women, 1746–1892* (Bloomington: Indiana University Press, 1993), 116–30.

5 Stuart Blumin, *The Emergence of the Middle Class: Social Experience in the American City, 1760–1900* (New York: Cambridge University Press, 1989).

6 Apart from consecutive entries in the Cincinnati city directory of the late 1850s, we have no information regarding Potter's date or place of birth or where she went after leaving the city in 1860. See Sharon Dean's introduction to *A Hairdresser's Experience in High Life* (1859; New York: Oxford University Press, 1991; subsequent page references will refer to this edition). Dean states that Potter was listed as owning $2000 worth of property. Until recently, only selections of the *Gazette*'s review were known to exist, and only because Alvin F. Harlow excerpted them in his twentieth-century (unfootnoted) book on Cincinnati, *The Serene Cincinnatians* (E. P. Dutton: New York, 1950), 171–75. The exact date of the publication of Potter's book in 1859 was unknown until I located the copyright application in the Library

of Congress (which led to the discovery of three Cincinnati reviews of the book). Because events are not arranged chronologically it is difficult to determine any conclusive sequence for them, but Potter's mention of particular events and locations—for example, Louis Kossuth's visit to Cincinnati, a fire in the St. Charles Hotel in New Orleans, and the description of resort hotels in Saratoga, New York—allow us to place her travels during the 1840s through the 1850s. Susan Graber, "*A Hairdresser's Experience in High Life* by Mrs. Eliza Potter: Cincinnati in the Mid-Nineteenth Century," *Bulletin of the Historical and Philosophical Society of Ohio* 25.3 (1967): 215–24.

7 To date, the body of critical work on *A Hairdresser* is limited to three relatively recent accounts, including Sharon Dean's introduction to the reprinted Oxford edition. Barbara T. Ryan discusses Potter in her dissertation's account of "kitchen testimony." See "'An Uneasy Relation': Servants' Place in the Nineteenth-Century American Home" (Ph.D. diss., University of North Carolina at Chapel Hill, 1994). Rafia Zafar's account, the most recent of the three, takes up many of the issues I discuss relating to this text's diverging narrating relations. See "Dressing Up and Dressing Down: Elizabeth Keckley's *Behind the Scenes* and Eliza Potter's *A Hairdresser's Experience in High Life*," in her book *We Wear the Mask: African Americans Write American Literature, 1760–1870* (New York: Columbia University Press, 1997), 151–84.

8 Zafar, *We Wear the Mask*, 160. Zafar views this tendency as pronounced enough to describe *A Hairdresser* as "a black autobiography without African Americans," 152.

9 *Cincinnati Daily Gazette*, October 19, 1859, p. 3.

10 "New Books," *Cincinnati Daily Commercial*, October 19, 1859, p. 1.

11 *Cincinnati Daily Commercial*, October 19, 20, 22, 1859.

12 The *Gazette* responded with a brief dismissive jab at the *Commercial*'s reviewer, which it entitled "Fits." October 21, 1859.

13 *Cincinnati Daily Commercial*, October 19, 1859, p. 1. The third review also corroborates that Potter was "well known in this city as an adept in the profession of which the book professes to give the experience." *Cincinnati Daily Enquirer*, October 23, 1859, p. 2.

14 Here, the dramatic censure that greeted black dressmaker Elizabeth Keckley's *Behind the Scenes* (1868) comes to mind. In this case, the employee was defending her employer, Mary Todd Lincoln, yet critics refused to take her at her word. For the publicity scandal surrounding this black work-

ing woman's narrative, see Foster, *Written by Herself*, 116–30, and Xiomara Santamarina, "Behind the Scenes of Black Labor: Elizabeth Keckley and the Scandal of Publicity," *Feminist Studies* 28.3 (Fall 2002), 515–36.

15 My understanding of the beauty industry derives in large part from Lois W. Banner's *American Beauty* (New York: Knopf, 1983) and Karen Halttunen, *Confidence Men and Painted Women: A Study of Middle-Class Culture in America, 1830–1870* (New Haven: Yale University Press, 1982).

16 Potter's representation of hairdressing thus revises perceptions of this relatively new skilled occupation as a form of manual labor. See Virginia Penny, *The Employments of Women: A Cyclopaedia of Woman's Work* (Boston: Walker, Wise & Co., 1863), for a listing that places hairdressing under the category of manual labor.

17 Potter's problematic status as female entrepreneurial laborer anticipates that of another successful black hairdresser's forays into the black public sphere: Madame C. J. Walker's success in selling haircare products and the economic and social independence it afforded her was perceived as challenging the patriarchal class prerogatives articulated by black business leaders of the early twentieth century, including, most notably, Booker T. Washington. See Noliwe M. Rooks, *Hair Raising: Beauty, Culture, and African American Women* (New Jersey: Rutgers University Press, 1996), 51–95, and A'Lelia Bundles, *On Her Own Ground: The Life and Times of Madam C. J. Walker* (New York: Washington Square Press, 2001).

18 Beth Lynne Lueck, *American Writers and the Picturesque Tour: The Search for National Identity* (New York: Garland Publishing, 1997).

19 Frances Trollope, *Domestic Manners of the Americans* (1832). For an analysis of the forms of cultural empowerment and rhetorical authority associated with travel writing, see William W. Stowe, *Going Abroad: European Travel in Nineteenth-Century American Culture* (Princeton, N.J.: Princeton University Press, 1994), 56–73. In this regard, *A Hairdresser's Experience in High Life* could also be read as a vernacular precursor to the text that would appear as the definitive ethnography of the upper classes, Thorstein Veblen's *Theory of the Leisure Class: An Economic Study of Institutions* (1899).

20 Sociologists use the phrase "anonymous friendship" to describe the asymmetrical relations of affect and confessional intimacy characterizing salon hairdressing. It is on this basis that the analogy between hairdresser and physician is often invoked today. As one study suggests, "The analogy rests on the recognition that both physicians and hairdressers experience a degree of physical and communicative intimacy that, in our culture, is rare

in a professional relationship. . . . Apparently, patrons who are solicitous of this form of intimacy are not deterred by the fact that the revealing of self that is involved is not reciprocal; in fact, they do not want it to be. It is the lack of reciprocity that makes the loving an illusion and the friendship anonymous. As a matter of principle, the stylists (and physicians) tend not to share their whole selves with clients." J. Greg Getz and Hanne K. Klein, "The Frosting of the American Woman: Self-esteem Construction and Social Control in the Hair Salon," in *Ideals of Feminine Beauty: Philosophical, Social, and Cultural Dimensions*, ed. Karen A. Callaghan (Westport, Conn.: Greenwood Press, 1994), 131–43, quotation 135.

21 This stance thus foregrounds Potter's efforts to overcome the prohibitions traditionally attached to the servant's gaze. In this way, sightseeing represents an enactment of "liberty" that marks, paradoxically, a break from the very domestic routine that provided the opportunity for Potter to see the sights "with my little responsibility at my side" (25). This framing of vision as a source of class conflict should not lead us to overlook many of the shared aesthetic goals of self-improvement that middle-class travelers and their servants associated with travel. See Karen L. Kilcup, "The Domestic Abroad: Cross-Class (Re)Visions of Europe and America," *Legacy* 16.1 (1999): 22–36.

22 The reviewer alludes here to a scene from Milton's *Paradise Lost* (Book IV). Ithuriel uses his spear to expose Satan, who, disguised as a toad, is whispering in Eve's ear: "Assaying by his devilish art to reach / The organs of her fancy, and with them forge / Illusions as he list, phantasms and dream / . . . Vain hopes, vain aims, inordinate desires" (801–3, 808). (Thanks to Nick Jones for identifying this reference.) The astonishing Miltonic parallel confirms that Potter's descriptions of her clients spoke to the reviewer's conception of this domain as an alluring, yet irremediably fallen, one. *Cincinnati Daily Gazette*, October 19, 1859, p. 3.

23 My account of the social implications of antebellum class formation is informed by Blumin, *The Emergence of the Middle Class*.

24 Marion Pullan, *Beadle's Guide to Dress-Making and Millinery* (New York: Beadle, 1860), cited in Lois Banner, *American Beauty*, 29. Banner's chapter "Beauty as Business: The Early Development of the Commercial Beauty Culture" speaks to the social/commercial ambiguity of beauty workers.

25 This phrase derives from the title of Bledstein's book. Burton Bledstein, *The Culture of Professionalism: The Middle Class and the Development of Higher Education In America* (New York: W. Norton, 1976).

26 Ibid., 100.

27 Halttunen, *Confidence Men and Painted Women*, 34.

28 Ibid.

29 In this regard, Potter emphasizes the incompatibility of theatricalized forms of status with the presumed "naturalness of gender." See Amy Schrager Lang, "Class and the Strategies of Sympathy," in *The Culture of Sentiment: Race, Gender, and Sentimentality in Nineteenth-Century America*, ed. Shirley Samuels (New York: Oxford University Press, 1992), 128–42.

30 Mary Ryan, *Women in Public: Between Banners and Ballots, 1825–1880* (Baltimore: Johns Hopkins University Press, 1990), 54.

31 "Dressing down" is the colorful phrase Rafia Zafar uses in *We Wear the Mask* to describe Potter's relation to her clients, 151.

32 Bruce Robbins, *The Servant's Hand: English Fiction from Below* (Durham, N.C.: Duke University Press, 1986), 41–43.

33 Bledstein, *The Culture of Professionalism*, x.

34 Though not present on the title page, Potter's name did appear on the back of the title page as the copyright holder. Potter's application for the copyright, on file at the Library of Congress, establishes the month (October) in which her book appeared. As mentioned previously, the publication of this book within a day of news of John Brown's raid on Harpers Ferry indicates that Potter's frankness was not framed as a racial problem calling for racial veiling or evasiveness. All reviews make it clear that the author's identity was well known and support Potter's claims about her popularity in Cincinnati. The *Daily Commercial* refers to the author as "a colored hairdresser, extensively known and patronised by the ladies of this city." October 19, 1859, p. 1.

35 Robbins, *The Servant's Hand*, 41–43.

36 References to this review derive from the *Cincinnati Gazette*, October 19, 1859, p. 3.

37 A third review that has recently come to light closely follows the *Gazette*'s critical logic: "We believe that the narrative, although not written in the most elegant English, is pregnant and interesting. . . . The writer makes a confident [*sic*] of her readers by taking them behind the scenes of fashionable life, and disclosing much of the hollowness and bitterness which is found there." *Cincinnati Daily Enquirer*, October 23, 1859, p. 2.

38 Bledstein, *The Culture of Professionalism*, x.

39 All subsequent references to this review originate from the *Cincinnati Daily Commercial*, October 19, 20, 22, 1859.

40 Getz and Klein, "The Frosting of the American Woman," 138.

41 Elizabeth Freeman, "'What Factory Girls Had Power to Do': The Technologic of Working-Class Feminine Publicity in *The Lowell Offering*," *Arizona Quarterly* 50.2 (Summer 1994): 109–28. See also Christine Stansell, *City of Women: Sex and Class in New York, 1789–1860* (Urbana: University of Illinois Press, 1987), 125–29. One recent and illuminating discussion on the similar negotiations of early twentieth-century shirtwaist workers can be found in Nan Enstad, *Ladies of Labor, Girls of Adventure* (New York: Columbia University Press, 1999).

42 Clearly, class impropriety was not the only connotation that a well-dressed working "girl" could bring to mind. A light-skinned mulatta, especially in the South, could be perceived as a concubine. But I would argue that for a freeborn independent working woman in Cincinnati such as Potter, the semiotic incongruity provoked by her dress pertains to her status as fashionably dressed worker. Freeman, "'What Factory Girls Had Power to Do,'" 115–16. As Nan Enstad explains in relation to twentieth-century factory women's own fashion consumption, "When working women purchased clothing, they exercised their new entitlement as workers. [These women] made clothing a badge of their own labor." *Ladies of Labor, Girls of Adventure*, 63–64.

43 This distinction is crucial inasmuch as it means that Potter cannot be confused with the "parvenu" whose buying power has nothing to do with her own labor power but instead represents her family's or husband's wealth.

44 Blumin, *The Emergence of the Middle Class*, 109, 121. Nicholas Bromell discusses antebellum writers' anxieties over the role and status that their (mental) labor played in a period of social and economic transformation. His study of Stowe, Emerson, and Thoreau (among others) concurs with Blumin's assessment on the symbolic dominance of the mental/manual binary and the division of labor to which it referred in an industrializing society. See *By the Sweat of the Brow: Literature and Labor in Antebellum America* (Chicago: University of Chicago Press, 1993).

45 Potter is echoing the concerns of workers who "while asserting that all value is created by labor and all labor is honorable, bitterly complained of the humiliation of workers." Blumin, *The Emergence of the Middle Class*, 122. This interpretation helps us account for the singularity of Potter's antislavery views, views that focus on slavery's undemocratic theft of labor and that reject outright the racializing logics of both proslavery and abolition. Potter's description of free black slaveowners' cruelty to their slaves pro-

vides an instance of this: "So you can see, color makes no difference, the propensities are the same, and those who have been oppressed themselves, are the sorest oppressors. . . . Those who are as black themselves as the ace of spades will, if they can, get mulatoes for slaves, and then the first word is 'my nigger'" (159).

46 In relation to the representation of working women in middle-class fiction, Amy Schrager Lang asserts, "To be poor, to struggle 'manfully,' to be ragged and dirty, to have a brown face, to be dangerous—to be all of these things is to be a millgirl, is to be a slave, is to be black." "The Syntax of Class in Elizabeth Stuart Phelps's *The Silent Partner*," in *Rethinking Class: Literary Studies and Social Formations*, ed. Wai Chee Dimock and Michael T. Gilmore (New York: Columbia University Press, 1994), 276.

47 Enstad, *Ladies of Labor*.

CHAPTER 4

1 Mary Clemmer Ames, *Evening Post*, April 18, 1862, p. 1, cited in Jennifer Fleischner, *Mrs. Lincoln and Mrs. Keckly* (New York: Broadway Books, 2003), 4.

2 Cited in Fleischner, *Mrs. Lincoln and Mrs. Keckley*, 324.

3 Elizabeth Keckley, *Behind the Scenes, or, Thirty Years a Slave and Four Years in the White House* (1868; New York: Oxford University Press, 1988), 330. Subsequent page references to this text will be appear in parentheses.

4 See Eric Foner, "Reconstruction and the Crisis of Free Labor," in *Politics and Ideology in the Age of the Civil War* (New York: Oxford University Press, 1980), for a discussion of the conflicts that erupted over freedmen's quest for autonomy and planters' need for labor during Reconstruction.

5 Critical publicity surrounded Mary Todd Lincoln (1818–82) throughout her tenure as First Lady: Kentucky-born, her loyalty to the Union was always questioned and she was constantly criticized for her extravagance. See Ruth Randall Painter's *Mary Lincoln: Biography of a Marriage* (Boston: Little, Brown & Co., 1953), 412–15. See also Ishbel Ross, *The President's Wife: Mary Todd Lincoln* (New York: Putnam & Sons, 1977) and Jean Baker, *Mary Todd Lincoln: A Biography* (New York: Norton, 1987). Baker, in particular, describes Keckley's text as a form of "retaliation" (280), uncannily echoing the review of *Behind the Scenes* that appeared in the *New York Citizen*, April 18, 1868, under the heading "Indecent Publications." See Fleischner, *Mrs. Lincoln and Mrs. Keckly*, for the most recent and authoritative account of Mary Lincoln and Elizabeth Keckley's relationship.

6 I derive my interpretation of deference from Stephanie Coontz's formulation of racialized patron-client working relations in *The Social Origins of Private Life: A History of American Families, 1600–1900* (London: Verso, 1988), 139.

7 The title of this obscure pamphlet, *Behind the Seams; By a Nigger Woman Who Took in Work from Mrs. Lincoln and Mrs. Davis* (New York: National News Co., 1868), bespeaks the illicit connotations associated with the public speech of black personal servants.

8 William Andrews counters "accommodationist" interpretations of Keckley's narrative by referring to her postbellum political priorities in "Reunion in the Postbellum Slave Narrative: Frederick Douglass and Elizabeth Keckley," *Black American Literature Forum* 23 (Spring 1989): 5–17. Justin G. Turner and Linda Levitt Turner, the editors of Mary Lincoln's letters, describe *Behind the Scenes* as "an early example of what has come to be a popular if questionable literary genre: a former employee's backstairs glimpse into the private lives of public figures." *Mary Todd Lincoln: Her Life and Letters* (New York: Knopf, 1972), 472. Frances Smith Foster corroborates most of Keckley's claims in her "Historical Introduction" to an edition of *Behind the Scenes* (Chicago: Lakeside Press, 1998), xix–lxxvii. Of special interest is the fact Foster uncovers regarding the identity of Keckley's last owner, Hugh Garland. Garland, to whom Keckley appealed for permission to buy her freedom, was the attorney who argued against the citizenship claims of slaves Hugh and Harriet Scott in the infamous Dred Scott case in 1857. For the most complete description of the publishing scandal, see Foster's *Written by Herself: Literary Production by African American Women, 1746–1892* (Bloomington: Indiana University Press, 1993), 126–30. See also the review of *Behind the Scenes* in the *New York Citizen*, April 18, 1868.

9 Deborah Gray White's *Ar'n't I a Woman: Female Slaves in the Plantation South* (New York: Norton, 1985) laid the groundwork for historical reevaluations of black women's labor in slavery. See also Jacqueline Jones's *Labor of Love and Labor of Sorrow* (New York: Random House, 1985) and Angela Davis, "Reflections of the Black Woman's Role in the Community of Slaves" (1971), reprinted in *The Angela Y. Davis Reader*, ed. Joy James (London: Blackwell Publishers, 1998), 111–28.

10 Ishbel Ross comments on Keckley's publishing motives when she states, "Lizzie was a century ahead of her time in turning her knowledge into profit, but it was not that she did not love Mrs. L. She, too, was malleable in the hands of others. . . . Her later years were not happy ones, and she died

obscurely in a shabby boarding house." *The President's Wife*, 267. In fact, Keckley worked at Wilberforce University in Ohio as a respected teacher for several years after the publication of her book. Jean Baker, who states incomprehensibly that the book was "subtitled a novel" expresses stronger distaste for Keckley. She sees *Behind the Scenes* as "retaliation" and as Keckley's "own means of repayment" for her work as agent in the Old Clothes Scandal. *Mary Todd Lincoln*, 280. Justin G. Turner and Linda Levitt Turner, editors of Mary Lincoln's letters, also subscribe to this popular view of Keckley's text: despite being "accurate," "*Behind the Scenes* was an early example of what has come to be a popular if questionable literary genre: a former employee's backstairs glimpse into the private lives of public figures." *Mary Todd Lincoln*, 472. Fleischner, *Mrs. Lincoln and Mrs. Keckly*, depicts the complex ambiguities at the heart of the part-employment, part-friendship dynamic between the two women.

11 Foster, *Written By Herself*, 130.

12 Suzanne Lebsock, *Free Women of Petersburg: Status and Culture in a Southern Town, 1784–1860* (New York: W. W. Norton, 1984), 180.

13 The *Oxford English Dictionary*'s definition of "modiste" (derived from *mode*, the French word for fashion) stipulates "one who makes, invents, or deals in articles of fashion; especially a maker of ladies' robes, millinery, etc." *OED* (compact edition, 1971), 577. This connection between fashion and labor thus reinforces the links between labor and status that Keckley takes such pains to describe. "Angry negro servant" is the phrase the reviewer of the *New York Citizen* used to describe Keckley.

14 William Andrews's analysis of Keckley's postbellum "materialism" highlights the difference between her discourse and Jacobs's earlier appeal to an "idealist" vision of "moral absolutism." But this analysis, which appears to historicize a significant discursive difference between the two, effectively flattens out or elides the significant interpersonal and gendered dynamics of Keckley's work relations. Framed within a "materialist" context, Keckley's single-minded concern with what Andrews terms her "career" makes her appear somewhat selfish to modern readers. As he describes it, "No one, least of all Keckley herself, is concerned about this slave woman's sexual respectability; at issue is something much more important—her financial reputation. . . . We may be sure that she wanted her *postbellum* audience to know of her unswerving fealty to the ethics of the marketplace. . . . Thus she links her sense of pride and respectability to an external stan-

dard—that of the marketplace—rather than an internal principle—what Jacobs would have called her 'virtue.'" "The Changing Moral Discourse of Nineteenth-Century African American Women's Autobiography: Harriet Jacobs and Elizabeth Keckley," in *De/Colonizing the Subject: The Politics of Gender in Women's Autobiography*, ed. Sidonie Smith and Julia Watson (Minneapolis: University of Minnesota Press, 1992), 229, 231, 233.

15 Keckley was not the first to describe the "bright side" of slavery. Before the war, former slave Lunsford Lane also used the phrase. See *The Narrative of Lunsford Lane* (Boston, 1842), iv. As Frances Smith Foster suggests, the multiple texts allow Keckley to "authenticate her account without resorting to a posture of self-defense." See "Autobiography after Emancipation: The Example of Elizabeth Keckley," in *Multicultural Autobiography: American Lives*, ed. James Robert Payne (Knoxville: University of Tennessee Press, 1992), 57.

16 The date of this letter, 1838, is significant because it suggests that Keckley's identification with paternalism is not merely a pragmatic a posteriori response to postbellum political realities. By alluding to Keckley's identification with paternalism I mean to foreground the feelings of obligation, dependency, and interdependence that she associates with her own southern history. Elizabeth Fox-Genovese and Eugene Genovese discuss southern paternalism and its many contradictions, including insight into the "contribution of blacks to the forging of . . . paternalism," in *Fruits of Merchant Capital: Slavery and Bourgeois Property in the Rise and Expansion of Capitalism* (New York: Oxford University Press, 1983), 117. As they observe, the "commitment" of slaves to a paternalist "dependency relationship" did not itself signify an endorsement of slavery. (Keckley's example supports their point that slaves "knew their white folks too well to see them as ten feet tall.") Rather, slaves appealed to these relations of interdependence as a form of protection.

17 This appeal is paradoxical, not only because a slave is "buying into" an ideology that mystifies slavery's power relations, but also because it inverts the paternalistic dynamic itself.

18 Lebsock, *Free Women of Petersburg*, 180, describes dressmaking and millinery as the most artisan-based and lucrative careers for antebellum women.

19 Arjun Appadurai describes the privileging dynamics of this deferential model of publicity as "mark[ing] the speaker as someone who knows something special and who has the privilege of passing it on." See "Topographies

of the Self: Praise and Emotion in Hindu India," in *Language and the Politics of Emotion*, ed. Catherine A. Lutz and Lila Abu-Lughod, (Cambridge: Cambridge University Press, 1990), 98.

20 For a perspective on the little-recognized *public* nature of intimacy, see Lauren Berlant, "Intimacy: A Special Issue," *Critical Inquiry* 24 (Winter 1998): 281–88.

21 Another striking instance of Keckley's mis/recognition of how her dresses circulate concerns a dress she makes for Varina Davis. Keckley's unironic description of her 1865 Chicago Fair encounter with a wax figure of Jefferson Davis wearing a dress displays complete unawareness of the role of this dress in the North's efforts to ridicule Mr. Davis's manhood. Instead of referring to the context of insult, Keckley describes the "pleasing discovery" (75) that the dress was one she had made. See Nina Silber, "Intemperate Men, Spiteful Women, and Jefferson Davis," in *Divided Houses: Gender and the Civil War*, ed. Nina Silber and Catherine Clinton (New York: Oxford University Press, 1992), 283–305.

22 Coontz, *The Social Origins of Private Life*, 139; David Roediger, *The Wages of Whiteness: Race and the Making of the American Working Class* (London: Verso, 1991), 47.

23 See Mary Romero, *Maid in the U.S.A.* (New York: Routledge, 1992), 123–26. *Like One of the Family* (New York: Independence Publishers, 1956) is the ironic title of Alice Childress's novel about domestic workers and their employers.

24 For a summary of the scandal, see Painter, *Mary Lincoln*, 405–15.

25 "Indecent Publications," *New York Citizen*, April 18, 1868, p. 4.

26 See Christine Stansell, *City of Women: Sex and Class in New York, 1789–1860* (Urbana: University of Illinois Press, 1987), 160.

27 The literature on the semiotic and social invisibility of domestic servants is wide ranging. See Faye Dudden, *Serving Women: Household Service in Nineteenth-Century America* (Middletown, Conn.: Wesleyan University Press, 1983), and Karen Halttunen, *Confidence Men and Painted Women: A Study of Middle-Class Culture in America, 1830–1870* (New Haven: Yale University Press, 1982), for accounts of the spatial divisions that helped obscure the presence of workers and their work in the middle-class household.

28 Both Andrews and Foster elaborate at length on the historical and political circumstances that govern this change in perspective from the antebellum

slave narrative. See Andrews, "Changing Moral Discourse," 237; and Foster, "Autobiography after Emancipation," 57.

29 Although Lincoln scholars inevitably attribute Keckley's at times unflattering depiction of Mary Lincoln to motives of revenge, others have stressed Keckley's psychological ambivalence toward the former First Lady. See Jennifer Fleischner, *Mastering Slavery: Memory, Family, and Identity in Women's Slave Narratives* (New York: New York University Press, 1996), 96–97. My analysis suggests that any consideration of this relationship must attend to the work-produced, or work-mediated, nature of this bond.

30 This understanding of the structural rhetorical asymmetries existing between worker and employer speech builds on, yet moves beyond, understandings of the aesthetic disadvantages commonly associated with "working-class" autobiography. That is, Keckley does not encounter a problem of literary standards per se. What she does is deploy wildly incompatible modes of representation that pit publicized labor against private subjectivity. See Regenia Gagnier, *Subjectivities: A History of Self-Representation in Britain, 1832–1920* (New York: Oxford University Press, 1991).

31 Eliza Potter, *A Hairdresser's Experience in High Life* (1859; New York: Oxford University Press, 1991), 68.

32 John E. Washington, *They Knew Lincoln* (New York: Dutton, 1942), 213.

CODA

1 Perhaps if Keckley had placed more emphasis on her reform work as founder and president of the Contraband Relief Association (later the Freedmen and Soldier Relief Association), her text might have been more readily perceived as referring to the abolitionist tradition of racial elevation. Keckley's depiction of some of the freedmen seeking refuge in Washington, D.C., differentiated them from her, despite her sympathy for their cause: "We make an appeal . . . on behalf of those freedmen whom . . . are seeking an asylum in our midst, and are in a situation demanding the sympathy and support of those of us who have been blest with a happier allotment in life. . . . Our society . . . was formed for the purpose, not only of relieving the wants of those destitute people, but also to sympathize with, and advise them" (*Christian Recorder*, March 14, 1863). See Lynn Domina, "I Was Re-Elected President: Elizabeth Keckley as Quintessential Patriot in *Behind the Scenes*," in *Women's Life-Writing: Finding Voice/Building Community*, ed. Linda Coleman (Bowling Green, Ohio: Bowling Green State

University Popular Press, 1997), 139–51, and Jennifer Fleischner, *Mastering Slavery: Memory, Family, and Identity in Women's Slave Narratives* (New York: New York University Press, 1996), 93–132.

2 Booker T. Washington, *Up from Slavery* (1901), ed. William L. Andrews (New York: W. W. Norton, 1996), 100.

3 Victoria W. Wolcott, *Remaking Respectability: African American Women in Interwar Detroit* (Chapel Hill: University of North Carolina Press, 2001); Farah Jasmine Griffin, *Who Set you Flowin'?: The African American Migration Narrative* (New York: Oxford University Press, 1995); Hazel Carby, "Policing the Black Woman's Body in an Urban Context," *Critical Inquiry* 18 (Summer 1992): 738–55.

4 Kevin K. Gaines, *Uplifting the Race: Black Leadership, Politics, and Culture in the Twentieth Century* (Chapel Hill: University of North Carolina Press, 1996), is one of the most recent and influential accounts of the dynamics of class and race in uplift: "Uplift ideology's argument for black humanity was not an argument for equality. . . . The shift from race to culture, stressing self-help and seemingly progressive in its contention that blacks . . . were assimilable into the American body politic, represented a limited conditional claim to equality, citizenship, and human rights for African Americans" (4).

5 Caroline H. Dall, *Woman's Right to Labor; or Low Wages and Hard Work* (Boston: Walker, Wise, and Co., 1860), 6–7.

6 *Sisters of the Spirit: Three Black Women's Autobiographies of the Nineteenth Century*, ed. William L. Andrews (Bloomington: Indiana University Press, 1986).

INDEX